Strategic Defense

Strategic Defense

"Star Wars" in Perspective

Library of Congress Cataloging in Publication Data

Payne, Keith B.
   Strategic defense.
   Includes bibliographical references and index.
   1. Strategic Defense Initiative.   I. Title.
UG743.P39   1986   358'.1754   85-29190
ISBN 0-8191-5109-2 (alk. paper)
ISBN 0-8191-5110-6 (pbk. : alk. paper)

All Hamilton Press books are produced on acid-free
paper which exceeds the minimum standards set by the National
Historical Publications and Records Commission.

*For my wife and parents, who continually demonstrate
that which is good and worthy of protection.*

Table of Contents

List of Figures

Acknowledgement

I would like to thank several individuals who provided valuable comments on parts of the early manuscript: Ms. Jill Coleman, Mr. Mike Ennis, Dr. Pat Friel, Mrs. Margot Glavis, Mr. Kurt Guthe, Dr. James Motley, Lt. Col. William Tuttle, and Dr. Barry Schneider. I also appreciate the work done by Mr. Guthe and Ms. Coleman on the subject of chapter ten. Thanks also are due to Captain Barbara Bennington (P) for her valuable assistance during the early stages of writing. In addition, I would like to express my deep appreciation to Ms. Beth Miller and Ms. Coleman for their patient and seemingly tireless efforts in the production of the manuscript; their assistance exceeded any rightful expectation, and I am grateful. Finally, I wish to recognize Dr. Colin Gray, and the late Col. Josephus Briggs, Jr. who provided the much-needed encouragement that led me to write this book.

Preface

This book is an examination of the Strategic Defense Initiative that was set into motion by President Reagan's so-called Star Wars speech of March 23, 1983. It also offers a look at the deeper and abiding issues of the relationship between strategic defense and theories of nuclear deterrence, strategy, stability, arms control, commitments to allies, and morality. These issues are not new; they have been debated for more than two decades. The Strategic Defense Initiative, or "Star Wars," has simply rendered them of much greater current interest. In this regard an intellectual debt is owed to those who, in decades past, covered much of the ground that we all are looking at anew—notably Herman Kahn and Donald Brennan. The current strategic debate suffers greatly by their absence.

A point should be made with reference to the shorthand use of terms in chapter ten. There is a diversity of views concerning the Strategic Defense Initiative in all of the major NATO countries. However, despite the certainty that generalization does damage to nuance I often have followed the standard form of referring to "Europeans" as shorthand for opinion trends in the Federal Republic of Germany, France, and Britain.

Finally, it should be noted that I have attempted to write this particular book for those people who do not have the time or the inclination to follow closely the strategic nuclear policy debate, but generally are interested in "Star Wars." When a choice between clarity and detail had to be made, I opted for the former—hopefully with some success.

Foreword

by

Zbigniew Brzezinski

When President Reagan announced the Strategic Defense Initiative (SDI) in a televised speech on March 23, 1983, he directed the U.S. technical community to investigate the potential for constructing a highly effective defense against ballistic missiles. The long-term goal of this investigation, as presented by the president, was to provide the technology necessary for nothing short of "rendering these nuclear weapons impotent and obsolete." Since that March 23rd presentation, labeled by the media as the president's "Star Wars" speech, there has been a deluge of articles and editorials on the subject of strategic defense. Despite the apparent general scarcity of understanding concerning what the SDI is and is not there has been no lack of commentary. This book provides an extremely useful guide to anyone interested in understanding the nature of the SDI and the debate surrounding it—a debate which may prove to be one of the most important of our times.

Current technical and political circumstances make the decision to proceed with an SDI eminently sensible. The development of ballistic missile technology has led to accuracies that could potentially enable Soviet offensive forces to pose a first-strike threat to an effective U.S. retaliatory response and to almost all U.S. command and control facilities. The fact that the Soviet Union has deployed large numbers of highly accurate offensive forces in its arsenal of ICBMs and continues to add to that arsenal, while the United States has not, is particularly disturbing. Indeed, even if the U.S. strategic modernization program were carried out over the coming decade as currently envisaged, our strategic arsenal would not possess "counterforce" capabilities equal to those of the Soviet Union.

It has long been held as a near-truth that as long as the U.S. could threaten to retaliate effectively the Soviet Union would be discouraged from contemplating a first strike. However, the Soviet strategic build-up and its ICBM deployments in particular constitute a danger to the continued effectiveness of the U.S. deterrent. Concern over the continuing build-up of the Soviet capability to destroy our retaliatory forces and command and control facilities in a first strike does not reflect an exaggeration of the threat to stability posed by these Soviet forces. Indeed, we have been watching the momentum of the Soviet counter-force build-up for years—realizing that if arms control negotiations could not provide a solution we would be compelled to provide for our security unilaterally. It is now possible to conceive of circumstances under which the Soviet Union could strike first and destroy most of our land-based retaliatory forces. Only those ballistic missile carrying submarines on patrol might survive the Soviet attack; and the doubtful ability to communicate with those surviving submarines following attack on our communications facilities would likely reduce their retaliatory potential.

The American hope has been that these destabilizing trends in offensive technology could be handled through a political process, i.e., arms control. However, it is doubtful that strategic arms control negotiations, as we have come to know them, possess the capacity to produce the expected stabilizing limitations on offensive counterforce weapons. The position adopted by the Soviet Union in the current talks at Geneva suggests that the political route will continue to be fruitless unless we go forward with a credible SDI program. Of particular importance is the emphasis the SDI places upon near-term defensive technologies appropriate for defense coverage of American retaliatory capabilities. A credible SDI emphasizing such a defensive potential will facilitate reductions in destabilizing offensive arms, such as the over 600 Soviet SS-18 and SS-19 ICBMs (and their successors). It will do so by allowing our negotiators to present their Soviet counterparts with two options, one mutually beneficial, the other particularly costly to the Soviet Union.

The first option would be to renegotiate ABM Treaty restrictions against the defense of retaliatory forces. In return for real reductions in modern counterforce-capable ICBMs, of which the Soviet Union possesses the vast majority, the United States would agree not to proceed with deployment of its strategic defense system. If the Soviet Union refuses this bargain the U.S. would declare that the continued Soviet offensive build-up has placed in jeopardy supreme American interests and that the U.S. consequently is compelled to withdraw from the ABM Treaty. Such an action would both reflect the truth concerning Soviet ICBM deployments and be consistent with Article 15 of the Treaty governing legal withdrawal. Following withdrawal from the Treaty the U.S. would deploy a BMD system for protection of its strategic retaliatory capabilities. This action would nullify the decade-long Soviet deployment of counterforce-capable ICBMs. If the Soviet response was to increase its ICBM arsenal in an attempt to reestablish its threat to our retaliatory forces, the Soviets would be engaging in a losing tailchase that would be excessively costly for them. It would be easier and cheaper for the U.S. to augment its defenses and restore the survivability of its retaliatory capability than it would be for the Soviet Union to attempt to overturn those defenses through an increase in its offensive threat.

In order to pursue such an approach to strategic defense and arms control the United States must revise the current orientation of the SDI. The Reagan Administration has focused the emphasis of the SDI on those "exotic" technologies that might one day provide effective protection for large urban areas. It has given less emphasis to the near-term potential for the defense of selected strategic retaliatory forces—although there is general agreement that such defensive capabilities are now or soon will be in hand. To provide the necessary impetus for real Soviet offensive arms reductions, the SDI must convince Moscow's leadership of our capability and willingness to deploy a strategic defense system soon if it continues to reject significant limitations on destabilizing offensive forces. The Soviet Union must also be convinced that we will be willing to forego BMD deployment if they are willing to make the stabilizing reductions in their offensive missile force we have long sought. It should be clear that to pursue such a meaningful negotiating posture and defense strategy the U.S. requires a credible near-term BMD program. Support for the SDI is thus support for any future prospects for real reductions through arms control.

In this book Keith Payne documents the case for the SDI and strategic defense in terms of arms control and strategic stability. Without making utopian claims for the potential efficacy of defensive systems, Dr. Payne provides an innovative strategy for increasing American security and obtaining genuine arms control through a combination of defensive and offensive modernization programs.

Dr. Payne's emphasis on the necessity for both defensive and offensive programs may prove controversial. Nonetheless, he provides a strong and balanced case for the integration of offensive and defensive systems in support of strategic stability and arms control. Indeed, because Keith Payne is able to weave offense, defense and arms control into a single strategy this book will prove to be a major contribution not only to the debate over the SDI, but also to the much larger debate over the general direction that American strategy should take in coming decades.

ONE
Chapter 1

"WELCOME TO THE TWENTY-FIRST CENTURY"

It is mid-May, the year is 2000. The United States and the Soviet Union have been involved in a military crisis for about one week. This military crisis soon will erupt into a shooting war, a war involving nuclear weapons for the first time since World War II.

It began when the Soviet Union started to mass soldiers at key points along its border with Iran. From the Soviet leadership's perspective it had no other choice. A bloody civil war in the Moslem state of Iran was threatening Soviet control of its own Moslem population. The civil war in Iran pitted the local Iranian Communist party, the Mujahadin-e-Khalq, in alliance with socialists and other nonreligious fundamentalists, against the fanatical Moslem followers of the late Khomeini. The civil war was having an effect within Soviet borders as Soviet Moslems became increasingly vocal in support of their fellow Moslems and in opposition to the "Godless" communist/socialist "United Front" which the Soviet government was supporting. The leadership in Moscow worried that if the civil war were not ended, open resistance to the Communist party leadership would spread to the Soviet Union itself. Given the troubles the Soviet Union was having in controlling many other ethnic groups within its own borders and Eastern Europe, it did not want to take any chance of appearing weak. What would happen if the Poles, the Czechs, the Hungarians, and the East Germans saw Soviet control challenged within the Soviet

Union itself? Might not even the Ukrainians begin to feel restive? No, decided the men in the Kremlin, this civil war could not be allowed to continue, this conflict on its southern border had to be stopped, and military power seemed the only sure solution. The Iranian civil war had placed the Soviet leadership in a position wherein the use of force appeared to be the "least miserable" of a set of miserable response options.

The U.S. responded to the massing of Soviet troops with repeated, stern, diplomatic warnings of "grave concern." But the U.S. had given such warnings before, over Angola and Afghanistan in the seventies and eighties, and elsewhere since. This tough talk was never followed by much action, or only of the symbolic sort such as the American boycott of the 1980 Moscow Olympics. This time, the Soviet leadership saw a developing threat to its own authority in the Soviet Union—whatever limited risk there was in confronting the U.S. over this affair had to be accepted.

The president had, of course, repeatedly warned the Soviet Union against direct military action in the Persian Gulf. America's European allies, Japan, and the entire industrialized economy of the West was dependent upon a regular supply of energy from the Persian Gulf. Allowing the Soviet Union to control the Persian Gulf could put America's allies at its mercy, maybe forcing some of them out of the NATO alliance; and despite Moscow's assurances of limited objectives, who could know where the Soviet Union might stop. Had not appeasement to Hitler only made Nazi Germany more aggressive, and led to World War II? No, the president reasoned, the U.S. could not allow the Soviet Union to dominate this area critical to Western economies, it had to draw the line for once and say, "no more."

On May 24, at 1:00 a.m. (Washington time), tens of thousands of Soviet troops started to move into the northern Iranian provinces of Azerbaijan and Khurastan as Soviet Airborne Guards landed in Tehran and the major provincial capitals of Tabriz and Qazvin to support the United Front and defeat local armed resistance. Soviet special operations forces, the SPETSNAZ, had carried out their assignment. Specifically, seven hundred of these highly trained elite fighters had entered Iran covertly with orders to assassinate key officials of the Iranian leadership, assume control of the radio and television stations, and destroy what remained of the Iranian air force. By early morning the fundamentalist government of Iran had been removed from power. The Soviet plan called for over 220,000 troops, including twenty-three armored and motorized rifle divisions, to gain control of cities, industrial areas, and major roads. Many Soviet officers, with experience in Afghanistan, were more than familiar with the tactics required to seize these objectives.

The president, when awakened and briefed of the situation, asked: "What are my options at this point?" The invasion had been expected—U.S. spy satellites had been monitoring the Soviet troop buildup for almost three weeks. A U.S. naval task force had been ordered to the area earlier as a precaution and a show of American will. A U.S. carrier battle group was within two days of the area, but the chief of naval operations was very reluctant to send a carrier battle group into the shallow waters and close quarters of the Persian Gulf. It was too risky at this point; those carriers represented major military assets. The president was told that the relatively small number of mountain passes and chokepoints through which the majority of Soviet ground forces had to move could be sealed if the president would authorize the use of nuclear weapons. It was not clear to the president what should be done, but it was quite clear what should not be done—the idea of starting a nuclear war was "crazy."

The president put U.S. military forces on DEFCON (Defense Condition) 2, "Worldwide Alert" and informed the Soviet leadership that the U.S. would oppose Soviet actions militarily if the Soviet advance was not halted immediately and a cease-fire called. The general secretary of the Soviet Communist party, who was also president of the Soviet Union, responded privately that Soviet actions were consistent with the UN Charter—had not the "legitimate" United Front government of Iran "invited" fraternal Soviet assistance to help put down civil unrest in Iran? And did not the 1921 Treaty of Friendship give the Soviet Union the legitimate right and even the responsibility to come to the assistance of the Iranian government? The Soviet president cautioned the U.S. not to interfere with this limited operation because supreme Soviet interests were involved and this was an obvious area of Soviet vital interest, well outside the zone of U.S. influence and power.

Further U.S. warnings received similar replies. The Soviet position came as little surprise; it was the same line Moscow had taken following the invasion of Afghanistan and Czechoslovakia back in 1979 and 1968. It appeared obvious to the president that diplomacy would not stop the Soviets, and that their objectives would more than likely include Iranian oil fields in Khuzestan and the refineries on the Persian Gulf. The U.S. could not allow Soviet troops to occupy those areas of vital interest— the credibility of the U.S. as an ally would evaporate and an oil crunch greater than that of 1972-1973 could result. Perhaps more dangerous, the Soviets would feel at greater liberty to challenge the U.S. around the world.

The president ordered the reestablished U.S. Rapid Deployment Force (RDF) into action. It had expected to go. The RDF was not expected to defeat Soviet forces in a head-on military confrontation, but to establish a defensive line that the Soviet Union would not cross for fear of the real U.S. threat— nuclear escalation. The RDF was ordered to establish a presence along the few arteries that run through the Zagros Mountains, just north of the Iranian oil fields. The difficulty of moving men and material thousands of miles, very rapidly, severely limited what could be done by the U.S. But within three days 3,500 men had assumed defensive positions, as planned, supported by light armor. In an unexpected display of support, the Americans were joined by 1,200 French paratroopers and legionnaires. No one expected this modest force to stop a Soviet advance should it come; but everyone assumed the Soviets would stop before meeting U.S. troops in combat.

For their part, as a precautionary measure, the Soviet leadership began to mobilize troops in Eastern Europe and in the western Soviet Military Districts. Not that an attack by the West in Europe was expected, but the Soviets wanted to tie down NATO forces in Europe and make them unavailable to the Persian Gulf. Moscow reasoned that a partial mobilization of the Warsaw Pact would keep U.S. troops in Europe. The plan worked well, NATO assumed a high state of alert, and what had been part of the U.S. contingency plan—to reinforce the RDF with American forces stationed in West Germany— was quickly forgotten.

The shaky situation in Europe changed abruptly when the Polish armed forces moved from uncooperative compliance with Soviet mobilization plans to openly hostile opposition. What started as scattered resistance among civilians spread to an increasing number of military units until actual firefights were taking place between Polish and Soviet military units. The Poles wanted to grasp what might be the only opportunity in a hundred years to break free from Moscow while the Soviets were occupied actually fighting against the Americans in the Persian Gulf.

The East German government expressed its solidarity with the Soviet Union and the Warsaw Pact allies, but open resistance, first civilian and then military, to Soviet military mobilization plans soon spread throughout East Germany and then into Czechoslovakia as well. Although the U.S. government was publicly declaring that it would not interfere in Eastern Europe, there was strong support in the U.S. for a policy that would assist the Eastern Europeans covertly, and many in Eastern Europe hoped for eventual NATO aid.

What had started as a crisis in the Persian Gulf had rapidly spread to Eastern Europe, and was no longer under the control of the U.S. or the Soviet Union. The Soviet leadership now had to consider how to handle the armed rebellion of three of its Eastern European satellites, the possibility of imminent direct military conflict with the U.S. in the Persian Gulf, and the fact that NATO was in the process of its own military mobilization. Matters became more complex when some units of the West German army, the Bundeswehr, began providing support to East German units fighting the Soviets. Pan-Germanism had experienced a renewal in West Germany in the late-1980s with increasingly enthusiastic support, and many East Germans had quietly supported the goal as well. Although the West German government was not officially supporting the rebellion in East Germany, it was not possible to control the enthusiasm of West Germans to assist in removing the wall that still separated the two German states.

Events in Eastern Europe shaped Soviet actions in the Persian Gulf. Whereas previously Soviet leaders wanted to tie U.S. forces to Europe, they now feared Western support for the Eastern Europeans; Moscow made a bid to draw U.S. attention, and possibly its forces, away from Europe. It decided to defeat the U.S. in the Persian Gulf quickly and destroy the Western will for any further confrontation. The leadership in the Kremlin further hoped that an open defeat of the U.S. in the Persian Gulf would demonstrate Soviet power and Western weakness, and thereby scuttle any Eastern European hopes of Western aid.

The Soviet advance against the RDF was successful, inflicting heavy casualties on the retreating remnants of U.S. and French forces. As these forces assumed new battle positions the president warned the Soviet Union that the United States would not tolerate any further Soviet advances, and, to this end, would employ "every means at its disposal" to forestall the Soviet advance. This, of course, was a thinly veiled nuclear threat. The president was not at all certain that nuclear weapons should be used—the move everyone except the U.S. ground force commander advised against—but the threat of nuclear use, accompanied by visible moves to make that threat credible, should deter the Soviets from any further advance if they had any sense.

The president directed the chairman of the Joint Chiefs of Staff to prepare for possible nuclear employment against selective Soviet ground targets. The smallest possible nuclear charges were readied for use against advancing Soviet tank columns. But the president waited to give the actual authorization for nuclear use, hoping the threat would work.

The Soviet Union responded promptly, although not as the Americans had hoped. Soviet spy satellites and other intelligence sources had warned that the U.S. was preparing to enforce its nuclear threats with real actions, and the chief of the Soviet General Staff was quite vocal about Soviet troops being on the receiving end of nuclear fire. Soviet leaders were not sure why the U.S. was hesitating but they decided to exploit the situation. Immediate strikes against all U.S. and French positions in Iran were ordered.

Rockets armed, not with nuclear, but with chemical weapons and conventional high-energy explosives, had been brought in with the invading forces. The Soviets wanted to defeat U.S. forces in Iran quickly and decisively, and if that could be done by using chemical rather than nuclear weapons of mass destruction, so much the better. The Soviet Union would not need to be the first to use nuclear weapons. A massive barrage of chemical and conventional warheads hit U.S. and French ground positions. Soviet bombers were also sent against some U.S. naval vessels suspected of carrying nuclear weapons. A message warned the Americans that any nuclear retaliation against the Soviet Union would lead to "devastating and worldwide consequences."

The Soviet attack, particularly the use of chemical weapons, had a horrible effect. The shaky perimeter U.S. military forces had established was full of gaping holes; units were decimated. It was obvious that the American nuclear deterrent threat had not worked, and defeat appeared to be at hand.

It was June 8, and the president was confronted with a dilemma: the U.S. nuclear deterrence threat had not worked and the Soviet Union had used "weapons of mass destruction"—chemical, nuclear, and biological weapons were so defined by the UN and international law—against U.S. forces. Yet it remained that the Soviet Union had not used nuclear weapons. The president weighed the options and alternatives: U.S. forces were not armed with modern chemical weapons, neither were American forces particularly well prepared to survive Soviet chemical attacks. So the U.S. could not respond in kind, even if it wanted to. Some nuclear weapons were still available, but the prospect of initiating a nuclear war was appalling to the president. Yet the secretary of state and the president's national security adviser warned that the Soviet Union could not only continue to use chemical weapons, but might begin to use biological weapons against the remaining U.S. forces and positions. The only option seemed to be to demonstrate that the U.S. would indeed use nuclear weapons and hope that the fear of escalation to an all-out nuclear war would be enough to induce the Soviets to accept a cease-fire and begin negotiations.

At this critical point, the events in Europe heightened the crisis. The Soviet Union warned that it would no longer allow West Berlin to be a refuge for renegade East German troops. It was clear that the Soviet Union was preparing to occupy West Berlin. It was also clear that the beleaguered French, British, and U.S. troops stationed in West Berlin could not hold the city for more than a few hours. They could die gallantly, but they could not stop the overwhelming number of Soviet forces in the area.

The secretary of state recommended that the president demonstrate U.S. resolve with a limited nuclear strike against

Soviet forces in Iran. Although this action might not save the U.S. survivors in Iran, it would demonstrate U.S. resolve and might deter the Soviets from attacking West Berlin. A Soviet attack on West Berlin would turn the crisis into a shooting war between NATO and the Warsaw Pact, and who knew where such a war might end? Would there be a rapid nuclear escalation if NATO and the Warsaw Pact began fighting? The secretary of state's advice—to use a few nuclear weapons now in the Persian Gulf—might force the Soviets to realize that the crisis was becoming completely uncontrollable. The president's national security adviser agreed and called the proposal a strategy for "restoring deterrence" through very limited nuclear use.

After great reluctance the president agreed. Nuclear strikes against Soviet military positions in Iran were ordered. The strikes were intended to serve both political and operational purposes. Politically, they would demonstrate that the U.S. was willing to escalate to nuclear war in the hope that this "shot across the bow" would convince the Soviets to halt their advance in Iran, and more importantly, to refrain from attacking the Western garrisons in West Berlin, lest the conflict escalate to full-scale nuclear war. Operationally, the strikes were intended to stop Soviet armor from advancing further into Iran.

Thirty relatively low yield nuclear artillery rounds were launched by U.S. M-110 A1 howitzers. Immediately following the strike the president sent a message to the Soviet general secretary specifying that the U.S. nuclear attacks were in retaliation for the Soviet use of chemical "weapons of mass destruction" and that this grave situation now threatened the future of mankind. The president suggested that all forces halt where they were and that there be a cease-fire on all fronts to avert disaster.

The U.S. nuclear strike was successful, halting the Soviet advance at least temporarily, and West Berlin remained free, although completely cut-off from the West. The president's fear, of course, was now that nuclear weapons had been used the Soviet response would involve multiple nuclear strikes against U.S. positions in Iran and against U.S. naval forces in the Persian Gulf and Indian Ocean, removing U.S. power from the area for at least the near term. But perhaps Moscow would recognize the danger of further escalation and agree to a cease-fire.

Soviet doctrine had always stressed that once the super-powers used nuclear weapons in conflict, all "the wraps were off"—the U.S. could expect massive nuclear strikes against its military forces, especially its nuclear forces, and against its military-industrial centers, which would include cities. But now that such a moment in history had arrived, the Soviet Politburo agreed to the Defense Council's recommendation that it disregard doctrinal admonitions and the urgings of the military leadership. "A full nuclear attack against the U.S. would be too dangerous," said the minister of defense, adding, "Of course the American nuclear strike must be answered, but why risk our own destruction in doing so?" But, he added, the Americans could not be allowed to believe that they had frightened the Soviet Union into submission. It would destroy Soviet military credibility at home and around the world, which was essential for maintaining domestic order and restoring control over the Eastern Europeans.

Soviet military advisers insisted that the U.S. would launch a full-scale nuclear attack in any event, and suggested that it would be wiser to strike hard now and destroy as many U.S. weapons as possible before they could be used against the Russian motherland. The military argued that such a strike might be so successful as to prevent the U.S. from retaliating massively. Russian casualties and the destruction of industry might be very low, and most importantly, Communist party authority would endure.

The general secretary disagreed. The U.S. had to be taught a lesson, but not one that would risk full-scale U.S. nuclear retaliation. This had to be handled more delicately than that. Nuclear strikes against all U.S. positions in Iran and U.S. naval forces in the region were ordered. Intermediate range ballistic missiles stationed in the Soviet Union were to be used.

In addition, to convince the U.S. once and for all that the Soviet Union would not be intimidated by nuclear threat or strikes, the Politburo ordered a very limited intercontinental ballistic missile (ICBM) strike against the United States itself. The attack was to serve both political and military purposes. About eighty ICBM warheads would be used in a selective attack on petroleum refinery facilities throughout the U.S. Because refineries are highly vulnerable to nuclear effects and geographically concentrated, a small attack could destroy approximately 64 percent of U.S. petroleum refining capacity. Washington was to be avoided—such an attack might provoke full retaliation. In any case, the feeling in the Kremlin was that the U.S. leadership would be paralyzed by such a limited strike against the U.S. homeland itself, particularly if the attack was accompanied by a severe warning that any further U.S. nuclear retaliation would result in a massive Soviet nuclear reply against U.S. cities. They pointed out that much of the American public, and Congress, was already calling for "an end to this madness." Evidence indicated that the Americans were increasingly asking why they should risk nuclear destruction because of an unpopular war, taking place in some "godforsaken" land 8,000 miles away from home. The Politburo was of the unanimous opinion that the U.S. would exercise great restraint in response to this nuclear attack; most Politburo members believed that the Americans would sue for peace. The minimum result would be a Western pull-out from West Berlin and Iran, the destruction of U.S. credibility worldwide, and more importantly, the exhibition of the Soviet Union's dominant power and resolve.

The Politburo had a rough idea of the probable effects of its nuclear attack. Some hasty civilian evacuations and makeshift civil defense preparations had already taken place in the United States as tensions mounted. Home basements, public shelters, and even subways had been transformed into shelters for people fearing the worst. But, the vast majority of the urban population living near the target areas had taken few precautions and were vulnerable. The direct effects of the nuclear attack and fallout would cause between 3 million and 5 million fatalities. Available medical aid would be inadequate. Many petro-chemical plants located near refineries would be destroyed. The fires at these plants would rage for days. The fires at refineries would be very difficult to extinguish because of local fallout, intense heat, and an inadequate supply of chemicals to douse the petroleum fires. Toxic chemicals would leak from petro-chemical plants. U.S. ports equipped to handle oil would be damaged, impairing U.S. capability to import petroleum. Railroads, pipelines, storage tanks, and other economic facilities associated with refineries would also be destroyed. Restoring an adequate supply of refined petroleum could take years. Buildings and other structures in urban areas close to refineries would also be damaged severely. For example, in Philadelphia, the local production, storage, and distribution of petroleum would be destroyed. There would be severe damage to the international airport, the railroad, and the highways, and sunken ships would block the channel. Hospitals within a 2-3 mile radius of the blast would be destroyed and naval shipyards damaged. This type of destruction would be repeated in all the cities around or near the selected targets, e.g., New York, Philadelphia, Chicago, Kansas City, New Orleans, Houston, Los Angeles, and San Francisco.

It would be the worst single disaster in U.S. history, and would shatter the American economy.[1] Still, the United States would have much more to lose if it retaliated and the Soviet Union made good its threat. The Soviet leadership was confident that this fear would minimize the U.S. response. On June 15, in the year 2000, at 2:00 a.m. (local Washington time), Soviet SS-24 ICBMs, each armed with about ten multiple nuclear warheads, were launched into the atmosphere en route to their targets. They streaked upward through the atmosphere in about four minutes and headed on their trajectories over the North Pole. A launch control officer responsible for firing several of the missiles, thinking about the unfortunate people near the selected targets, muttered with some sympathy, "Privet dvadtsat-pervomu veku," ("Welcome to the twenty-first century").

BACK TO THE PRESENT

How this Soviet nuclear attack might end is the subject of this book. Although it may come as a surprise, a conclusion very different from a stark listing of deaths and destruction might be possible. For example, by the twenty-first century the United States could have the defensive capability to intercept and destroy attacking ballistic missiles, whether coming from the Soviet Union or elsewhere. Of course, if the U.S. possessed some defense against ballistic missiles the Soviet Union would be unlikely to launch a selective strike against the U.S. in the first place—if nuclear missiles are likely to be intercepted, the result would only demonstrate an attacker's weakness. Thousands of nuclear weapons would be much harder to counter with limited defenses than a mere "demonstration of will" employing a handful of missiles. Yet the fear of a full-scale U.S. nuclear retaliation against limited Soviet defenses would be a powerful disincentive to any Soviet leader contemplating the massive use of nuclear weapons. That is what deterrence has been about for two decades—deterring attack by threatening nuclear retaliation.

If the scenario sketched above for the outbreak of nuclear war seems tragic and unbelievable, that is because all scenarios for nuclear war seem unrealistic. It is simply too difficult to imagine leaders making such awesome decisions. History, however, is filled with "unbelievable" events. Who would have believed that a world war could have been triggered by the assassination of an Austrian archduke—and that the assassin would have stumbled upon the archduke's automobile while it was enroute to a hospital to visit the survivors of an unsuccessful assassination attempt that took place earlier the same day? Or that Soviet Premier Khrushchev would secretly place nuclear-tipped missiles in Cuba in October 1962 shortly after the Cuban revolution? Or, for that matter, that in 1941, the Japanese would bomb the American Navy at Pearl Harbor in a surprise attack? The routine of international politics occasionally is broken by incredible events.

The limited options of the U.S. suggested in the present scenario are quite realistic. Indeed, the reason the U.S. and its allies place such reliance on the nuclear threat is because the U.S. really has very limited options of response in many areas of vital interest. The behavior of the U.S. in the nuclear war outlined above is, in general, not inconsistent with actual U.S. policy. The U.S. (and NATO) use the threat of nuclear "first use" in response to a Soviet conventional attack to compensate for Soviet advantages in conventional forces in many regions of the world. Unfortunately for the U.S. and its allies those regions include such areas of U.S. vital interest as the Persian Gulf, Northern Europe, Western Europe, Japan, and Korea. Geopolitics gives the Soviet Union an inherent advantage in and around Eurasia: the Soviet Union is located in Eurasia and occupies more than one-third of the entire continent, whereas, the U.S. is separated by vast oceans and is roughly three to eight thousand miles away from its periphery. The proximity of the Soviet Union allows relatively easy access for the Soviet land army. Soviet leaders (as the czars before them) have seen the value in maintaining a massive land army. The U.S. and its NATO allies have responded by using the nuclear threat as a "great equalizer." Consequently, as suggested above, if war occurs, the U.S. would be forced to decide relatively early whether to withdraw or use nuclear weapons. Following the Soviet invasion of Afghanistan in 1979 the U.S. implicitly threatened nuclear war if the Soviet Union were to push into the Persian Gulf.

General Bernard Rogers, commander of NATO forces, laments the fact that because of the relative weakness of Western non-nuclear forces, NATO would be forced to the early use of nuclear weapons in the event of war; and Western Europe is the area of the world where the West is best prepared to defend itself against Soviet attack without employing nuclear weapons. As General Rogers has observed:

> because of the failure to meet commitments in the conventional area..., we have mortgaged our defense to the nuclear response.

And;

> it is not being able to fight more than X number of days that has put us into the position of having to ask for the release of nuclear weapons fairly quickly.[2]

General Rogers summarized the essential problem of relying upon nuclear deterrence to compensate for an inadequacy in real military capabilities: "The continually widening gap between NATO and Warsaw Pact conventional capabilities impacts the credibility of NATO's deterrence because it compels the alliance to rely excessively on the early first-use of nuclear weapons."[3]

The U.S. and its NATO allies have by and large not been willing to spend the money and human resources needed to build adequate non-nuclear defenses. Consequently, we continue to rely, to a large extent, upon the threat of nuclear first use to safeguard our vital interests. If deterrence fails, U.S. options will be extremely limited. Acceptable options are virtually nonexistent—accept defeat (and the loss of vital assets), or start a nuclear war that could not be in the U.S. interest.

Would the American president be willing to accept the defeat of American forces and Soviet occupation of an area of vital interest, or would the president actually be willing to start a nuclear war to try and halt an otherwise unstoppable Soviet conventional attack? Knowing that nuclear war could result in 100-160 million American casualties would be a powerful incentive for any president to disregard U.S. nuclear use guarantees and commitments if provoked by the Soviet Union. Although the outbreak of nuclear war described above may seem unbelievable, it does illustrate the incredible risk the United States accepts by its continuing heavy reliance upon a nuclear threat to protect vital interests around the globe.

Until very recently American presidents reportedly endorsed this reliance upon the nuclear threat, despite the risk to the American people, and perhaps the entire world. Then on March 23, 1983, President Reagan delivered a televised speech to the nation in which he questioned the very basis of the U.S. nuclear deterrence policy. He asked:

> Would it not be better to save lives than to avenge them? Are we not capable of demonstrating our peaceful intentions by applying all our abilities and our ingenuity to achieving a truly lasting stability? I think we are—indeed we must.

> After careful consultation with my advisers, including the Joint Chiefs of Staff, I believe there is a way....It is that we embark on a program to counter the awesome Soviet missile threat with measures that are defensive. Let us turn to the very strengths in technology that spawned our great industrial base....I know this is a formidable technical task, one that may not be accomplished before the end of the century. Yet, current technology has attained a level of sophistication where it is reasonable for us to begin this effort.

That speech resulted in the Reagan administration's Strategic Defense Initiative, generally known as the "SDI." The program was immediately labeled "Star Wars" by its critics; the name stuck and is now the media title for the President's initiative. Labels aside, the program is intended to answer many questions surrounding the concept of defending against nuclear attack. Is technology capable of an effective defense, even against large-scale nuclear attack? Would such a defensive coverage be affordable? How would our defenses affect U.S. - Soviet relations? The SDI is the most serious attempt by the U.S. government to answer those questions in two decades.

Although the label "Star Wars" encourages visions of laser cannons and starfighters, we are a long way from the type of weapon systems brought to us via Hollywood imaginations. In any case, before a decision is made to build defenses against nuclear weapons, the hard questions of effectiveness and cost must be addressed. Otherwise, it would be akin to taking a cruise in a ship that no one is sure will float, and without knowing what the ticket will cost. The ship could float, even cruise, but the ticket may be too expensive; or worse yet, the ticket could be horribly expensive, and the ship would sink anyway. If we have little idea of how effective defenses against nuclear weapons might be, or how much they might cost, then a responsible decision on whether to build them cannot be made.

Ever since President Reagan introduced the SDI, it has been controversial. American and Soviet newspapers have been filled with commentaries. Community forums and television documentaries ask (more often instruct): is the SDI defensive or provocative, "stabilizing" or "destabilizing," clever or foolish, right or wrong? Whatever the SDI is, everybody is interested. Such interest is not surprising."Star Wars" addresses the key concern of our time—the fear of nuclear holocaust. The possibility of defending against nuclear weapons is so attractive that any suggestion to that end strikes a deep-felt response in Americans. Indeed, in numerous national opinion surveys, before and after President Reagan's March 23 speech, Americans overwhelmingly favored the idea of strategic defense.

This book is an assessment of the SDI: what it is; where it came from; why it is here now; where it is going; and how it might affect U.S. -Soviet relations. The SDI may result in nothing but disappointment, or it may remove the greatest threat of our time...or perhaps it will lead to something in between. This book is intended to facilitate an understanding of what the SDI is and is not, and the important debate that it has initiated.

ENDNOTES

1. The basis for this attack scenario is, Office of Technology Assessment, *The Effects of Nuclear War* (Washington, D.C.: USGPO, May 1979), pp. 64-75.
2. See, respectively, George Wilson, "Nunn To Broaden Debate on NATO By Arguing War Plans Are Flawed," *Washington Post*, Feb. 21, 1985, p. 8; and, William Beecher, "General Outlines Plan to Avert Nuclear War," *Boston Globe*, Dec. 16, 1984, p. 26.
3. Quoted in *Soviet Aerospace*, Vol. 43, No. 8 (March 11, 1985), p. 59.

TWO
Chapter 2

THE SDI: IS IT "STAR WARS"?

P resident Reagan's "Star Wars" speech of March 23, 1983 seemed clear and straightforward. Following the speech, however, numerous interpretations emerged concerning what the president "really meant." One of the recurring criticisms of the SDI is that the Reagan administration has been ambiguous about its purpose. For example, almost two years after the president's "Star Wars" speech Les Aspin (D-Wisconsin), the chairman of the House Armed Services Committee, criticized the administration concerning the ambiguity of the SDI's purpose. Congressman Aspin (no stranger to military issues) said,

> Here are some of the questions I hear from my colleagues as well as some of my own. One question is: where are we going with the SDI? The Administration says at various times that it is an R&D program, that it is a population defense system to replace deterrence. Which is it? And, if we don't know now, how will we determine the answer and when will we get it?[1]

In fact, there has been a great deal of misunderstanding about the SDI. Much of the commentary following President Reagan's speech implied that the president had called for the immediate deployment of "death rays in the heavens." But note the primary focus of President Reagan's now-famous "Star Wars" speech:

> I call upon the scientific community in our country, those who

gave us nuclear weapons, to turn their great talents now to the cause of mankind and world peace, to give us the means of rendering these nuclear weapons impotent and obsolete.[2]

This focus was repeated at the inaugural address on January 21, 1985, when the president said, "I have approved a research program, to find, if we can, a security shield that will destroy nuclear missiles before they reach their target. It wouldn't kill people; it would destroy weapons. It wouldn't militarize space; it would help to demilitarize the arsenals of Earth."

The president called upon the scientific community to examine the feasibility of defenses against nuclear weapons. That may not seem like such a radical idea—poll data suggest that most Americans think the United States already is defended against nuclear attack and are concerned when informed of the truth (see Appendix, Tables 1-4)—but it should be recalled that for nearly twenty years established wisdom ordained that defenses against nuclear weapons were infeasible, and probably undesirable. The president did not claim in his "Star Wars" speech that this wisdom was necessarily wrong, or that effective defenses of any type were now possible. Nor was the speech a call to deploy defensive arms. Rather, the speech reflected a profound dissatisfaction with the continuing nuclear threat, and, in consequence, directed the technical and scientific communities to explore an alternative—a defensive solution to the nuclear problem.

As with most challenges to conventional wisdom, the president's speech was met with a great deal of skepticism and criticism, even ridicule. It was suggested, repeatedly, that the president was foisting a cruel hoax upon the American people—a fantasy of security behind a defensive shield. Although no defensive system of any type was mentioned, the president's "vision" of defenses against nuclear arms was attacked immediately as a proposal to place "death rays in the heavens." Where the defenses might be based—on Earth, in the air, or in space—was never even suggested. Nor did the president mention whether defenses might use interceptor rockets, or exotic laser and particle beams to intercept an enemy's nuclear attack. Nevertheless, much of the initial derogatory labeling of "Star Wars" centered around "Death Stars" and "Darth Vader"

BMD = Ballistic Missile Defense
ICBM = Intercontinental Ballistic Missile
Def

was meant to discredit the program by making it seem fanciful, even silly. The label stuck and may have had some of its intended effect of discouraging public support for the program.[3] On the other hand, most Americans enjoyed the movie *Star Wars*, believe that the Soviet Union is indeed an "Evil Empire," and, according to recent poll data, believe that American technology can make defense against nuclear weapons possible (See Appendix, Table 5).

In short, what the president called for was a bold new effort by the scientific community to examine the feasibility of using defensive forces to remove the threat of nuclear ballistic missiles. The speech noted that such a task would be extremely difficult, and could take decades to achieve; but it reflected a basic optimism about the capacity of U.S. science to handle any technological problem. The March 23 speech was the initial critical step in what came to be known as the "Star Wars" program—the Strategic Defense Initiative (SDI).

Following his speech, the president directed two studies to be conducted—one to examine the technology necessary for ballistic missile defense (BMD), the other to assess the strategic and arms control policy implications of BMD. These classified studies were conducted from June through October 1983.

The technology study, called the Defensive Technologies Study, was conducted by over fifty scientists and engineers, and called on the technical aid of hundreds of individuals from academia and industry. The Defensive Technologies Study team was led by Dr. James Fletcher, former head of the National Aeronautics and Space Administration (NASA). An assessment of BMD policy implications was conducted under the auspices of the Future Security Strategy Study. It was led by Fred Hoffman, who is director of Pan Heuristics, a policy "think tank" based in Los Angeles. The conclusion of the policy study was that strategic defenses, even if less than perfect, could still help stabilize the U.S.-Soviet relationship.

The conclusions of the Defensive Technologies Study set the basis for the SDI program. The study concluded that "powerful new technologies are becoming available that justify a major technological development effort offering future technological options to implement a defensive strategy."[4] The study team outlined a long-term technology approach for BMD on a scale similar to that of the Apollo lunar-landings program.

It recommended a long-term research and development plan to evaluate and demonstrate the feasibility of key BMD technologies. The outcome of that research would in turn facilitate informed decisions on whether engineering, and later deployment, of effective BMD systems would be feasible. The Defensive Technologies Study Team also concluded that the most effective systems for BMD would use multiple layers, or tiers, and that a strong central management was needed to focus the development of technology for a comprehensive BMD capability.

The notion of multiple layers or tiers of defenses can be understood by thinking of an artichoke that has layer upon layer protecting the vulnerable center. Just so, a multitiered defense would use layer upon layer of defenses to intercept attacking missiles at various points along the missile's trajectory. Multiple layers would allow each tier to be less than perfect and still be useful. That is, if the first or second tier of defense fails to perform flawlessly, a third, fourth, or fifth tier would still have an opportunity to intercept the nuclear weapons that had penetrated the initial layers.

Following the Defensive Technologies Study's recommendation for a strong central management, the U.S. structured a focused research and technology program to pursue the new technologies concepts emphasized by the study. The program established by the Department of Defense continued the work of the technologies and policy studies and combined previously planned R&D into a single Strategic Defense Initiative. On January 6, 1984, the president reportedly signed National Security Decision Directive-119, authorizing a national research program to assess and demonstrate the technological feasibility of intercepting attacking nuclear missiles.

There was some difference in the emphasis of the policy and technology studies. The technology study apparently stressed the need for futuristic defenses, such as beam weapons located in space, to achieve a comprehensive defense capability, which would destroy all but .025 percent of attacking ballistic missile warheads (i.e., one in 5,000). The policy study reportedly emphasized the role that less effective "intermediate" defenses could play in stabilizing U.S.-Soviet relations. The difference concerned whether near-term BMD technology, which could provide only limited coverage, should be emphasized, or long-term "exotic" defenses, which might provide a comprehensive defense capability.]

The friction between long-term and near-term defense objectives, reportedly reflected in the Fletcher and Hoffman reports, has been obvious in various seemingly inconsistent statements made by administration officials concerning the SDI. For example, immediately after the president's March 23 speech, Secretary of Defense Weinberger clarified the goal of the SDI:

> The defensive systems the president is talking about are not designed to be partial. What we want to try to get is a system which will develop a defense that is thoroughly reliable and total.

> I don't see any reason why that can't be done.[5]

Yet months later statements by administration officials concerning the objective of the SDI began to focus increasingly upon intermediate goals involving limited defense objectives. Officials suggested that strategic defense during the 1990s could be used to protect the U.S. retaliatory deterrent capability (and ICBMs in particular) and that later, as the technology matured, the defense would include cities.[6] While acknowledging the possibility of intermediate objectives, Secretary of Defense Weinberger kept the focus on the long-term objective:

> What is being said is that as you proceed along that road [i.e., to strategic defense] there will be various steps that you attain, one after the other. And what some people are now saying is we can put in a transitional phase some of those additional protection steps. Some could protect cities, some could protect missile sites. But the goal is not that, the goal is to destroy missiles."[7]

President Reagan continued to endorse his long-term "vision" by saying: "It's [i.e., strategic defense] not going to protect missiles, it's going to destroy missiles."[8] Elsewhere he stated that the SDI "is not, and should never be misconstrued as, just another method of protecting missile silos."[9] Secretary Weinberger noted that "point defense [i.e., a partial defense for military forces] is not what the strategic defense initiative is all

21

about." Rather, the goal is a "thoroughly reliable, non-nuclear" defense that could "protect the entire nation and Europe."[10] Weinberger seemed to clarify the administration's preference concerning defensive objectives (that is, do we focus upon trying to protect retaliatory deterrent forces such as missiles, or do we focus upon the defense of cities?) by concluding:

> ...we would not want to let our efforts toward a transitional defense [i.e., limited defenses] exhaust our energies or dilute our efforts to secure a thoroughly reliable, layered defense that would destroy incoming Soviet missiles at all phases of their flight....It would not raise the question of whether we were trying to defend missiles or cities. We would be attempting to destroy Soviet missiles by non-nuclear means before Soviet missiles could approach any targets in the United States or the territory of our allies. The choice, therefore, is not one of defending people or weapons.[11]

Interestingly, prior to the March 23 "Star Wars" speech, both the president and Secretary of Defense Weinberger had talked of BMD in terms of its promise for defending ICBMs. Most recently, National Security Decision Directive 172 (NSDD 172), released May 30, 1985, reportedly is said to endorse the notion of a comprehensive defense as a long-term prospect. It also reportedly emphasizes the need to maintain deterrence during the interim period and addresses the potential role of BMD in protecting U.S. retaliatory forces from Soviet attack.[12]

The seeming inconsistency in administration statements concerning the objectives of strategic defense is more apparent than real—the difference being how far into the future one looks. Obviously, a "thoroughly reliable and total" defense cannot be available immediately; perhaps it will never be available. But it remains the overall, long-term goal...if the SDI proves that the technology is feasible. However, there are less demanding but still important objectives that could be achieved in the near future. Defending certain U.S. military facilities would be just such an objective. Why that "intermediate" objective may or may not be a good idea is considered in chapters five and six. It is sufficient to note here that there is no necessary inconsistency between an intermediate goal of partial defenses for strategic retaliatory forces, and a long-term goal of rendering nuclear weapons obsolescent. Indeed, whether defenses are initially intended to protect military and/or civilian targets, *both* types of protection would be critical to the eventual obsolescence of nuclear weapons.

It is likely that the administration has continued to talk of the long-term objective of defending people and cities for two reasons. First, it is reasonable to maintain a long-range goal if that goal is important enough, even though it is unclear whether it can ever be achieved. Given that the long-term objective of the SDI could literally make the difference between the extinction or preservation of human life on Earth, it is, surely, more important than any other pursuit. We hold many long-term objectives, to which we devote time, energy, and money even though we do not know whether they will ever be fully realized. For example, even though a reliable cure for the different types of cancer is not around the corner, the goal is so important that it is reasonable to pursue the cure or cures. Every "intermediate" success that reduces the death rate by some modest percentage is welcome. Similarly, the defense "cure" to the nuclear threat may be very distant, perhaps impossible; nevertheless, the goal is so important that research to that end is reasonable and partial steps welcome.

There probably is a second, more political reason why the administration continues to focus upon the long-term, though uncertain, goal of the SDI. The support of the American people for the government to defend them in the event of war is very high. We generally approve of the idea of survival, and if there is a war we would prefer to be defended. Almost all national opinion polls have indicated that approximately 75 percent to 85 percent of the population supports the concept of protection against nuclear attack with "Star Wars" weapons. (See for example Appendix, Tables 6-12; for an exception see Appendix, Tables 13, 14.) Indeed, self-identified Democrats, Republicans, and Independent voters support strategic defense as a concept with almost equally strong enthusiasm. (See Appendix, Tables 15, 16.) Even under less than ideal conditions public support for strategic defense remains high. (See Appendix, Tables 17-22.)

Consequently, the Reagan administration may not want to dilute the basis of popular support for "Star Wars" by focusing too much on the defense of military targets, though some national opinion poll data suggest the public would support the defense of military forces as well.

But the administration's commitment to the long-term objective of defending people certainly is not limited to rhetoric. The budget for the SDI requested by the administration appears to place great importance, in terms of research dollars, on the more futuristic defensive weapons. Indeed, some proponents of intermediate defense objectives have complained that the administration has done so at the expense of "more realistic" near-term systems of limited effectiveness.

The SDI research program was appropriated approximately $1.4 billion for fiscal year 1985; the administration has requested $3.7 billion for fiscal year 1986, which it almost certainly will not receive in full from Congress. The majority of the money will go toward research and development of the more advanced technologies to provide, if successful, very effective defenses. The total expected budget requests for the SDI between 1985 and 1989 is expected to amount to approximately $26 billion. It should be noted that those dollars are for research on defensive technologies and will not support the deployment of any forces. For fiscal year 1986 the budget request of $3.7 billion is broken down along the following lines:

	Fiscal Year 1986 Request
Sensors	$1,386 million
Directed Energy	966
Kinetic Energy	860
System Analysis and Battle Management	243
Survivability, Lethality, Space Power and Logistics	258
Management	9
TOTAL	$3,722

The amount of money envisioned for the SDI obviously is large anyway one looks at it. But even $26 billion should be put into context. Over a five-year period it averages to about $5 billion per year, or less than 2 percent of the current defense budget. By way of comparison, Americans spent over $53 billion on alcoholic beverages and over $30 billion on tobacco in 1984 alone, which totals to over $410 billion over a five-year period. Put another way, the money requested to investigate the capability to defend against nuclear weapons, averaged over a five-year period, will amount to about one-sixteenth of what Americans spent on tobacco and alcohol in 1984.

Surprisingly, too, the level of SDI funding that has caused so much controversy is not extraordinarily higher than would have been spent on research into defense technologies had the *somewhat* president never initiated his strategic defense program. The *a few billion dollars* Departments of Defense and Energy would have requested $15- *dollars* 18 billion, in any case, for R&D on some of the relevant new *here or there?* technologies.

Numerous cost estimates have been offered for strategic defenses. According to some estimates, deployment of a par- tially effective defense—one that could be available in the 1990s and would intercept 90 percent of attacking Soviet nuclear warheads—would cost about $60 billion. Other estimates for a partial system range between $60 and $90 billion; and es- timates for a complete defensive "architecture" using space- based lasers run as high as $500 billion.[13] What has been done differently under the "Star Wars" program, in addi- tion to the increment of R&D spending, is the uniting of various on-going research programs under a single umbrella organization—the Strategic Defense Initiative Organization— which began its difficult task in April 1984, headed by General James Abrahamson. General Abrahamson was a logical choice. He is personable, has a degree from MIT, a masters degree in Aeronautical Engineering, and a history of successfully direct- ing large important programs, including the Space Shuttle and F-16 fighter aircraft programs.

What is the SDI all about? Is it "just" research and develop- ment? Is it for the purpose of defending the American people or U.S. military forces? In a strict sense, the Reagan administra- tion's SDI program is "just" research and development; there is little if any possibility that any such defensive weapons will be deployed during the tenure of Ronald Reagan. What his administration can do is start the basic research and develop- ment necessary to permit a future president and Congress— possibly in the early 1990s—to make an informed decision con- cerning whether or not to deploy defenses. The SDI should help answer such questions as: are defenses against the Soviet nuclear threat feasible, and if so, how effective would they be, and how much would they cost to deploy and maintain? At the same time the administration must choose which types of BMD technology to emphasize and where the bulk of SDI dollars should go—toward the research of futuristic multilayered concepts with possible high levels of effectiveness, or toward systems probably less effective, but available sooner and adequate for defending military forces. The priorities of the research and development budget will reflect the ascendancy of one goal over the other. Consequently, in putting together the SDI research and development program, the administration must posit some goals—such research and development on BMD technology cannot take place in a vacuum of purpose.

In short, the SDI is, in a sense, "simply" a research and development program. But it includes some mid- and long-term goals—to defend U.S. military forces and provide more comprehensive protection for the American people. To note that the SDI so far is just research and development is not to downplay the major change in thinking that the president's speech initiated. Before the Reagan administration reopened the issue of deploying strategic defenses for the American people the subject was virtually closed; the established wisdom had been against BMD deployment for over a decade. Following the March 23, 1983 speech, strategic defense and the potential for BMD became respectable subjects once again. The SDI research and development requested by the president may provide the answers necessary for a future administration and Congress to make a reasoned, informed decision about whether the United States should spend the needed money to protect the American homeland from nuclear attack.

ENDNOTES

1. Quoted in *Aerospace Daily*, Jan. 22, 1985, p. 111.
2. For the text of the speech see, "A Decision Which Offers a New Hope for Our Children," *Washington Post*, March 24, 1983, p. A12.
3. The level of popular support reportedly decreases considerably when the label "Star Wars" is used to describe the program. See "The High Frontier," *Washington Times*, June 25, 1985, p. 3-A.
4. U.S. Department of Defense, *The Strategic Defense Initiative, Defensive Technologies Study* (March 1984), p. 4.

5. Charles Corddry, "Weinberger Says Total Defense is Sought for U.S.," *Baltimore Sun*, March 28, 1983, p. 1.
6. See Bill Keller, "Pentagon Aid Calls Antimissile Plan Central to Military Outlook," *New York Times*, Feb. 22, 1985, p. 15; and William Broad, "Reduced Goal Set On Reagan's Plan for Space Defense," *New York Times*, Dec. 23, 1984, p. 1.
7. Bernard Gwertzman, " 'Star Wars' Is Not a Bargaining Chip, U.S. Says," *New York Times*, Dec. 24, 1984, p. 7.
8. Ibid.
9. David Hoffman, "Reagan Seeks to Link SDI, Missile Cutbacks," *Washington Post*, March 30, 1985, p. A-13.
10. Quoted in Charles Mohr, "Capital Hill Gets A War Plea On MX," *New York Times*, March 14, 1985, p. A-8.
11. Caspar Weinberger, *Annual Report to Congress Fiscal Year 1986* (Washington, DC: USGPO, Feb. 4, 1985), p. 55.
12. Reported in Jim Klurfeld, "Star Wars Plan Is Modified," *Long Island Newsday*, June 14, 1985, p. 5.
13. See, respectively, Zbigniew Brzezinski, Robert Jastrow, Max Kampelman, "Defense In Space Is Not 'Star Wars'," *New York Times Magazine*, Jan. 27, 1985, p. 29; Pat Friel, "An Exchange on BMD Technology," *Comparative Strategy*, Vol. 5, No. 2 (1985), p. 216; *Defense Daily*, Nov. 29, 1983, p. 137; and *Soviet Aerospace*, October 18, 1983, p. 43.

THREE

Chapter 3

MUTUAL VULNERABILITY = "HOSTAGES FOR PEACE"?

T he SDI, even as "just" a research program, challenges conventional wisdom in the United States concerning deterrence and nuclear strategy. That, of course, is why the SDI has generated so much controversy.

THE MUTUAL VULNERABILITY
APPROACH TO DETERRENCE

The traditional U.S. understanding of nuclear deterrence policy (challenged by the SDI) is based on the assumption that effective defenses against nuclear attack are impossible,[1] and that there is little point in spending money in a futile attempt to reduce vulnerability. Strange as it may seem, this constitutes the basic starting point for U.S. established thought regarding deterrence and arms control.

In the area of deterrence policy, our presumed unalterable vulnerability to nuclear attack has been turned into a type of blessing. The logic is quite simple: if both sides are vulnerable to nuclear attack, then neither will be willing to engage in such behavior as might lead to nuclear war. Mutual vulnerability came to be seen in the United States as the guarantee of "stability" in U.S.-Soviet strategic relations. As long as the U.S. could retaliate against the Soviet Union with "catastrophic consequences," the Soviet Union would never strike first, since to do so would be suicidal. Similarly, as long as the Soviet Union was confident that it could retaliate against a vulnerable

United States, it would not be overly concerned about a U.S. first strike. From this basic reasoning emerged the approach to deterrence called "mutual assured destruction."

There were few requirements, demanded by this mutual vulnerability approach to deterrence—indeed, part of its attraction is its simplicity. The United States would have only to maintain a nuclear retaliatory threat, a so-called "strike-back" or "second strike" capability, to ensure deterrence stability. The offensive force requirements of mutual vulnerability were endorsed specifically by Secretary of Defense McNamara. During the early 1960s Robert S. McNamara did not talk in terms of mutual vulnerability; but by 1964 Soviet strategic forces were increasing and McNamara apparently concluded that attempting to limit damage from a nuclear attack was no longer useful.[2] In 1965 Secretary McNamara stated publicly that defense against nuclear attack had become a secondary objective; the primary objective of U.S. strategic forces was now deterrence, based upon a "second strike" capability which could inflict "intolerable" punishment on the Soviet Union.[3] McNamara defined the offensive capability necessary to support such a threat: the capacity to retaliate and destroy one-fifth to one-fourth of the Soviet population and one-half of Soviet industry.

Those who viewed mutual vulnerability as "stabilizing" reasoned that a capability to destroy Soviet strategic forces before they could be used, or developing an adequate defense of the American homeland, would be "destabilizing." If, the reasoning continued, the Soviet Union believed that its deterrent was threatened by a U.S. defensive capability, then the Soviet Union might consider a first strike in a crisis lest the United States use its nuclear weapons first.

For example, if the combination of U.S. defensive and offensive forces gave the United States the capability to strike first, destroy many Soviet nuclear forces, and defend itself against the "surviving" nuclear weapons, then the U.S. president might have an incentive to strike first. Under such conditions, the Soviet Union, fearing a U.S. first strike in an acute military crisis, might decide to strike first in order to beat the United States to the punch. An opponent's "first strike" threat was considered a cause of "instability" in U.S.-Soviet strategic relations. This instability would be minimized as long as each side could be confident of its ability to retaliate effectively. In short, mutual vulnerability came to be seen as the basic ingredient for deterrence stability. As Secretary of Defense Harold Brown observed in 1979:

> In the interests of stability, we avoid the capability of eliminating the other side's deterrent, insofar as we might be able to do so. In short, we must be quite willing—as we have been for some time—to accept the principle of mutual deterrence, and design our defense posture in light of that principle.[4]

As a consequence, strategic programs which threatened to destroy the opponent's nuclear retaliatory capability, or defend against that capability, came to be regarded as "destabilizing" because they might call into question the vulnerability upon which stability was thought to be based. Stability and mutual vulnerability became synonymous; anything that might upset vulnerability became inconsistent with deterrence and stability. Thus, programs that might defend the United States from nuclear attack were considered undesirable because they might prove "destabilizing." Commenting on this approach to deterrence, Henry Kissinger lamented that during the 1960s,

> the historically amazing theory developed that vulnerability contributed to peace and invulnerability contributed to risks of war.

> Such a theory could develop and be widely accepted only in a country that had never addressed the problem of the balance of power as a historical phenomenon. And, if I may say so, only also on a continent that was looking for any excuse to avoid analysis of the perils it was facing and that was looking for an easy way out.[5]

Ironically, under such a view of deterrence, strategic forces are to be protected from nuclear attack, but people are not. In effect, the mutual vulnerability theory is based upon the assumption, as one of its proponents put it, that the "populations of both countries are hostages for peace."[6] Amazing as it may seem, this view dominated declared U.S. policy from the early 1960s until the mid-1970s, and American strategic programs were defined as "stabilizing" or "destabilizing," depending upon whether they continued a condition of mutual vulnerability or threatened that condition.

Ballistic missile defense (BMD) intended to protect people obviously violates the mutual vulnerability concept of deterrence. Indeed, defending the American homeland against nuclear ballistic missiles is considered destabilizing precisely because it might weaken the Soviet deterrent threat. With this understood, it should not come as a surprise, given the mutual vulnerability orientation of many of the academic and media commentators, that the president's March 23, 1983 speech calling for accelerated BMD research was criticized as inconsistent with deterrence. The SDI represents a challenge to the notion that mutual vulnerability is an unavoidable but useful condition. It suggests, rather, that if vulnerability can be reduced or eliminated, the United States should proceed full steam ahead.

Vulnerability, it is believed, also serves the interest of America's NATO allies. The prospect that a Soviet attack on Western Europe might "escalate" to general nuclear war, with catastrophic consequences for the Soviet Union as well as the United States, was considered to be grim enough to keep the Soviets from either a conventional or a nuclear attack against NATO. The capability to threaten the Soviet Union with strategic nuclear forces is thought to permit the U.S. to "extend deterrence" coverage to its NATO allies.

The mutual vulnerability concept of deterrence, although certainly never entirely the basis for U.S. nuclear strategy, has had a profound impact upon U.S. strategic programs. For example, Donald Hornig, science adviser to Presidents Eisenhower, Kennedy, and Johnson, suggested that a primary reason for the U.S. refusal to proceed with the Nike-X BMD program of the mid-1960s was that:

> To the extent that [Nike-X] might threaten to be effective against a Soviet second strike, it would be provocative by suggesting we were aiming at a first strike capability. It would therefore put a premium on a Soviet first strike in the event of a tense international situation.[7]

Similarly, David Packard, as deputy secretary of Defense, observed that the United States decided against the Sentinel BMD program of the late 1960s, in part,

> because if we deployed this system around our cities....you

give the impression that you are trying to build up a first strike capability, and in my view you reduce your deterrence.[8]

According to Secretary of Defense Laird, the U.S. BMD program of the early 1970s (also canceled) consciously envisaged placing interceptor batteries at remote distances from urban centers to demonstrate to the Soviet Union that the United States would not defend its cities, "to show plainly that we do not threaten their deterrent."[9] As Henry Kissinger observed in 1979:

> When the administration with which I was connected sought to implement an anti-ballistic missile program inherited from our predecessors, it became the subject of the most violent attacks from the theory that it was destabilizing, provocative, and an obstacle to arms control...because opponents of BMD saw in the strategic vulnerability of the United States a positive asset.[10]

This sort of criticism of BMD—that defense is inconsistent with deterrence—is also often used to criticize the SDI.

The mutual vulnerability notion of deterrence affected other U.S. programs for strategic defense. The United States virtually eliminated other types of strategic defense during the 1960s and 1970s, notably defenses against Soviet bombers. For example, the number of U.S. interceptor aircraft plummeted from 1,200 in 1966 to the current force of under 300; by 1975 the U.S. had deactivated the last of its 135 antibomber surface-to-air-missile (SAM) batteries. Since these reductions, the Soviet Union has begun to increase its long-range bomber threat to America.

In the area of offensive forces, the United States has avoided giving its ICBMs a significant capability to destroy Soviet ICBM silos for fear that the Soviet Union might be concerned over its ability to retaliate effectively should there be a U.S. strike. Indeed, one of the most influential arguments, most often repeated, against deployment of the new U.S. MX ICBM is that the MX would threaten Soviet ICBMs and therefore be "destabilizing."[11]

Despite the general influence of the mutual vulnerability notion of deterrence, official policy, even prior to President Reagan's March 23, 1983, speech, had given rhetorical support to the goal reducing America's vulnerability to nuclear attack.

For example, the Carter administration's Presidential Directive-41 (PD-41, September 1978) directed the U.S. civil defense program to "...enhance the survivability of the American people and its leadership in the event of nuclear war."[12] A later National Security Decision Directive of the Reagan administration reportedly states that

> ...it is a matter of national priority that the United States have a civil defense program which provides for the survival of the U.S. population in the event that a nuclear war were to be thrust upon the United States.[13]

But despite such "pre-SDI" rhetoric about strategic defense, neither the Carter nor the Reagan administrations followed through with civil defense programs that could live up to their declared objectives. Consequently, when President Reagan rejected the condition of vulnerability and called for a serious national effort to investigate the feasibility of rendering strategic missiles "obsolete," it was properly labeled as a first step in reorienting American strategic thought. Where conventional wisdom claimed that vulnerability to nuclear attack was inevitable, and that deterrence based on mutual vulnerability was "stabilizing," President Reagan suggested in his speech that condoning one's vulnerability and threatening nuclear retaliation as the means of preserving security was dangerous and immoral. He suggested that a defensive alternative would be superior. The president, in short, threatened to turn the established strategic dogma on its head. The SDI called into question concepts of strategic "stability" that had dominated the field since the mid-1960s. And public opinion, it was soon apparent, enthusiastically supported the president. (See Appendix, Table 23.)

MUTUAL VULNERABILITY AND ARMS CONTROL

The SDI called into question not only the established policy concerning deterrence and stability, it also challenged a great deal of previous U.S. strategic arms control policy, because the mutual vulnerability approach to strategic stability had been a basis for arms control policy since the beginning of the SALT I negotiations in 1969.[14] Rightly or wrongly, many believed that mutual vulnerability was the best available method of preserving stability. Arms control was therefore used as a means of facilitating that stabilizing condition of mutual vulnerability.

For example, the Anti-Ballistic Missile (ABM) Treaty, signed as a part of SALT I (as signed in 1972 and amended in 1974), prohibits U.S. or Soviet deployment of more than 100 BMD interceptors. Such strict restrictions on BMD were sought, in large part, to facilitate a continuing condition of mutual vulnerability and thereby promote the conventional understanding of "stability."[15] A strict limitation on capabilities to intercept strategic ballistic missiles obviously is consistent with an understanding of deterrence that equates stability and the condition of mutual vulnerability. In the case of the United States, the mutual vulnerability approach to stability contributed significantly to the desire for an ABM Treaty.

Mutual vulnerability deterrence also shaped U.S. objectives in the area of offensive force limitations. The general objective at SALT I was not to reduce offensive weapons so as to protect people against nuclear attack—the U.S. could not hope to reduce the number of Soviet strategic nuclear weapons enough to protect American cities, people, and industry, since the Soviet Union possessed far too many weapons already. Rather, a more modest objective, mandated by the mutual vulnerability approach to deterrence, was to reduce the Soviet offensive first-strike threat to U.S. retaliatory forces by placing limitations on the capacity of Soviet ICBMs to target U.S. ICBMs. The purpose of this objective, of course, was to help ensure that vulnerability remained mutual—that the Soviet Union could not destroy U.S. retaliatory forces in a first strike. The U.S. specifically stated that the purpose of further SALT negotiations would be to reduce offensive first-strike capabilities in order to preserve strategic retaliatory capabilities.[16]

It is clear from U.S. SALT I objectives, both in the area of offensive and defensive limitations, that American arms control objectives were entirely compatible with the mutual vulnerability approach to stability: defenses against nuclear weapons should be limited so as to preserve unquestioned mutual vulnerability, and offensive first strike capabilities should be limited so as to ensure the "survivability" of retaliatory capabilities. Incredible as it seems, strategic arms control has been viewed in the United States in part, as a mechanism for ensuring the vulnerability of the United States and the Soviet Union to nuclear attack. This hard-to-believe fact is reflected in a remark by Dr. Herbert Scoville, the president of the Arms Control Association and former assistant director of the Arms Control and Disarmament Agency: "Star wars will put an end to any hope for progress in arms control. It will also destroy the best arms control agreement we have, the ABM Treaty, which by forbidding defense ensures that every retaliatory warhead is able to reach its target."[17] In the bizarre logic of the mutual vulnerability approach to deterrence, arms control became a means by which to ensure continuing vulnerability to nuclear attack.

Just as the SDI challenges the mutual vulnerability orientation of U.S. deterrence policy, so also it challenges the mutual vulnerability orientation of U.S. strategic arms control policy. The president could have done little more to call into question established wisdom about deterrence and arms control than to mandate the SDI.

WHY THE SDI?

Why did the president decide to pose such a direct challenge to conventional wisdom about arms control and strategic relations? Obviously, an endorsement of strategic defense—given traditional views concerning mutual vulnerability—would be controversial.

It is difficult to piece together the exact sequence of events that led to the president's SDI, or to know the true importance played by particular individuals in his decision. What is clear is that the SDI is an example of a president leading the bureaucracies and services—making policy—not being led by it or by the mindless creep of technology. The president appears to have made a direct decision and was not simply persuaded by clever advisers. Nevertheless, it appears that a number of converging influences and factors helped result in the March 23 speech.

Although several advisers appear to have played important roles in initiating the SDI proposal, it is clear that President Reagan was sympathetic to the notion of strategic defense long before the SDI speech. During his bid for the Republican presidential nomination in 1976, candidate Reagan voiced a hope to his military adviser, General Daniel Graham, of finding a way out of the "trap of deterrence based on mutual vulnerability."[18] He likened the U.S.-Soviet strategic relationship to two men aiming cocked pistols at each other— a prelude to catastrophe. During his 1980 presidential campaign, Ronald Reagan commented on a visit to NORAD (the North American attack warning center located inside Cheyenne Mountain, Colorado):

> NORAD is an amazing place—that's out in Colorado, you know, under the mountain there. They actually are tracking several thousand objects in space, meaning satellites of ours and everyone else's, even down to the point that they are tracking a glove lost by an astronaut that is still circling the earth up there. I think the thing that struck me was the irony that here, with this great technology of ours, we can do all of this yet we cannot stop any of the weapons that are coming at us. I don't think there's been a time in history when there wasn't a defense against some kind of thrust, even back in the old-fashioned days when we had coast artillery that would stop invading ships if they came.[19]

The seeds of the SDI clearly existed before Ronald Reagan became president. Indeed, his concern with the strategic relationship extends back at least to 1967, when as the new governor of California he visited the Lawrence Livermore weapons laboratory located in Livermore, California. He was the first governor to do so. According to Dr. Edward Teller, then director of the laboratory, Governor Reagan at that time revealed a concern for and understanding of strategic matters. Ronald Reagan's deep dissatisfaction with a deterrence policy based upon mutual vulnerability, and his faith that American technology could lead to a way out of mutual vulnerability, provided fertile ground for what came to be the SDI.

By the early 1980s, events were taking place that would increase the president's appreciation for a dramatic change in strategic policy. First, it had become overwhelmingly clear that the long-term trends in strategic offensive forces were running against the United States. Further, the public mood seemed to be moving in an increasingly "anti-nuclear" direction. The "nuclear freeze" movement was mounting significant grassroots support, including a draft of the American Catholic Bishop's Pastoral Letter on nuclear war that criticized U.S. offensive force programs and endorsed a freeze. The arms control negotiations in Geneva did not appear to offer great hope for a serious reversal of these distressing trends, nor did they provide a solution to the "trap of mutual vulnerability." Finally, several advisers and influential scientists suggested to the president that technology had advanced to the point where an effective BMD was a real possibility.

These factors combined to convince Ronald Reagan that the strategic dilemma could not be solved by continuing to travel along the same old path. That path—trying to compete with the Soviet Union in offensive arms to maintain the deterrent, while attempting to negotiate limits on the same arms—had only led to ever-increasing numbers of nuclear weapons and offered no hope of moving away from the mutual vulnerability "trap." But now a potential solution had appeared in the form of new technologies for defending against ballistic missiles —a potential solution to the unfavorable long-term trend in offensive forces, and a potential avenue leading away from mutual vulnerability. In presenting the SDI, the president also addressed the concern of the antinuclear movement, i.e., the threat of nuclear war. He was able to respond to the "freeze" and antinuclear groups in a new way—not just by explaining that the United States required new forces to maintain deterrence (an explanation that had become increasingly unpersuasive), but by proposing the possibility of countering the nuclear threat directly. It also responded to criticisms that the administration was somehow cavalier to the threat of nuclear war and offered a more hopeful vision than permanently relying upon mutual vulnerability to nuclear attack to preserve stability.

ADVISERS

One of the influential scientists who appears to have played a key role in the origin of the SDI is Dr. Edward Teller. Dr. Teller, one of America's most distinguished scientists, had for years been keenly interested in finding an effective counter to ballistic missiles. He opposed mutual vulnerability as "immoral," yet was a demanding critic of most

BMD concepts on grounds of infeasibility and/or ineffectiveness. However, new laser beam technology—reportedly tested successfully in 1980—persuaded Dr. Teller of the potential for effective defenses against ballistic missiles. Dr. Teller expressed the view, in March 1985, that with recent and expected advances, "defense can prevail—although I did not believe that until about five years ago."[20] According to Dr. Teller, since the potential for effective BMD now exists, the mutual vulnerability approach to deterrence has become both "immoral and not now necessary."[21]

Dr. Teller reportedly met with the president in September 1982 to present his views about the potential for defending against ballistic missiles. Following this meeting the president began asking scientific and technical advisers about the feasibility of BMD. Dr. Teller, a colleague from Lawrence Livermore Laboratory, Dr. Lowell Wood, and other influential scientists and aerospace experts had been meeting at the Heritage Foundation in Washington, D.C., since 1981 with members of President Reagan's "kitchen cabinet," to consider the future prospects for BMD. Members of this group also met with the president several times before the March 23, 1983 speech to discuss BMD.

One member of the group meeting at the Heritage Foundation was General Daniel Graham. Toward the end of the 1980 campaign, General Graham had become convinced that BMD deployed in space was both possible and the proper solution to the nuclear threat. He went to the Heritage Foundation for help in sponsoring a space defense study; the project began in January 1981 and led to the "High Frontier" study. General Graham spoke to both the president and Secretary of Defense Weinberger about the basic idea of space-based defense on separate occasions in early 1981.[22] General Graham, who describes himself as "the midwife, but not father" of the SDI, took the case for space-based defenses to the public—through books and extensive public lectures—with a resultant deluge of letters to the Pentagon concerning the "High Frontier." But General Graham personally delivered his High Frontier ideas to General John Vessey, who was to become chairman of the Joint Chiefs of Staff (JCS), and who, as General Graham commented, "was pretty positive from the very beginning." General Graham also briefed Admiral Watkins, the chief of Naval Operations and member of the JCS. Admiral Watkins was, in the general's words, "very supportive" of the idea of defending against ballistic missiles. Nevertheless, General Graham notes that between March 1982 and March 1983 he spent a great deal of time arguing with influential individuals in the Pentagon who opposed the "High Frontier" because they feared that it would draw funds away from their own budgets, or because it had originated from outside the Pentagon.

The JCS played an important role in the origins of the SDI; apparently no single presidential adviser or BMD advocate held so much sway as it did. On February 11, 1983 the President, Robert McFarlane (who became National Security Adviser eight months later), and the JCS met to discuss offensive force modernization. The discussion, however, moved toward strategic defenses, and when asked whether advances in defense technology were promising the JCS apparently responded unanimously and affirmatively. Evidently, Admiral Watkins played a key role in support of strategic defense during that discussion.

In commenting on this critical meeting, President Reagan has said:

> At one of my regular meetings with the [Joint] Chiefs of Staff, I brought up this subject about a defensive weapon....and I asked them, 'Is it possible in our modern technology of today that it would be worthwhile to see if we could not develop a weapon that could perhaps take out, as they left their silos, those nuclear missiles?'...And when they did not look aghast at the idea and instead said yes, they believed that such a thing offered a possibility and should be researched, I said, 'Go.'[23]

Then-Chairman of the JCS General John W. Vessey has stated that the JCS, although recognizing the technical uncertainties, did indeed endorse a new policy direction toward defense and away from dependence on the threat of nuclear retaliation.[24]

Robert McFarlane was present at the February JCS meeting; he apparently had consulted informally earlier with Admiral Watkins, who shared his moral distaste for a purely offensive-oriented deterrent. Following that JCS meeting, McFarlane helped draft the presidential endorsement for increased research into BMD. That endorsement was to be delivered during the president's next defense speech on March

23, 1983. The president's science adviser, Dr. George Keyworth (who was strongly endorsed by Dr. Teller for the position), reportedly helped in drafting the March 23 speech. That speech, which led to the Fletcher and Hoffman studies (as discussed in chapter two), came as a surprise to much of the Washington defense and foreign policy bureaucracy. In fact, it was not until mid-March that even some senior officials and advisers knew that the speech would contain the SDI proposal.

The idea of strategic defense was so inconsistent with the reigning wisdom that the SDI proposal almost certainly would not have survived the usual bureaucratic process. It is for this reason that the SDI is a good example of "top-down" leadership—the president leading the bureaucracies in the development of policy. It certainly appears that the president was predisposed toward strategic defense. Consequently, when advisers and influential scientists became convinced that BMD could work, the president agreed that research into defense technology should be pursued. Interestingly, in a recent interview, when asked about the origins of the SDI, the president responded, "It kind of amuses me that everybody is so sure I must have heard about it, that I never thought of it myself. The truth is I did..."[25]

The thought that technology had advanced to the point where effective BMD was a real possibility had also been presented to several key senators well before the president's speech. In 1979, four technical experts from aerospace industry joined in briefing various senators, including Senators Jackson, Warner, Garn, Hollings, Moynihan, and Wallop. Maxwell Hunter of the Lockheed Corporation was a member of this industrial "Gang of Four." Hunter, an expert on BMD systems, had worked on defensive technology going back to the Nike-Zeus program in 1961. The Gang of Four managed "almost by accident" to brief 10 percent of the Senate within a few days on the BMD potential of space-based lasers. Several of the senators were quite enthusiastic about the prospect for defending against ballistic missiles—especially Senator Wallop, who became a key proponent of BMD in Congress.[26] Consequently, by the time the president delivered his televised SDI proposal, there were some important figures on Capitol Hill ready to provide enthusiastic support.

SUMMARY AND CONCLUSION

In summary, President Reagan's SDI proposal challenges conventional wisdom regarding deterrence and stability. The U.S. approach to deterrence has centered on a condition of mutual vulnerability, and the capabilities for mutually assured destruction. Actual U.S. strategy never entirely followed mutual vulnerability reasoning—U.S. offensive forces have been targeted against Soviet military capabilities and not simply against cities and industry. Nevertheless, U.S. capabilities to defend against bomber attack were dismantled during the 1960s and 1970s, and U.S. BMD programs were rejected repeatedly and criticized throughout the 1960s and early 1970s, in large part on the grounds that attempting to reduce U.S. vulnerability would be destabilizing. In addition, U.S. offensive forces have been limited in their "counterforce" potential on the grounds that it is destabilizing to "threaten the Soviet deterrent."

U.S. strategic thought has been heavily influenced by the mutual vulnerability notion of deterrence, and U.S. strategic forces and arms control policy illustrate that influence. They have reflected two objectives: (1) not threatening the Soviet deterrent (i.e., the Soviet capability to destroy the United States); and, (2) maintaining a "second-strike" capability to threaten the Soviet Union with "intolerable damage."

The March 23, 1983 speech in which the president presented his SDI proposal challenged the shibboleth surrounding mutual vulnerability. Any suggestion that technology might offer a way out of the "mutual vulnerability trap" and that the United States ought to investigate such a possibility was sure to spark considerable controversy in a defense and foreign policy establishment that had become accustomed to the notion that mutual vulnerability means deterrence stability.

Nevertheless, Ronald Reagan appears to have hoped for a way out of the mutual vulnerability "trap" for many years. When influential scientists and advisers suggested to the president that the potential for effective BMD had arrived with recent technological advances, he said, "go." He appears to have acted very much from his own predisposition, which viewed mutual vulnerability as courting disaster. A combination of influences appears to have led President Reagan to make the SDI speech, and the gauntlet was flung at a policy that had dominated strategic thought for almost two decades.

ENDNOTES

1. For a relatively recent rendition of this view see Sidney Drell and Wolfgang Panofsky, "The Case Against Strategic Defense," *Issues in Science and Technology* (Fall 1984), pp. 45-65.
2. See U.S. Senate, *Statement of the Secretary of Defense, Robert S. McNamara, before the Senate Armed Services Committee and the Senate Subcommittee on Department of Defense Appropriations on the Fiscal Year 1965-1966 Defense Program and the 1965 Defense Budget* (Washington, D.C.: USGPO, Jan. 27, 1964), p. 31.
3. See U.S. Senate, Committee on Armed Services, Committee on Appropriations, Subcommittee on Department of Defense, *Hearings on Military Authorization and Defense Appropriations for Fiscal Year 1966*, 89th Cong., 1st sess. (Washington, D.C.: USGPO, Feb. 24, 1965), pp. 43-46.
4. Harold Brown, *Department of Defense Annual Report FY 1980* (Washington, D.C.: USGPO, Jan. 25, 1979), p. 61.
5. Henry Kissinger, "The Future of NATO," in *NATO The Next Thirty Years*, Kenneth Myers, ed. (Boulder, Colo.: Westview Press, 1980), p. 6.
6. Statement by Wolfgang Panofsky, in U.S. Senate, Committee on Foreign Relations, *Strategic Arms Limitation Agreements, Hearings*, 92nd Cong., 2nd sess. (Washington, D.C.: USGPO, 1972), p. 368.
7. See his testimony in U.S. Senate, Committee on Armed Services, *Authorization for Military Procurement, Research and Development, FY 1971, Hearings*, Part I, 91st Cong., 2nd sess. (Washington, D.C.: USGPO, 1970), p. 2296.
8. U.S. Senate, Committee on Foreign Relations, Subcommittee on International Organizations and Disarmament, *Strategic and Foreign Policy Implications of ABM Systems, Hearings*, Part I, 91st Cong., 1st sess. (Washington, D.C.: USGPO, 1969), p. 289.
9. See U.S. Senate, Subcommittee of the Committee on Appropriations, *Department of Defense Appropriations for Fiscal Year 1971, Hearings*, Part I, 91st Cong., 2nd sess. (Washington, D.C.: USGPO, 1970), p. 306.
10. Kissinger, op. cit., p. 6.
11. See, for example, Daniel Patrick Moynihan, *Loyalties* (New York: Harcourt Brace Jovanovich, 1984), pp. 15-19.

12. Quoted in U.S. Senate, Committee on Armed Services, *Research and Development, Civil Defense*, 96th Cong., 2nd sess. (Washington, D.C.: USGPO, 1980), p. 3549.

13. Quoted from the statement by Louis Giuffrida, Director, Federal Emergency Management Agency, in U.S. Senate Committee on Armed Services, *Department of Defense Authorization for Appropriations for Fiscal Year 1983, Hearings*, Part 7, *Strategic and Theater Nuclear Forces*, 97th Cong., 2nd sess. (Washington, D.C.: USGPO, 1982), p. 4929.

14. This mutual vulnerability basis of arms control is clearly reflected in the "quasi-official" history of SALT I. See, John Newhouse, *Cold Dawn: The Story of SALT* (New York: Holt, Rinehart and Winston, 1973); it is also reflected pervasively in the open record of Congressional hearings concerning SALT I.

15. For example, Gerard Smith, the head of the U.S. SALT I delegation suggested before Congress that the mutual vulnerability promoted by BMD limitations would make a first strike "inconceivable." See U.S. Senate, Committee on Armed Services, *Military Implications of the Treaty on the Limitations of Anti-Ballistic Missile Systems and the Interim Agreement on Limitations of Strategic Offensive Arms, Hearings* (Washington, D.C.: USGPO, 1972), p. 286.

16. U.S. Unilateral Statement A attached to the SALT I ABM Treaty states that the purpose of future negotiations should be, "to constrain and reduce on a long-term basis threats to the survivability of our respective strategic retaliatory forces." U.S. Arms Control and Disarmament Agency. *Arms Control and Disarmament Agreements*, 1980 Edition (Washington, D.C.: USGPO, 1980), p. 146.

17. Quoted in "Is There A Way Out?" *Harper's* (June 1985), p. 41.

18. Interview with General Daniel Graham, March 26, 1985.

19. Quoted in Robert Scheer, *With Enough Shovels: Reagan, Bush and Nuclear War* (New York: Random House, 1982), p. 104 (Advance Reader's Edition).

20. Interview with Dr. Edward Teller, March 19, 1985.

21. Ibid.

22. Interview with General Daniel Graham, March 26, 1985.

23. Quoted in "The President's View," *Newsweek*, March 18, 1985, p. 21.

24. See the statement of General John W. Vessey in, U.S. Senate, Committee on Armed Services, *MX Missile Basing System and Related Issues, Hearing*, 98th Congress, 1st Session (Washington, DC: USGPO, 1983), pp. 164-165.

25. Ibid.

26. Interview with Maxwell Hunter, March 21, 1985.

FOUR
Chapter 4

THE SOVIET UNION AND STRATEGIC DEFENSE

T he preceding chapters have examined the origins, scope and purpose of the Strategic Defense Initiative. Before proceeding, however, it is of critical importance to understand the Soviet view on strategic defense in general, and ballistic missile defense in particular. The strategic balance is largely a two-sided affair, and how the Soviet Union views defense against nuclear attack and "Star Wars" will be an important factor in determining U.S. behavior.

If the Soviet Union decides to oppose American strategic defenses, such as building additional offensive forces as a counter, the United States will find it more difficult to achieve its near- or long-term defensive objectives. On the other hand, if the Soviet Union endorses the concept that it and the U.S. move away together from ever-increasing numbers of offensive forces and toward a more defensive-oriented relationship, then limits on offensive forces, which would ease the move to effective defenses, may be easier to negotiate. In general, the lower the number of offensive forces the easier it will be to provide useful defenses.

Whether the Soviet Union eventually will agree to such a "cooperative" approach to strategic defense is an important question that is open to debate. Consequently, consideration of the Soviet perspective on strategic defense is an important step in understanding the SDI and its likely future.

THE SOVIET VIEW OF STRATEGIC DEFENSE

The Soviet Union has approached strategic defense in a far different manner than has the United States. Until recently the U.S. had officially endorsed the notion of leaving itself vulnerable to Soviet nuclear attack "in the interests of stability."[1] But the Soviet Union appears not to share that particular American view; instead, the Soviet Union has maintained a long and steady commitment to the "defense of the Motherland." While the United States pursued a policy of deterrence that accepted its vulnerability, the Soviet Union believed that its survival in case of war, even nuclear war, was an extremely important objective. The difference in the Soviet and U.S. views concerning the importance of strategic defense could not have been more striking.

Soviet strategic doctrine has long emphasized the need of surviving, possibly "winning," a nuclear war. That is not to say that Soviet leaders are anxious to fight a nuclear war, nor do they take the consequences of nuclear war lightly. Rather, the Soviet Union views the possibility of nuclear war so seriously as to prepare as best it can to survive the worst. This approach to nuclear war is almost completely foreign to the American view, which, because of the bleak outlook, has endorsed no serious preparation for survival.

Interestingly, in the early 1970s some in the American defense intellectual community believed that Soviet talk of fighting and surviving nuclear war was either the "primitive" and "unsophisticated" thinking of the Soviet military, or propaganda intended to scare the West. A theory emerged that the Soviets might reject their own "primitive" views about survival in nuclear war once they were educated to the American view that survival was basically impossible. Paul Warnke, chief U.S. arms control negotiator for the Carter administration, viewed Soviet thinking on fighting, surviving, and winning a nuclear war in such a light:

> This kind of thinking is on a level of abstraction which is unrealistic. It seems to me that instead of talking in these terms, which would indulge what I regard as the primitive aspects of Soviet nuclear doctrine, we ought to be trying to educate them into the real world of strategic nuclear weapons, which is that

nobody could possibly win.

And,

> In my view the Soviets have always lagged behind the United
> States in their appreciation of the realities of nuclear logic.[2]

Yet despite such efforts, while the United States, in effect, continued to reject the notion of survival, the Soviet Union continued its traditional efforts to "defend the Motherland." The basic difference in views led to different levels of effort on programs designed for defense in the event of war. For example, in the late 1960s the U.S. virtually dismantled its programs for intercepting attacking bombers while the Soviet Union continued to modernize its bomber defense systems. These include radars, interceptor aircraft, and surface-to-air missiles (SAMs). The U.S. civil defense program has been very modest and has focused primarily on protection against natural disaster; the Soviet civil defense program is enormous and involves training for millions of civilians in basic civil defense procedures. The Soviet program of preparing and hardening leadership bunkers for protection against nuclear war is also enormous. For example, the construction and equipment alone for Soviet political leadership relocation sites over the past 25 years may have cost up to $56 billion (over twice the anticipated cost for SDI research through 1989).[3] The comparable U.S. program is much smaller. Only neutral Switzerland has a civil defense program comparable to the Soviet Union's. (See Figures 1-3 for a comparison of U.S. and Soviet strategic defense programs.)

These Soviet programs have not diminished, despite their expense. Soviet expenditures on defense against U.S. strategic bombers are much greater than the cost of the U.S. bombers. Indeed, over the past decade the Soviet Union has spent more on strategic defense than the United States has on strategic offense,[4] and all the while the United States has allowed its strategic defenses to dwindle to virtual nonexistence.

This review of U.S. and Soviet defense programs is not intended to suggest that the Soviet Union can be confident of surviving a nuclear war. It is unclear how effective all these current Soviet defensive programs might be under actual con-

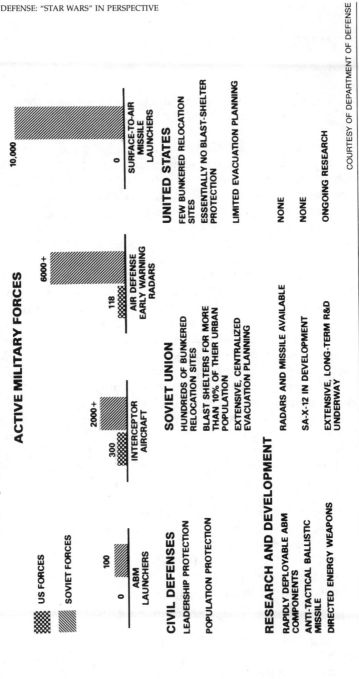

FIGURE 1

A Comparison of Strategic Defense Efforts

COURTESY OF DEPARTMENT OF DEFENSE

FIGURE 2

USSR—U.S. Strategic Defense Programs

	U.S.S.R.	U.S.
BMD LAUNCHERS	100	0
INTERCEPTORS	1200	279
STRATEGIC DEFENSE RADARS	~7000	~100
SAMs	10,000	0
HARDENED BUNKERS FOR POLITICAL LEADERSHIP	~1500 Identified	<100
FULL–TIME CIVIL DEFENSE PERSONNEL	150,000+	~7000
CIVIL DEFENSE SPENDING PER YEAR	$3–4 Bil.	$.17 Bil.

FIGURE 3

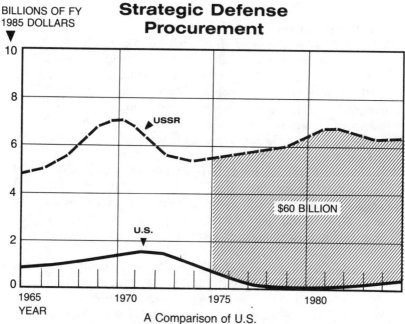

BILLIONS OF FY 1985 DOLLARS

Strategic Defense Procurement

A Comparison of U.S.
Strategic Defense Procurement Expenditures
with Estimated Dollar Cost of
USSR Procurement

ditions of nuclear conflict. However, the vast differences in U.S. and Soviet programs for strategic defense do imply that there is a major difference in views—the Soviet Union spending substantial amounts of money and manpower on defense against nuclear arms while the United States essentially gives up all efforts at defense.

The Soviet approach to strategic defense cannot be understood apart from the overall objectives of Soviet strategic doctrine. The various programs for defense against nuclear attack would play an important role in meeting the political and military objectives of Soviet strategic doctrine. These objectives include:[5]

1. the destruction of the U.S. (and allied) will and capability to fight,

2. the maintenance of authority and control over the country,

3. the preservation of the economic and industrial basis for reconstitution and reconstruction of war damage,

4. the assurance of a preponderance of military power after the war.

The Soviet Union pursues a "combined arms" approach to these objectives; that is, both offensive and defensive forces are critically needed for their achievement. Strategic nuclear offensive forces would be employed to destroy as much as possible of the U.S. retaliatory capability before it could be used. For example, Soviet missiles might be fired against U.S. ICBMs and bombers, and missile-carrying submarines that were known to be in port. The Soviet Union can have little confidence that it would disarm the United States in such a first strike, but it could greatly reduce the U.S. retaliatory capability. The Soviet offensive strategic force would fulfill two primary roles: (1) it would destroy U.S. will and capability to carry on the conflict; and, (2) it would help reduce U.S. retaliatory capabilities and thereby limit the damage that could be inflicted upon the Soviet Union.

The role of Soviet defenses would be to complement the offense in limiting damage to the Soviet Union. It would further reduce the U.S. retaliatory capacity. Indeed, Soviet offensive forces might well degrade much of the U.S. retaliatory capability except for that of the at-sea submarine launched missile force. Defending against a U.S. retaliatory force composed primarily of submarine launched missiles would significantly reduce Soviet defense requirements. In addition, the defense would not have to function perfectly against this residual U.S. force to meet Soviet requirements—Soviet doctrine does not anticipate coming through a nuclear war unscathed. Rather, the mixture of defensive programs—bomber defense, missile defense, and civil defense—would absorb enough of the U.S. retaliatory capability to ensure that, although damaged, the Soviet Union could survive and recover politically, economically, and militarily.

The Soviet understanding of limited defenses being "good enough" appears to reflect a major distinction between current Soviet and traditional American thinking about BMD. In the Soviet view, absolute protection, while ideal, is not considered essential. Other defensive measures, notably civil defense, would help compensate for a partially effective BMD system. On the other hand, much of the U.S. discussion of BMD focuses upon the requirement for a nearly-leakproof "astrodome" over the United States. The Defensive Technologies Study which helped to establish the SDI, for example, reportedly placed its sights on a defense that would be 99.975 percent effective. There is little American discussion of a mixture of defensive measures that are "leaky" but good enough to protect the country. As a foremost American expert on Soviet BMD noted, "what might appear useless to the United States, with its much more demanding perceptions of what ballistic missile defense must provide, might have significant incremental value in Soviet eyes."[6] In short, the Soviet doctrine prescribes offensive and defensive means to meet its political and military objectives: the combination of offensive "counterforce" strikes to destroy U.S. retaliatory capabilities, and defensive preparations to reduce the damage from those U.S. forces that might be used after surviving the Soviet first strike.

Soviet strategic doctrine does not suggest that the Soviet Union would in any way prefer to fight a nuclear war, or prefer war to peace. Rather, the Soviet Union appears to prefer to avoid war while achieving its foreign policy objectives— which include the extension of Soviet influence and power. The doctrine does suggest that the Soviet Union views nuclear war as a real possibility, and thus seeks to limit the damage it would suffer. Soviet doctrine also suggests the view that the preparations and programs to limit damage could eventually make a difference in the outcome of the war.

It is clear that Soviet strategic nuclear offensive forces have been designed to destroy U.S. retaliatory capabilities. For example, a primary objective of Soviet ICBM modernization has been to acquire the combined explosive power and accuracy necessary to destroy U.S. ICBMs in their silos. This apparently was accomplished by the mid-1980s. Soviet defensive programs are particularly oriented toward the protection of Communist party, state, and military leadership and facilities, and "essential" portions of the workforce and industry.

In short, it is clear that the Soviet Union is very interested in defending itself against nuclear attack. Limiting damage in the event of war, and particularly protection of political and military authority, are principal objectives in Soviet doctrine. The SDI indicates a new direction for the United States; but the Soviet Union has been pursuing its strategic defense as a matter of course for over two decades. Perhaps the terrible wartime destruction suffered during World Wars I and II has made the Soviet leadership more sensitive than American leaders to defending the homeland in the event of war. Whatever the reason, it is clear from Soviet doctrine and programs that, unlike the United States, it has a long historical attachment to a policy of defending against nuclear attack.

SOVIET BMD

Ballistic missile defense is the single "missing link" in the Soviet defense effort. True, the Soviet Union has deployed the single BMD site permitted under the SALT I Anti-Ballistic Missile (ABM) Treaty signed in 1972—the world's only operational BMD system. But that BMD system, centered around Moscow, could not provide nationwide protection against U.S. nuclear forces. Although the Soviet Union has nationwide bomber defense and civil defense programs, the deployment of BMD has been limited to the single Moscow site. Nationwide BMD appears to be the missing element in Soviet defenses. One must wonder why the Soviet Union—with its emphasis on the need to limit damage in a nuclear war—would sign a treaty limiting its capability to deploy BMD legally.

The Soviet Union appears to have decided, even before the SALT I negotiations began, to curtail deployment of its Moscow BMD system, construction on which had begun in the early 1960s. The Soviet leadership probably recognized that the system's technological limitations would render it ineffective against modern U.S. forces. And at the time the treaty was signed, the U.S. was perhaps ten years ahead of the Soviet Union in BMD technology. Since the signing of the treaty the Soviet Union has steadily increased its research and development for BMD, but it had not, until recently, modernized its deployed BMD system.

In 1980, however, the Soviet Union began a major improvement program for its Moscow BMD system. The original Moscow system involved a single defensive layer of long-range BMD rockets of limited capability. Rather than for citywide defense, the Moscow system provides a layer of defense against ballistic missiles for political and military authorities in the area. Sixty-four above-ground launchers and nuclear-armed interceptors, and a handful of radars were located at four complexes around a ring 40-50 miles from the center of Moscow. Much larger radars (dubbed "Hen House" radars by the Pentagon) are located on the periphery of the Soviet Union and two additional immense radars ("Dog House" and "Cat House" radars) lying southwest of Moscow completed the system.

The upgraded and expanded Moscow system will involve two layers of defense, including both long- and short-range, silo-based, nuclear-armed interceptors. The number of deployed interceptors and launchers will be increased to the 100 permitted by the SALT I Treaty. (Hundreds more could be built and stockpiled without violating the ABM Treaty.) Three new large BMD radars (120 ft. high and 500 ft. wide) reportedly are being constructed (called "Pushkino" radars), one just north of Moscow. These new radars when complemented by new interceptors could enable the Moscow system to provide some defense coverage for a large portion of the western Soviet Union. The upgraded Moscow BMD system will probably be fully operational by 1987.

There apparently is some evidence that the Soviet Union is stockpiling BMD components that could be integrated with the Moscow system. This has led to the fear that a Soviet

BMD system could be rapidly deployed to provide much wider area coverage than that of the current Moscow BMD.[7] In recent Congressional testimony, the chairman of the National Intelligence Council, Robert M. Gates, observed:

> The potential exists for the production lines associated with the upgrade of the Moscow ABM system to be used to support a widespread deployment. We judge they could undertake rapidly paced ABM deployments to strengthen the defenses at Moscow and cover key targets in the western U.S.S.R., and to extend protection to key targets east of the Urals, by the early 1990s.[8]

Other significant BMD developments in the Soviet Union have led the U.S. to conclude that the Soviet Union is rapidly developing the capability to deploy a nationwide BMD system.[9] In addition to the new large "Pushkino" radars under construction, at least six even larger Pechora-class radars (300 ft. wide/500 ft. long) are under construction. These Pechora radars may be capable of tracking several thousand attacking ballistic missile "warheads" simultaneously.[10] A complete BMD infrastructure of Pushkino, Pechora, and older Hen House radars—the long lead-time elements of a BMD system—could be operational by the late 1980s. This, naturally, has intensified the U.S. concern that the Soviet Union is preparing the necessary infrastructure for the rapid deployment of a nationwide BMD system. (See Figure 4)

The Soviet Union also reportedly has in production the BMD elements that could be integrated with the radar infrastructure described above to provide a nationwide BMD system. For example, the new interceptors for the Moscow system may, if matched with the developing radar infrastructure, constitute a two-tiered defensive system. (To provide a nationwide defense these new interceptors and the large Pushkino, Pechora, and Hen House radars would have to be augmented by other "tracking" and interceptor guidance radars.) The Soviet Union has two such radars—the "Flat Twin" and "Pawn Shop"—reportedly in production, but not in deployment. These are designed modularly and around trailers, thereby rendering them transportable and facilitating rapid assembly, intensifying concerns about a Soviet capability to "break out" of the SALT I ABM Treaty constraints and rapidly

FIGURE 4

Approximate Coverage of Soviet Large Array Antennas

This map illustrates the geographic coverage of large Soviet phased-array radars. Note that the new Soviet radar located in central Siberia fills a previous gap in Soviet radar coverage. This radar, located about 450 miles inland is, according to the U.S., a violation of the ABM Treaty because the treaty specifies clearly that such radars must be located on the country's periphery and oriented outward.

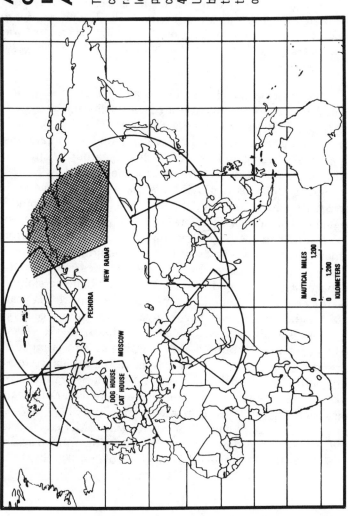

deploy a nationwide system.

Why would the prospect of the rapid deployment of a Soviet nation-wide BMD system cause American concern? The concern of the U.S. is, of course, that the Soviet Union, given its advanced capability for BMD deployment, could have a nationwide system in place well before the United States could deploy anything like a similar defensive capability. A *unilateral* capability for defense could give the Soviet Union a significant strategic advantage over the United States. As one Defense Department official observed:

> We might find this year that we have zero time to respond to an ABM Treaty breakout by the U.S.S.R. with no way to provide in a timely way a parallel capability. There is no way to accelerate a defensive initiative in the U.S. to duplicate the Soviet capability.[11]

The Soviet capability to intercept ballistic missiles is not limited to those systems identified as specifically designed for the purpose of ballistic missile defense. That is, some Soviet surface-to-air missiles (SAMs) have antibomber and antimissile capabilities. This could be extremely dangerous because these SAMs have not been constrained by the SALT I ABM Treaty. The Soviet Union is deploying a surface-to-air missile system, the SA-10, which may have the potential to intercept some U.S. strategic ballistic missiles. First operational in 1980, the Soviet Union now has over sixty operational SA-10 sites, and work is underway on at least thirty more.[12] In keeping with the priority of defending political and military authorities, more than half of these sites are located near Moscow. A mobile version of the SA-10 is being developed and may be operational this year.

Another mobile SAM with a capability to intercept ballistic missiles will soon be operational, the SA-X-12. The SA-X-12 has a truck-mounted radar. Missiles and launchers are carried by a second truck. It may have the capability to intercept both strategic ballistic missiles and shorter-range systems such as the now-famous Pershing II intermediate-range ballistic missiles being deployed in relatively small numbers in Western Europe.[13] The deployment of SAMs with BMD capabilities is particularly worrisome because the existing infrastructure of more than 10,000 deployed SAMs and over 1,000 SAM radars could provide the basis for a significant BMD capability that would complement the BMD systems discussed above, and would, moreover, be unconstrained by the ABM Treaty.

To put together the puzzle of Soviet BMD capabilities and BMD potential is to conclude that the Soviet Union is intensely interested in upgrading its Moscow BMD system and developing as rapidly as possible its potential to deploy an extensive BMD system. Whether the Soviet Union intends to break out of the SALT I ABM Treaty and deploy a nationwide BMD system is not known at this point. The U.S. probably would be uncertain of the Soviet intention to do so until the first signs of nationwide construction were seen.

SOVIET "STAR WARS" PROGRAMS

The Soviet Union also is well advanced in the area of "Star Wars" technology. For example, Soviet laser weapon programs date back to the mid-1960s and are much larger than the U.S. effort;[14] and since the early 1970s the Soviet Union has had a research program to explore the feasibility of placing particle beam weapons in space. Soviet programs to develop "directed energy weapons" (DEW) for strategic defense —including BMD, antibomber and antisatellite weapons—have been in the past and will continue to be pursued vigorously. U.S. programs for directed energy weapons are much smaller, and may trail the Soviet Union by years.[15] The Soviet laser program alone, if replicated in the U.S., would cost approximately $1 billion per year.[16]

Although it is difficult to know much, if any, precise detail about Soviet DEW programs, given the secrecy that surrounds them, the Soviet Union appears to be developing an arsenal of laser weapons that could be used for BMD, antibomber, and antisatellite missions during the 1990s. For example, by the late 1980s the Soviet Union may have built ground-based laser BMD test models, and testing of components for widespread system deployment could begin in the early 1990s. Widespread deployment of an operational system is not likely to occur during this century; but if the Soviet Union decided to skip some testing steps it could be ready to field a ground-based laser BMD system by the early-to-mid-1990s.[17]

In addition, the Soviet Union is developing multiple types of laser weapons for use against aircraft. For example, it is possible that a laser which could be used in conjunction with SAMs against U.S. strategic bombers could be operational by the late 1980s. Another laser, probably operational in the 1990s, would be placed on board ships to defend ships at sea. And, airborne laser weapons could be deployed beginning in the early 1990s for use against cruise missiles, satellites, and possibly submarine launched ballistic missiles.

The Soviet Union is even more advanced in the development of antisatellite laser weapons. In fact, the Soviet ground-based antisatellite laser program has developed to the point where they *already have* a test model system which has been *used* to interfere with U.S. satellites.[18] Construction on these facilities at operational sites could begin immediately and become operational by the end of the 1980s. The Soviet Union could have a test model of a space-based antisatellite laser by the late 1980s or early 1990s; and it may be deployed as an operational space-based system in the 1990s. Development of a space-based laser for BMD will most probably ensue, with deployment after the year 2000.

The Soviet particle beam program may be somewhat less advanced; particle beams appear more difficult to develop than lasers. Nevertheless, the Soviet Union has a vigorous program for particle beam development. A space-based particle beam test model for BMD could even be ready for testing by the late 1990s. A test model of a space-based particle beam weapon intended to disturb a satellite's electronics could be tested in the early 1990s, and a system to destroy satellites could be tested in the mid-1990s.

In short, it is clearly evident that the Soviet Union is conducting vigorous programs of research and development in the area of "Star Wars" defenses. This review of Soviet programs is not meant to overstate the case or paint lurid pictures of Soviet "death rays." But the American public, in pondering the SDI and strategic defense in general, should be at least aware that the Soviet Union has been pursuing this area of defensive weapons development vigorously, and will continue to do so regardless of what the U.S. does or does not do. It also should keep in mind that survival of nuclear attack is a key goal of the Soviet leadership and the Soviet Union has worked doggedly toward that end for years. As Robert Gates observed, "the Soviets have a large program to provide protection for their leadership. We judge that, with as little as a few hours warning, a large percentage of the wartime management structure would survive the initial effects of a large-scale U.S. nuclear attack...Deep underground facilities for the top national leadership might enable the top leadership to survive—a key objective of their wartime management plans."[19]

SUMMARY

There is no doubt the Soviet Union has had a most serious interest in strategic defense for many years. This interest is reflected in Soviet strategic doctrine, which focuses on minimizing the damage the Soviet Union would suffer in a nuclear war. Under the Soviet plan, offensive strategic nuclear weapons and defensive forces would combine to limit damage by destroying as many U.S. strategic forces as possible before they could be used, and absorbing those weapons that survive and are used in retaliation. Soviet strategy does not call for "perfect" defenses; it appears willing to settle for partially effective defenses.

Soviet offensive nuclear forces have been designed to maximize the destruction of U.S. retaliatory capabilities. Soviet defenses against nuclear forces, in combination with offensive strategic forces, are conceived to ensure that the Soviet Union survives a nuclear war. According to two of America's foremost experts on the Soviet Union:

> There is no certainty that any group governing a large, heterogeneous population can design controls that would be effective throughout a nuclear war and in its aftermath. If such a system could be perfected, it probably exists in the Soviet Union. There are many statements in the Soviet Press about how the Armed Forces, the national economy, and the population must be prepared for the eventuality of a nuclear war. This requirement is a basic tenet of Soviet military doctrine.[20]

Indeed, Soviet strategic defense programs include the world's most extensive protection against strategic bombers, an extensive civil defense program, and the world's only operational BMD system. And each one of these defenses is being upgraded and modernized. For example, the Moscow BMD system has undergone extensive upgrading and expansion since 1980. Yet the Moscow system is only one element of the Soviet BMD potential; in addition, some Soviet surface-to-air missiles (SAMs) have the potential to intercept both bombers and ballistic missiles. The Soviet development, production, and construction of new BMD components, including new interceptors, a network of huge new radars, and new transportable radars, has led the U.S. to suspect that the Soviet Union is preparing the basis for the rapid deployment of a nationwide BMD system.

Finally, the Soviet Union is quite advanced in the area of "Star Wars" weapons. It is years ahead of the U.S. in some development programs for "exotic" directed energy weapons, including several laser weapon development programs for BMD, antibomber and antisatellite defense that could lead to deployed weapon systems in the next decade.

ENDNOTES

1. As stated by Harold Brown, *Department of Defense Annual Report Fiscal Year 1980* (Washington, D.C.: USGPO, January 25, 1979), p. 61.
2. Cited in Richard Pipes, "Why the Soviet Union Thinks It Could Fight and Win a Nuclear War," *Commentary*, 64 (July 1977), p. 21; and U.S. Senate, 92nd Cong., 2nd sess. (Washington, D.C.: USGPO, 1972), p. 181.
3. Department of Defense, *Soviet Military Power 1985* (Washington, D.C.: USGPO, April 1985), pp. 51-52.
4. Richard DeLauer, statement by the Under Secretary of Defense, Research and Engineering, *The FY 1986 Department of Defense Program for Research, Development and Acquisition*, 99th Cong., 1st sess. (Washington, D.C.: USGPO, March 7, 1985), p. IV-7.
5. See the discussions in John Dziak, *Soviet Perceptions of Military Doctrine and Military Power* (New York: National Strategy Information Center, 1981), p. 28; Joseph Douglas and Amoretta Hoeber, *Soviet Strategy for Nuclear War* (Stanford, CA: Hoover Institution Press, 1979), p. 17; and Sayre Stevens, "The Soviet BMD Program," in *Ballistic Missile Defense*, Ashton Carter and David Schwartz, eds. (Washington, D.C.: The Brookings Institution, 1984), p. 188.
6. See Stevens, op. cit., p. 188.

7. David Rivkin and Manfred Hamm, *In Strategic Defense, Moscow Is Far Ahead, Backgrounder*, No. 409 (Feb. 21, 1985), p. 8.

8. See Robert M. Gates and Lawrence Gershwin, *Soviet Strategic Force Developments*, Testimony before a Joint Session of the Subcommittee on Strategic and Theater Nuclear Forces of the Senate Armed Services Committee, and the Defense Subcommittee of the Senate Committee on Appropriations, June 26, 1985, pp. 5-6.

9. See *Soviet Military Power*, op. cit., pp. 46, 48.

10. See, for example, Ted Agres, "Soviets Building ABM Radar System," *Washington Times*, April 14, 1984, pp. 1, 12A.

11. See Clarence Robinson, "Soviets Accelerate Missile Defense," *Aviation Week and Space Technology* (January 16, 1984), p. 16.

12. See, *Soviet Strategic Defense Programs* (Washington D.C.: USGPO, October 1985), p. 20; and *Soviet Military Power*, op. cit., p. 50.

13. Gates and Gershwin, op. cit., p. 5.

14. See, *Soviet Strategic Defense Programs*, op. cit., pp. 12-13. See also George Wilson, "Soviets Reported Pushing Laser Arms," *Washington Post*, April 3, 1985, p. 1.

15. See the testimony of Richard DeLauer in U.S. Senate, Committee on Armed Services, *Department of Defense Authorization for Appropriations for Fiscal Year 1985, Hearings*, Part 6, 98th Cong., 2nd sess. (Washington, D.C.: USGPO, 1984), pp. 2928-2929.

16. *Soviet Strategic Defense Programs*, op. cit., p. 13

17. *Soviet Military Power*, op. cit., p. 44

18. Reported in, "Pentagon says USSR tested lasers against US satellites." *Christian Science Monitor*, October 2, 1985, p. 2.

19. See Gates and Gershwin, op. cit., p. 6.

20. See Harriet Fast Scott and William F. Scott, *The Soviet Control Structure: Capabilities for Wartime Survival* (New York: Crane Russak, National Strategy Information Center, 1983), p. 129.

FIVE
Chapter 5

"HEAVIER-THAN-AIR FLYING MACHINES ARE IMPOSSIBLE"

T he question of the technical feasibility of defending against ballistic missiles is at the heart of the ongoing SDI debate. Much of the criticism of the SDI is based upon the judgment that a comprehensive BMD capability is not possible, and almost certainly never will be. Indeed, some technical analyses support such a judgment.[1] For example, in April 1984 a paper prepared by Dr. Ashton Carter for the Office of Technology Assessment concluded with the following "principal judgment":

> The prospect that emerging "Star Wars" technologies, when further developed, will provide a perfect or near-perfect defense system...is so remote that it should not serve as the basis of public expectation or national policy about ballistic missile defense (BMD).[2]

Similarly, Dr. Harold Brown, former Secretary of Defense, stated in a paper for the Johns Hopkins School of Advanced International Studies that, "Technology does not offer even a reasonable prospect of a successful population defense."[3]

On the other hand, other highly credible scientists and technical analyses have been much more optimistic. For example, in 1983 the Defensive Technologies Study team was composed of over fifty scientists and engineers who came together to examine emerging BMD technologies. The technology study team consulted with hundreds of technical experts, and following 100,000 man-hours of study, the team reached optimistic conclusions regarding the potential for effective defense. The head of the study, Professor James Fletcher, described the conclusions of the technology study as follows:

> ...although enormous hurdles remain; the technological advances of the past two decades show great promise for ballistic missile defense...In the Defensive Technologies Study, we took an optimistic view of the emerging technologies and concluded that, "a robust, multi-tiered ballistic missile [defense] system can eventually be made to work."[4]

Professor Fletcher's own conclusions are optimistic about BMD technology:

> A complete four-phase system....has the potential for protecting nearly all of the population—perhaps even greater than 99 percent, in my opinion—against massive nuclear attacks.[5]

Similarly, Professor Robert Jastrow, founder of NASA's Institute for Space Studies, has testified before the U.S. Senate that the United States by the early 1990s could have a two-layered BMD system for about $60 billion; and that a conservative estimate of such a system would place its effectiveness against Soviet ballistic missile attack at 90 percent.[6]

Obviously, there is some debate within the scientific community concerning whether or not the potential exists for an effective and comprehensive BMD system. Some respected members of the "scientific community" have stated that a comprehensive BMD capability is virtually impossible. In contrast, other equally respected members of the same community are confident that there is a great potential in the emerging technologies for highly effective BMD.

It is reasonable, therefore, to be cautious in anticipating what technology can achieve. However, one also should be reluctant to accept the judgment, even from experts, that a particular technological task is "impossible," particularly in reference to a decades-long project such as building a comprehensive defense system. Expert opinion in the past concerning "the impossible" can be quite humorous. Several examples should be instructive:

> "Rail travel at high speed is not possible because passengers, unable to breathe, would die of asphyxia."[7]

Dr. Dionysus Lardner (1793-1859)
Professor of Natural Philosophy and
Astronomy at University College, London

"Heavier-than-air flying machines are impossible."[8]

Lord Kelvin
British mathematician, physicist, and
President of the British Royal Society. c. 1895

"It is apparent to me that the possibilities of the aeroplane, which two or three years ago was thought to hold the solution to the [flying machine] problem, have been exhausted, and that we must turn elsewhere."[9]

Thomas Alva Edison
1895

"To affirm that the aeroplane is going to 'revolutionize' naval warfare of the future is to be guilty of the wildest exaggeration."[10]

Scientific American
July 16, 1910

"I can accept the theory of relativity as little as I can accept the existence of atoms and other such dogmas."[11]

Ernst Mach
Professor of Physics,
University of Vienna, 1913

"This is the biggest fool thing we have ever done...The bomb will never go off, and I speak as an expert in explosives."[12]

Admiral William Leahy,
advising President Truman on the
impracticality of the atomic bomb, 1945

"The people who have been writing these things that annoy me, have been talking about a 3,000 mile high-angle rocket shot from one continent to another, carrying an atomic bomb and so directed as to be a precise weapon which would land exactly on a certain target, such as a city."

"I say, technically, I don't think anyone in the world knows how to do such a thing, and I feel confident that it will not be done for a very long period of time to come....I think we can leave it out of our thinking. I wish the American public would leave that out of their thinking."[13]

Dr. Vannevar Bush
Former Dean of Engineering at the
Massachusetts Institute of Technology
and President of the Carnegie Institution
of Washington, 1945

There is surely some basis, given historical precedent, to be skeptical of those in the scientific community who stamp "impossible" on future technology. Current skepticism concerning the impossibility of an effective BMD may, in the twenty-first century, appear as short-sighted as past statements concerning the impossibility of flying machines, rail travel, ICBMs, and the atomic bomb. Indeed, according to some scientists close to the SDI, the people most familiar with the emerging technologies tend to be optimistic about the potential for BMD.[14] This is *not* to endorse every new claim for a technically "exotic" BMD concept. It is to suggest that, though there is at the present no consensus concerning the future potential for BMD, this is not a conclusive indictment against the SDI. Professor Fletcher put the technical critique of the SDI in the proper perspective when he observed that, "there are many uncertainties as the United States embarks on its strategic defense effort. We could not now with confidence construct effective ballistic missile defenses. Conversely, we have not been presented with any compelling technical means that show that such defenses are not possible. The technical issues surrounding the development of effective defenses have many possible solutions and should not at this stage be the primary focus of the debate."[15]

There has, moreover, recently been some basis for optimism about the prospect for BMD. In a test on June 10, 1984, the U.S. Army successfully intercepted a dummy ICBM warhead that had been launched from Vandenberg Air Force Base, California. The test program was designed to validate some of the technology necessary for a *non-nuclear* capability to intercept

FIGURE 5

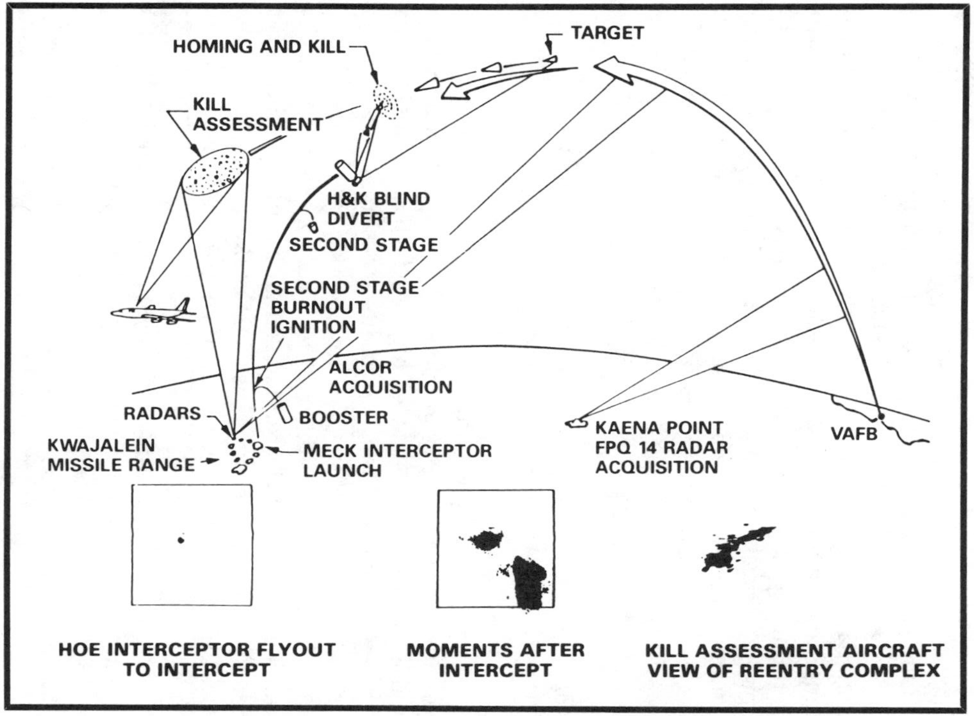

Homing Overlay Experiment

Illustration of the U.S. Army's successful Homing Overlay Experiment (HOE). This experiment was a test of a non-nuclear ballistic missile interceptor. In this test, conducted on June 10, 1984, a ground-based missile carried a small heat-seeking rocket which intercepted a dummy warhead at an altitude of approximately 100 miles.

COURTESY OF DEPARTMENT OF DEFENSE

an attacker's warheads outside the atmosphere. The successful non-nuclear intercept was the world's first as far as is known. While the ICBM warhead was high above the atmosphere the interceptor's sensors locked onto it and the interceptor rocketed toward the mock warhead. The BMD flight vehicle unfurled a metal umbrella-like net in the path of the warhead, and at an altitude of 100 miles the warhead was destroyed in the ensuing collision with the metal net. Destruction of the warhead was confirmed by sensors on the Kwajalein atoll in the Marshall Islands, and by specially instrumented aircraft.[16] This successful experiment represented a decade of research in BMD technology begun by the U.S. Army's BMD Advanced Technology Center in Huntsville, Alabama.

One successful test, of course, does not in any way prove that BMD "will work" as a comprehensive system. The Soviet Union may be expected to take offensive countermeasures in an attempt to counter U.S. BMD systems. But recognition now of uncertainty concerning future defense effectiveness is not appropriate criticism of the SDI. The SDI is, after all, a research program intended to help determine whether emerging technologies will provide the potential for successfully intercepting a massive nuclear ballistic missile attack and overcoming Soviet offensive countermeasures.

BUT WILL IT WORK?

To answer the question, "will it work," depends primarily upon how "it" and "work" are defined. If the question refers to a multilayered BMD system—a highly effective defense against all potential Soviet offensive countermeasures —the general consensus is that "it" would not "work" with current technology. There are a number of technical issues that must be researched before a clear understanding can be achieved of whether emerging technologies will make a highly effective BMD feasible. That research is, of course, the purpose of the SDI.

The fact that technical problems exist concerning the feasibility of a comprehensive BMD capability does not in any way undercut the SDI. On the contrary, it illustrates the importance of SDI research. The point should be made clear for those critics who charge that, since a highly effective BMD is impossible, the president should drop the SDI. The SDI is not a program to deploy any type of BMD. Its purpose is to help address the question of the technical feasibility. Judgments concerning the wisdom of comprehensive BMD deployment should not precede the research that will determine its feasibility.

If the question, "will it work," refers to a more limited one- or two-layer BMD system that is intended to protect selected military forces and facilities, then the answer is less ambiguous. Both skeptics and optimists concerning the prospects for a comprehensive BMD capability agree that a limited BMD capability suitable for protecting selected strategic retaliatory assets is feasible *with known technology*.[17] Defense for a selected set of strategic retaliatory assets would be easier to accomplish than protection of cities and people. For example, effective BMD coverage for ICBMs would be made easier by the high levels of hardness built into American ICBM silos, and by the fact that even a modest percentage of ICBMs protected against an attack could be considered a "good enough" level of defense. Consequently, it appears that current technology could not support the objective of a highly effective defense for the entire American population. However, it could support a more limited defensive objective such as enhancing deterrence by reducing the prospects for any useful Soviet first strike against U.S. retaliatory forces.

A limited defense capability is not, of course, the ultimate hope for defense presented in the president's March 23 speech or in subsequent policy statements. But protecting U.S. strategic retaliatory forces would certainly be the first defensive mission following a decision to deploy BMD, even if it were intended eventually to provide comprehensive protection for cities and people. A limited defense capability en route to comprehensive protection certainly could be useful by helping to reduce any Soviet first-strike incentives. Such a defense capability would contribute to the enhancement of deterrence—an initial objective in any decision to deploy BMD.[18]

In short, whether defending against ballistic missiles "will work" depends upon the time frame in question and what is meant by "work." Current technology could support less than comprehensive defense objectives; emerging BMD technologies may hold the potential for a future comprehensive defense capability. Determining the potential of those emerging BMD technologies is what the SDI is all about.

SDI'S 100 PERCENT TECHNICAL PROBLEM

A repeated technical criticism of the SDI is that any defense must work perfectly because even one nuclear warhead penetrating to a city target would devastate that city. Thus, given the vast arsenal of Soviet nuclear weapons, a U.S. defense that was "only" 99 percent effective would not be "good enough." As several well-known critics of the SDI and strategic defense in general have observed:

> Mr. Reagan's dream and his historical argument completely neglect the decisive fact that a very few nuclear weapons, exploding on or near population centers, would be hideously too many....only a kill rate closely approaching 100 percent can give protection.[19]

This wide-spread technical criticism is based upon an almost certainly mistaken assumption regarding Soviet strategy. It assumes that in the event of nuclear war the Soviet Union would mass its strategic nuclear forces against U.S. cities. The important question is not whether one out of a hundred nuclear weapons would penetrate, but *where* that penetrating weapon would detonate. Obviously, if that one weapon hit an American ICBM silo, it would not have nearly the same devastating effect as if it hit an American city. This is important, because if the Soviet Union were to launch an attack it almost certainly would use its weapons against U.S. military forces, and particularly strategic retaliatory capabilities; it would not mass all of its forces against U.S. cities. Soviet strategic doctrine clearly focuses upon the military mission of destroying U.S. military capabilities, because those forces pose a direct retaliatory threat to the Soviet Union, particularly given its own "leaky" defenses. The deployment of defenses by the U.S., and more defenses by the Soviet Union, should not alter the Soviet objective of limiting damage to itself in the event of war; it should, in fact, reinforce the logic of Soviet thinking. There is little reason to assume, as do those who claim that anything short of a perfect defense is worthless, that the Soviet Union will revise its nuclear targeting strategy away from the fundamental offensive objective of reducing U.S. retaliatory capabilities. U.S. military capabilities, including leadership centers, and particularly the U.S. nuclear retaliatory potential, are very likely to remain the most important and valuable targets in Soviet strategic doctrine.

Although speculation about future Soviet targeting objectives does not permit certainty on either side of the argument, critics of the SDI reveal an ignorance of strategy and Soviet doctrine and targeting objectives when they argue that:

> ...to the extent that defenses pose a serious threat to the "assured destruction" capability of either side, they invite retargeting to retain such destructive capacity. The fewer warheads the Soviets can expect to arrive on U.S. territory, the more likely these warheads are to be assigned to the softest and most valuable targets—major urban areas. Warhead accuracy would become less important, and sheer destruction, with maximum collateral damage, more important, thus reversing the priorities associated with limited war strategies.[20]

But using large numbers of Soviet nuclear forces to threaten American cities would draw thousands of weapons away from the Soviet Union's primary purpose, reducing U.S. nuclear capabilities. More likely, the Soviet Union would concentrate its forces to gain the maximum military effect from a small number of penetrating weapons. For this, it would need to target the most valuable and vulnerable American retaliatory assets, not indulge in a gratuitous attack on American cities. Either way, there would be some level of urban damage. But the level of civil destruction would be less than if the Soviets concentrated their warheads and penetrated the "leaky" defense against U.S. cities...and considerably less than in our current state of defenselessness.

Consequently, it seems that even imperfect defenses could be extremely helpful if they compelled the Soviet Union to consume its limited number of penetrating forces to attack U.S. retaliatory capabilities instead of cities. In addition, because defending retaliatory forces would be relatively "easy," even "leaky" defenses would help deter the Soviet Union from any first strike because of the uncertainty of success. As Professor John Erickson, one of the West's foremost experts on

Soviet strategy, has observed, "Soviet military opinion cautions against any 'adventurist strategy' which might prematurely initiate a total struggle, when the requisite 'correlation of forces' (*sootnoshenie sil*) cannot assure a favorable outcome (even victory) in such a struggle."[21]

Perhaps even more important than the utility of a limited U.S. defense against a large Soviet attack is that which it might have against other types of threats. For example, our current defenselessness leaves America extremely vulnerable to the unauthorized launch of nuclear weapons, an "accident" involving the launch of nuclear weapons, or a small attack from a third party. No helpful U.S. option is available today in the event the president is informed by the Kremlin of an accidental or unauthorized launch because the U.S. could do nothing to stop the resultant destruction. This situation becomes even worse when one considers the probability that additional states or organizations could come into possession of a nuclear-armed intercontinental ballistic missile over the course of coming decades. The prospect of continued U.S. defenselessness in such a future is truly frightening. Even an extremely limited BMD capability could provide protection against such unauthorized, "accidental," or third-party threats.

Herman Kahn often noted that strategic defenses would be valuable for two mutually supporting reasons: they could provide "deterrence plus insurance." Defenses should enhance deterrence, thereby reducing the probability of war; and if deterrence ever fails, defenses would help reduce the resultant level of destruction—even if they were not "perfect."

GENERIC SDI CONCEPTS

Although it is uncertain what types of future systems would constitute a comprehensive BMD "architecture," the potential components of a more limited, near-term BMD are better known.[22] A limited defense could include three tiers or layers of defense. The first layer could consist of approximately 100 satellites armed with numerous small, heat-seeking rockets. These non-nuclear rockets would attack Soviet ICBMs in the "boost phase" of their flight. The boost phase would be the first of four distinct phases of a Soviet ICBM's flight toward the

United States. During the 3-5 minute boost phase the ICBM's rocket engines burn and "boost" the missile's payload until it leaves the atmosphere. The intense heat produced by the rocket engines during the boost phase provides U.S. space-based infrared sensors with a means of detecting the Soviet launch.[23]

Interception during the boost phase is important to the effective functioning of even a limited BMD system because the Soviet ICBM would not yet have released its complement of multiple warheads (multiple independently targeted reentry vehicles-MIRVs). Consequently, a single intercept could destroy numerous warheads. For example, if the largest Soviet ICBM, the SS-18, could be destroyed during its boost phase, all of its potential 20-30 warheads (and possible "decoys" designed to confuse the U.S. BMD) would be neutralized. A capability for boost-phase intercept would give defensive interceptors important leverage because a single interceptor could destroy many offensive warheads—in theory, it could give BMD a 100 to 1 advantage over the offense.[24]

A second defensive layer could consist of ground-based non-nuclear BMD interceptors. This second layer would be derived from the BMD technology tested successfully by the U.S. Army in June 1984. These non-nuclear "exoatmospheric" interceptors could be launched from the United States and would operate in outer space during the long mid-course of an attacking missile's flight trajectory. Active and passive sensors based in space would observe the separation of the warheads from the MIRV bus and facilitate midcourse interception by ground-based, non-nuclear interceptors. This second layer of defense would further "thin-out" the attacking force and reduce the number of offensive weapons against which the next layer of defense would have to contend.

The third layer in this hypothetical limited BMD system would attack Soviet warheads in their last phase of flight. This is the terminal phase (lasting about 1 minute) when the warhead reenters and then descends through the atmosphere on the final leg of its ballistic trajectory toward the intended target. Terminal phase BMD would intercept warheads within the atmosphere, i.e., it would employ "endoatmospheric interceptors." This defensive layer could utilize ground-based BMD missiles with non-nuclear homing interceptors.

A comprehensive BMD architecture would likely incorporate interceptor systems to attack Soviet ICBMs and warheads throughout their entire flight path. In addition to intercept during the boost, midcourse and terminal phases, a comprehensive defense could strike at the "bus" that carries and releases a missile's MIRVs following the boost phase. Interception during this 3-5 minute "postboost phase" of flight could also provide defensive leverage if the defense can destroy the bus before it has released all of its MIRVs. Following the boost and postboost phases the released warheads, decoys, and other "penetration aids" intended to counter defenses travel along the midcourse of their trajectories above the atmosphere.In this midcourse phase the warheads rise over a long arc to an altitude of about 1,000 kilometers. The midcourse phase of flight lasts 20-30 minutes. Comprehensive defense could have more than one tier of interceptors ready to destroy attacking warheads during the midcourse, given its relatively long duration.

The "exotic" means for intercept in a future comprehensive defense might include directed energy weapons (DEW), such as laser or particle beams. DEW components could be space-based, utilizing satellite platforms to strike at Soviet ICBMs as they rise in their boost phase from their launch sites in the Soviet Union. Ground-based (or space-based) lasers could use space-based relay and "battle" mirrors to direct the beam to Soviet boosters. Space-based weapons capable of propelling small homing interceptors at speeds far greater than the 10,000 mph of current rockets might also provide an effective boost, postboost, and midcourse means of intercept. This would be an "electromagnetic railgun" which would use an intense magnetic field to propel a homing interceptor at a Soviet missile or warhead at speeds greater than 50,000 mph. Railgun tests already have exceeded speeds of 10,000 mph.[25]

Although it is far from clear at this point, given the early stage of SDI research, a comprehensive defense probably would include multiple defensive tiers and multiple means of intercept. A defensive architecture for comprehensive protection might include ground-based interceptors such as the one tested by the U.S. Army in June 1984, ground- and space-based lasers, space-based laser relay mirrors, space-based homing rocket interceptors, and space-based particle beams and electromagnetic railguns.

In short, a limited system could include three layers of non-nuclear homing interceptors—a space-based tier for boost phase intercept and a ground-based layer for midcourse exoatmospheric and terminal endoatmospheric intercept. A more distant comprehensive defense might include several additional tiers of interceptors making use of space-based DEWs and electromagnetic railguns.

Near term limited or more distant comprehensive BMD architectures would rely on air, ground- and space-based devices to provide a limited or a global warning network. Space-based sensors would be essential to detect the launch of Soviet ICBMs or submarine-launched ballistic missiles (SLBMs). This area of "boost-phase surveillance" is a key element in SDI research. Satellite active and passive sensors, possibly complemented by ground-based rocket "probes" carrying sensors, would also perform midcourse surveillance and tracking. Midcourse sensors could permit the defense system to discriminate between nuclear warheads in the "threat cloud" that must be intercepted and the nonthreatening objects intended to confuse the defense, such as decoys and debris. These sensors would track objects in the threat cloud and hand information over to other sensors to improve the effectiveness of the various defensive tiers. The terminal defensive layer could use information from midcourse sensors, in addition to ground-based radars and possibly long-endurance aircraft equipped with infrared sensors, to determine objects leaking through previous defensive layers and to identify threatening warheads.[26]

Space-based sensors also would contribute to an effective "battle management." A layered battle management system would monitor the threatening situation and distribute information to authorities, identify defensive resources, including sensors and interceptors, and allocate them in the most effective fashion. Obviously, an effective battle management system would require highly advanced data processing (hardware and software) and communication systems.

It should be noted that advanced warning and surveillance systems are important for non-BMD functions as well. For example, future space arms control agreements would likely require an enhanced capability for space surveillance for verification purposes. Improvement of U.S. space-based sensors is important regardless of the SDI.

There are, of course, uncertainties involved in a number

of SDI technical areas. For example, the unclassified summary of the Defensive Technologies Study noted, "There are several critical technological issues that will probably require research programs of ten to twenty years." These issues include:[27]

— will it be possible to intercept missiles in their boost and postboost phase?

— will midcourse discrimination become sufficiently precise to permit useful distinction between warheads and penetration aids?

— can defense systems be rendered sufficiently survivable to counter Soviet defense suppression tactics?

— will defenses be able to achieve a sufficiently favorable cost ratio vis-à-vis Soviet offensive countermeasures?

— can a battle-management system be effective, survivable, and capable of rapid response?

THE IMPORTANCE OF LAYERED AND PREFERENTIAL DEFENSE

At this point it appears important that a future BMD system include multiple tiers. Multiple tiers or layers of defense would be designed to intercept ballistic missiles and MIRV buses during their boost and postboost phases of flight. This type of defense also would intercept warheads during their long midcourse and short terminal phases of flight. This "birth to death" defensive coverage of attacking missiles should provide a more effective defense at less cost than concentrating all defensive resources in an attempt to achieve a near-perfect single layer of defense. Multiple layers would permit each tier to be far less than "perfect" while providing an overall high level of defense effectiveness. The benefits of multiple defensive tiers can be seen in the example of a hypothetical defensive architecture that includes five defensive tiers. This hypothetical system would incorporate layers of defense to intercept in the boost, post- boost, early and late midcourse, and terminal phases of an attacking ballistic missile's flight trajectory. If each layer of defense was 85 percent effective, the overall level of effectiveness would permit .01 percent "leakage" of offensive warheads.

In a Soviet attack of 10,000 warheads, only one would be likely to penetrate. Under current defenseless conditions *all* attacking warheads except those that malfunctioned would detonate on or over the United States.

A multilayered system also allows the defense to take advantage of those characteristics of each flight phase that are beneficial for the defense. As mentioned above, *boost* and *postboost* intercept could catch the attacking ballistic missiles and buses before they could release their host of deadly MIRVs and penetration aids. The relatively long duration of the *midcourse* may provide sufficient time to discriminate between real warheads and the "pen aids," thereby allowing the defense to strike only at real warheads and conserve its assets. As the "threat cloud" of warheads and pen aids reenters the atmosphere during the terminal phase, the lighter pen aids would be stripped away because they would descend through the atmosphere at a different rate than the heavier warheads. Consequently, although the time available for terminal intercept is quite short, the atmosphere helps to filter out the threat cloud exposing the real warheads to the defense.

Obviously, if all missiles could be intercepted during their boost phase, an ideal situation, then the rest of the defensive architecture would be unnecessary. But Soviet offensive countermeasures might degrade the effectiveness of even a very robust boost phase defense system. Consequently, it would be important to "backstop" even an exceptionally good boost phase defense. Fortunately for the defense, the offensive countermeasures that could be effective against the first layer of defense may not be effective against the second or third layers. Indeed, the offensive countermeasures designed to defeat particular layers of defense generally are incompatible with the offensive countermeasures needed to penetrate all other layers of defense. Thus the use of multiple defensive layers increases the attacker's difficulties in designing a successful offensive strategy. For example, adding shielding to an ICBM to reduce the effects of boost phase lasers would add weight to the attacking missile; the added weight would in turn reduce the number of warheads and pen aids that the missile could carry, thereby easing the defense's burden during the midcourse and terminal stages. Similarly, the added shielding to protect an ICBM from laser beams would not easily protect against particle beams, which could pass through shielding and disrupt the complex electronics of the ICBM.

Since SDI research is necessary to determine the technical feasibility of a comprehensive defensive architecture, it is not possible to specify in other than a general way the systems that might be used if a decision were made to deploy comprehensive defenses. However, the advantages to the defense of multiple types and tiers of BMD suggest that any future comprehensive defense against ballistic missiles would consist of multiple layers and types of intercept systems.

An additional advantage for the defense could come from a tactic for interception called "preferential defense." It could be especially useful for a limited defensive system. Preferential defense would assign interceptors to defend highly valued assets preferentially. For example, U.S. sensors would detect the Soviet ballistic missile launch; following MIRV separation, U.S. sensors would help determine the points in the United States scheduled for destruction by the attacking nuclear warheads. This would permit the U.S. BMD system to allocate interceptors to defend *only* those points under attack, and to defend the most valued points with the most interceptors. Thus, if the Soviet Union launched a large attack against U.S. strategic retaliatory forces and military-industrial centers, the United States could decide to defend some assets, move some retaliatory forces, and leave undefended those particularly hard to destroy or of less value. The United States could concentrate interceptors against those nuclear weapons headed toward military-industrial centers with large nearby civilian populations. Soviet offensive planners, not knowing what the United States would defend, or with how many interceptors, would have great difficulty in overwhelming the U.S. defenses at those points defended preferentially. Preferential defense tactics, then, would permit the United States to obtain maximum defensive leverage from a limited BMD system.

Preferential defense tactics obviously require that the U.S. defense system have a good capability for determining the aim points of the attacking warheads following their release from the MIRV bus. This would necessitate effective sensors for midcourse discrimination—one of the more difficult technical problems. An effective preferential defense also would necessitate a layer of midcourse interceptors. A ground-based interceptor capable of destroying Soviet warheads in midcourse would provide defensive coverage for a very large area. Only a few BMD sites would be needed to cover most of North America. Consequently, the Soviet Union would not be able to determine what the United States was intending to defend by examining the location of U.S. interceptors.

In short, preferential defense tactics and multiple layers of interceptors, including some space-based components, could characterize a future BMD architecture. Be that as it may, it should be remembered that the SDI is a plan to examine the emerging technologies that may eventually contribute to such a defensive system; it is not a program to build any specific BMD architecture.

Of course, to achieve comprehensive protection against nuclear weapons, even a highly effective defense against ballistic missiles would have to be complemented by air defenses against bombers and cruise missiles. Fortunately, the West has a number of air defense systems in production and deployed in Western Europe, and some of the systems useful for BMD would also contribute to air defense. In addition, recent policy developments indicate that the U.S. recognizes the need for increased air defense as the Soviet bomber/cruise missile threat grows, and as a complement to any future comprehensive BMD program.

SUMMARY AND CONCLUSION

In summary, there is no certainty concerning the technological feasibility of a highly effective BMD. Numerous scientists familiar with emerging BMD technologies are optimistic about their potential; other respected scientists have announced their deep skepticism. In contrast, there is little debate concerning the feasibility of a limited defense system capable of protecting a selected set of assets. The value of such a system against a number of potential threats could be great indeed. The fact that some technical issues are in doubt concerning the potential for a comprehensive defense in no way reduces the value of the SDI. On the contrary, it underscores the importance of pursuing the necessary research to help address these important issues. A limited BMD architecture could consist of boost, midcourse and terminal layers of defense. A comprehensive BMD system probably would require postboost and possibly multiple midcourse defensive layers as well. The means used to destroy attacking Soviet missiles and warheads might include a combination of rockets armed with non-nuclear homing interceptors, laser and particle beams, and electromagnetic railguns. Some of these components might be ground-based, others space-based.

There are two primary technical criticisms of the SDI: (1) the potential for a comprehensive defense is very low ("impossible"), therefore the SDI should be curtailed; and, (2) anything less than perfect defense would not be useful, therefore the SDI should be curtailed.

Both of these charges against the SDI are unpersuasive. Given the potential for a highly effective defense many scientists see in the emerging BMD technologies it hardly seems reasonable to curtail the SDI, particularly since BMD's potential value, if realized, would be enormous compared to the relatively modest cost of the research program.

The second charge is generally based upon the presumption that the Soviet Union views city destruction as the highest goal of strategic doctrine. Consequently, the reasoning goes, imperfect defenses would compel the Soviet Union to use its strategic forces to saturate the American BMD to ensure the destruction of U.S. cities. But to assume that the Soviet Union would concentrate its forces against U.S. cities almost certainly reflects a misunderstanding of Soviet doctrine, which emphasizes the importance of targeting U.S. nuclear forces in order to change decisively the "correlation of forces." In the Soviet view, nuclear weapons should concentrate on military objectives, such as destroying enemy nuclear forces. The gratuitous destruction of population centers does not appear to play a role in Soviet military doctrine. Consequently, even a less than perfect BMD, rather than causing the Soviet Union to turn toward a "city-busting" targeting policy, should deny the Soviet military planner the ability to design or conduct successfully a nuclear first strike.

There is almost no debate concerning the merit of the president's long-term hope for strategic defense. The debate concerns the technical potential for moving from the current condition of virtual defenselessness to a future condition of "defense dominance." Those who see little or no potential for such a move caution that SDI research is destined to be a failure and a waste of resources. Those who believe that emerging BMD technologies offer the potential for an effective defense are, of course, anxious to get on with the necessary research.

One need not endorse a particular side of the technical debate to consider the issue. Indeed, it may be easier to consider the basic question from an agnostic perspective: does the uncertain potential for comprehensive BMD warrant the cost of pursuing the research program necessary to address questions of feasibility? In short, should we as a nation be willing to pay the costs to find out whether effective defense against nuclear missiles is feasible? Given the undistinguished history of technological skeptics concerning many successful projects in the past, the less than two percent of the defense budget that would be devoted to the SDI research program, and the escape from the nuclear threat that might be set in motion by the SDI, it certainly seems reasonable to answer, yes.

ENDNOTES

1. See, for example, Union of Concerned Scientists, *Space-Based Missile Defense* (Cambridge, MA: Union of Concerned Scientists, March 1984).
2. Ashton B. Carter, *Directed Energy Missile Defense in Space—A Background Paper* (Washington, D.C.: U.S. Congress, Office of Technology Assessment, OTA-BP-ISC-26, April 1984), p. 81.
3. Harold Brown, *The Strategic Defense Initiative: Defensive Systems and the Strategic Debate*, unpublished paper for the Johns Hopkins School of Advanced International Studies, The Johns Hopkins University, 1984, p. 4. For a similarly negative view see Richard Garwin's prepared statement, "The President's Strategic Defense Initiative," Testimony for the Senate Armed Services Committee, April 24, 1984, p. 4.
4. Quoted in James C. Fletcher, "Technologies for Strategic Defense," *Issues In Science and Technology*, Vol. 1, No. 1 (Fall 1984), pp. 15, 25.
5. Ibid., p. 26.
6. See Robert Jastrow, *How To Make Nuclear Weapons Obsolete* (Boston, MA: Little, Brown, and Company, 1985), pp. 100-106; see also *Soviet Aerospace*, Vol. 43, No. 16 (April 29, 1985), p. 1.
7. Quoted in Christopher Cerf and Victor Navasky, *The Experts Speak* (New York: Pantheon Books, 1984), p. 232.

8. Ibid., p. 236.
9. Ibid., p. 236.
10. Ibid., p. 246.
11. Ibid., p. 299.
12. Ibid., p. 252.
13. See the comments of Robert Jastrow, quoted in *Soviet Aerospace*, op. cit., p. 1.
14. Ibid., p. 250.
15. James C. Fletcher, op. cit., p. 29.
16. For an official description of this test see Office of Assistant Secretary of Defense (Public Affairs), News Release, No. 311-84 (June 11, 1984).
17. See Jastrow, op. cit., pp. 41-43; Patrick Friel, "U.S. Ballistic Missile Defense Technology: A Technical Overview," *Comparative Strategy*, Vol. 4, No. 4 (1984), pp. 319-347; Harold Brown, op. cit., pp. 13-16; Harold Brown, "The Strategic Defense Initiative: Defensive Systems and the Strategic Debate," *Survival* (March/April, 1985), pp. 59-60; see also Union of Concerned Scientists, op. cit., p. 61.
18. See *The President's Strategic Defense Initiative* (Washington, D.C.: USGPO, January 1985), p. 3. Defense of retaliatory forces is endorsed in what is reported to be the most recent National Security Decision Directive (NSDD) on the SDI, i.e., NSDD 172. See Jim Klurfeld, "Star Wars Plan Is Modified," *Long Island Newsday*, June 14, 1985, p. 5.
19. See McGeorge Bundy, George Kennan, Robert McNamara and Gerard Smith, "The President's Choice: Star Wars or Arms Control," *Foreign Affairs*, Vol. 63, No. 2 (Winter 1984/85), pp. 266, 267.
20. Union of Concerned Scientists, op. cit., p. 83.
21. John Erickson, "The Soviet View of Deterrence: A General Survey," *Survival*, Vol. 24, No. 6 (November-December 1982), p. 246.
22. See, for example, the specific proposal in Jastrow, op. cit., pp. 100-106.
23. Ibid., pp. 103, 114.
24. See Department of Defense, *The Strategic Defense Initiative–Defensive Technologies Study* (Washington, D.C.: USGPO, April 1984), p. 6.
25. Jastrow, op. cit., p. 92.
26. See *The Strategic Defense Initiative–Defensive Technologies Study*, pp. 7-8; and Department of Defense, Strategic Defense Initiative Organization, *Report to Congress on the SDI* (Washington, D.C.: USGPO, 1985), p. 24.
27. These issues are derived from *The Strategic Defense Initiative–Defensive Technologies Study*, pp. 11-12; and Fletcher, op. cit., pp. 23-25.

FIGURE 6

Artist's Conception of Space-Based Non-Nuclear Rocket Defense System

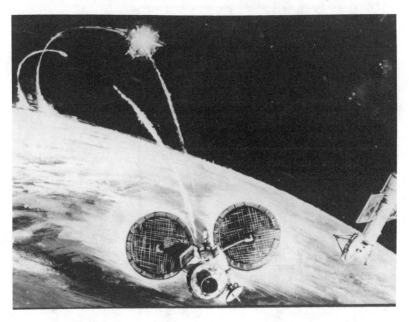

This BMD system would be intended
to intercept ballistic missiles warheads
through the use of homing rockets
based in space.

COURTESY OF DEPARTMENT OF DEFENSE

FIGURE 7

Defense Intercept Phases

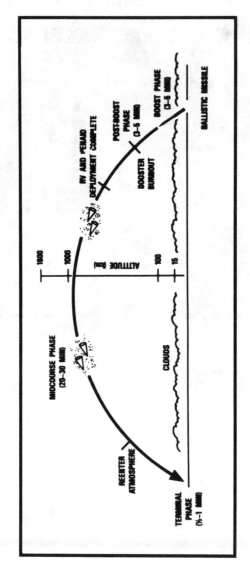

Illustration of the boost/post-boost, mid-course, and terminal stages of an ICBM's flight trajectory. This illustration indicates the importance of boost phase intercept to prevent the release of MIRVs and pen aids.

FIGURE 8

Neutral Particle Beam

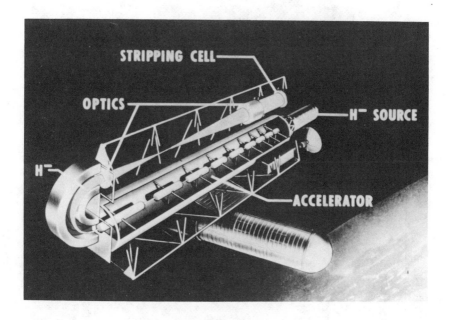

An artist's conception of a space-based neutral particle beam and its main components. Such system would shoot hydrogen molecules at about 60,000 kilometers per second.

FIGURE 9

Directed Energy Weapons: Neutral Particle Beam

PRESENT ▼   ▼ FUTURE

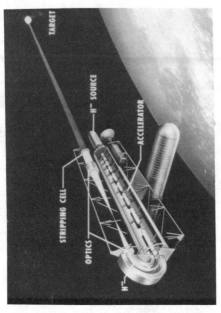

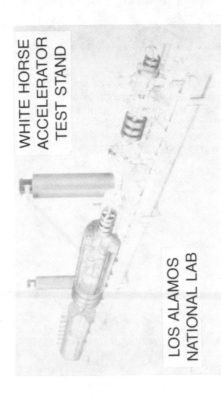

LOS ALAMOS
NATIONAL LAB

WHITE HORSE
ACCELERATOR
TEST STAND

- LABORATORY (Scaleability)

- SPACE BASED OPERATIONAL SYSTEM

An artist's rendering of the *current* laboratory particle beam
test stand called "White Horse" located at the Los Alamos
National Laboratory (left); and an artist's conception of a
future space-based, particle beam BMD system (right).

FIGURE 10

"White Horse" Neutral Particle Beam Test Stand

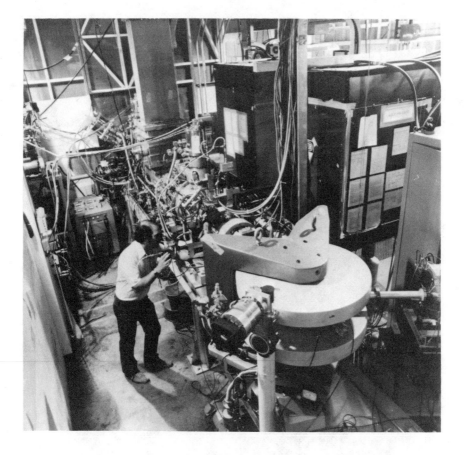

Picture of the "White Horse" Neutral Particle beam test stand located at the Los Alamos National Laboratory.

FIGURE 11

Artist's Conception of Space-Based Electromagnetic Railgun

The railgun would fire small projectiles at a rate greater than one per second and at speeds of thousands of meters per second.

FIGURE 12

Aluminum Block Test

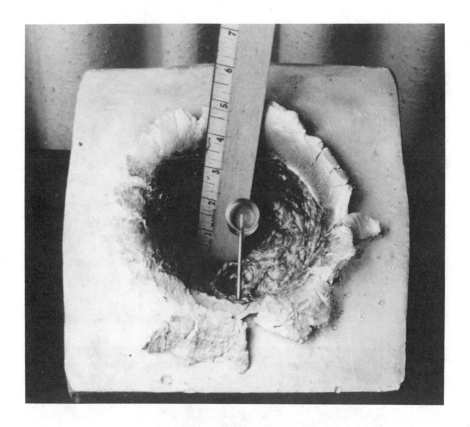

The aluminum block in this picture was struck by a 1/3 ounce projectile the size of the plastic object at the center. The projectile was traveling at about 15,000 miles per hour. The high speed collision resulted in a 4-inch deep blast in the aluminum block.

COURTESY OF DEPARTMENT OF DEFENSE

Artist's Conceptions of Ground-Based Laser Systems

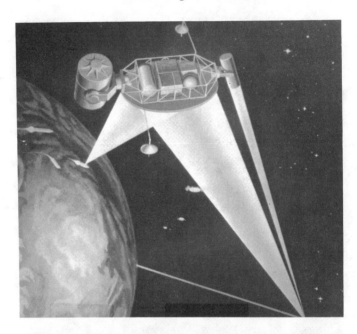

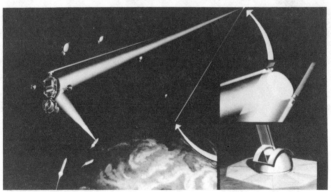

A high energy laser would intercept attacking ICBMs at the speed of light — about 300,000 kilometers per second. Note that the laser itself would be ground-based — facilitating ease of maintenance. Mirrors to relay the laser beam to target would be located in space.

FIGURE 15

Test Results of MIRACL

Picture of test results of the U.S. Navy's large chemical laser named MIRACL. It was able to burn off the tail of a drone aircraft in several seconds. In the case of an ICBM, a fraction of a second would be required.

FIGURE 16

Boost Surveillance and Tracking System

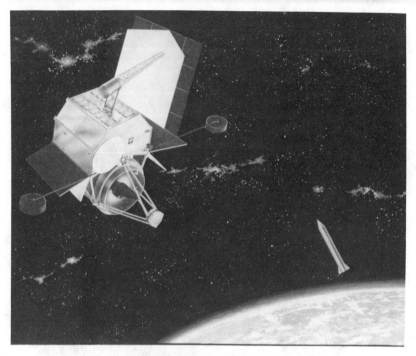

Artist's conception of a boost-phase surveillance satellite. Such a satellite would detect ballistic missile launches, track missiles during the boost phase of their flight, and relay firing information to interceptor components.

FIGURE 17

Notional Multiple Layered SDI

An illustration of multiple defensive layers intended to intercept attacking ballistic missiles and nuclear warheads along their entire flight path. Notice the combination of ground-based and space-based BMD components, and the importance of attacking ballistic missiles in their boost and post-boost phases of flight to preclude the release of thousands of warheads and pen aids.

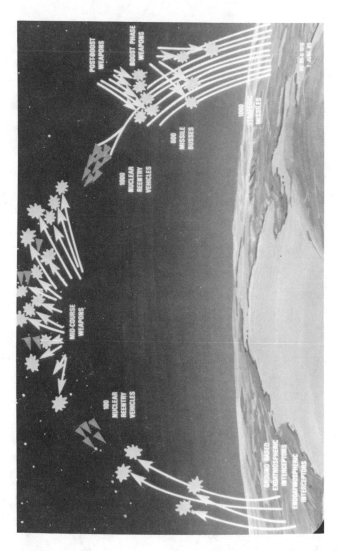

SIX

Chapter 6

STABILITY: THE SDI AND STRATEGIC DEFENSE

O ver the last two decades "stability" has become a magic word in U.S. strategic debates, both for those opposing and those supporting new weapon programs. Critics of new strategic forces tend to characterize them as "destabilizing," while their proponents claim that "stability" will be strengthened by their deployment. Unless a weapon system can be both stabilizing and destabilizing simultaneously, something is amiss. What is amiss is that to characterize a system as "stabilizing" or "destabilizing" is now generally done for political effect with little regard to logic. Whether spoken by proponents or critics of a program, the words have come to be used as political incantations.

During earlier debates in the United States, BMD programs were criticized as "destabilizing" by opponents. For example, Dr. Hans Bethe, an eminent physicist and critic of the current SDI program, argued before Congress in 1969 that the U.S. *Safeguard* BMD program "would indeed make it [deterrence] much less stable."[1] More recently the SDI has similarly been labeled "destabilizing." Yet the Reagan administration has observed that "providing a better, more stable basis for enhanced deterrence is the central purpose of the SDI program."[2] This chapter will look at the various stability/instability claims about the SDI and try to shed some light on their meaning and validity.

STRATEGIC STABILITY: WHAT IS IT?

Strategic stability concerns the probability of strategic nuclear war—if an arms control agreement or a weapon system is "stabilizing," it reduces the probability of war. In theory, the concept of stability is understood to involve the incentives and disincentives to use (or continue to use) strategic nuclear weapons, or to take provocative actions that might lead to the use of those weapons. But it is not limited to nuclear considerations. Strategic stability is linked directly to the probability of conventional war because such a conflict, in Europe for example, could provoke the use of nuclear weapons. This also applies to any acute crisis – recall the Cuban Missile Crisis of 1962. There is a continuum from crisis, to large-scale conventional war, to nuclear war, because even an initially low-level crisis could erupt into nuclear war. Stability encompasses this entire continuum ranging from events that might lead to the consideration of nuclear use, to actual strategic nuclear war. Under perfect stability the Soviet Union, for example, would not have sufficient incentives to strike the United States with nuclear weapons, attack Western Europe with conventional forces, or engage in other highly provocative acts that might lead to an "escalation" to nuclear war. In theory, *stability refers to that condition which minimizes the probability of nuclear war or the highly provocative behavior that might lead to nuclear war.*

As discussed in chapter three, over the past two decades many Americans came to view stability as synonymous with a condition of mutual vulnerability to nuclear retaliation. The theory was that if both sides were vulnerable to nuclear retaliation, neither would launch a first strike against the other, nor would either side behave in too provocative a manner (such as a conventional attack against an ally of the opponent).

As a result of this theory—that a condition of mutual vulnerability is an effective way to maintain stability—weapon systems that might appear to alter the condition of mutual vulnerability were tagged as "destabilizing"; in contrast, weapons that helped ensure the preservation of mutual vulnerability were labeled "stabilizing." For example, ICBMs that combined the accuracy and explosive power necessary to destroy the opponent's missiles in their silos have been considered destabilizing because destroying an opponent's means of retaliation could help alter the condition of mutual vulnerability. Similarly, defenses that might reduce the vulnerability of cities, people, and industry have been considered destabilizing. In the seemingly bizarre world of this strategic logic, the capability to threaten Soviet cities with nuclear destruction is good (i.e., stabilizing) but preparations to counter the Soviet threat and protect American cities are bad (i.e., destabilizing).

INSTABILITY AND THE SDI

Given the prevailing assumptions about stability described above, it is not difficult to understand why the deployment of strategic defenses, such as BMD, has been criticized as destabilizing. Of course, the SDI is a research program and should not be considered anything like destabilizing. But critics nonetheless oppose SDI research because it might, one day, lead to the deployment of defenses.[3]

The Soviet Union, for its part, must not consider BMD research and development destabilizing given its vigorous and expansive BMD R&D program. Indeed, it would be extremely destabilizing if the Soviet Union were to achieve a BMD R&D breakthrough of which the United States was unaware. If the Soviet Union were capable of providing a nationwide defense *unilaterally*, it might perceive less risk in using nuclear weapons or engaging in provocative actions. For that reason alone, U.S. R&D on ballistic missile defense is important, for it helps to ensure that the United States will not be surprised by a Soviet R&D breakthrough.

Is the SDI research program in the U.S. interest, or is it destabilizing as some critics assert? The question almost answers itself when put in perspective: should the United States permit the possibility of a surprise Soviet BMD breakthrough? Should the United States be ignorant of the future technical prospects for defense against ballistic missiles? The answers are clearly no. U.S. R&D on ballistic missile defense is important, and stabilizing (to use the term properly).

A more sensible concern vis-à-vis the SDI and stability is: if SDI research leads to a decision to deploy BMD, is that deployment likely to be destabilizing as opponents of the SDI charge?[4] There are three separate types of instability charges leveled against BMD deployment: (1) crisis instability, (2) transition instability; and, (3) post-transition instability. Each of these is first explained and then assessed below.

CRISIS INSTABILITY

The crisis instability charge follows directly from the mutual vulnerability notion of deterrence. The concern is that U.S. BMD deployment would cause the Soviet Union to question its own deterrent capability.[5] Consequently, in a military crisis the Soviet Union, unsure of the power of its deterrent, would fear a U.S. first strike. In dreaded anticipation of this, the Soviet Union might decide to beat the United States to the punch so that Soviet forces could not be destroyed on the ground. Crisis instability can be abbreviated simply to: "use'em" before "losing'em." The Soviet leadership would not have to believe that its first strike would mean victory, just that it might reduce the damage that it would be certain to suffer in any event. And the damage would be reduced because the United States would be able to retaliate only with those forces that survived the Soviet first strike. In short, the concern is that U.S. defenses might lead the Soviet Union to anticipate a U.S. first strike in a crisis, and thereby give the Soviet Union an incentive to strike first itself. As Strobe Talbott, a noted commentator on arms control, has observed:

> It has long been part of the dogma of the nuclear age that the best defense is a good offense. That is what deterrence is all about: the other side is less likely to attack if its leaders know they will prompt a vastly destructive counter-attack. A corollary to the dogma of "offense-dominated" deterrence is that there is nothing more provocative and destabilizing than strategic defense....Nixon was aware of the paradox that Reagan has overlooked: one side's quest for safety can heighten the other side's insecurity.[6]

Critics of ballistic missile defense argue that crisis instability would be especially dangerous if deployed ballistic missile defenses are imperfect and "leaky." For example, in a crisis the Soviet Union might presume that the United States would be under pressure to strike first because leaky defenses might only defend American cities effectively against an enfeebled Soviet nuclear capability, one that had been weakened by a U.S. first strike. In effect, a U.S. first strike would reduce Soviet offensive capabilities to the point where "leaky" U.S. defenses could "handle" the remaining Soviet offensive forces. Consequently, the Soviet Union would have an incentive to strike against U.S. nuclear forces before they could be used. As one critic of "Star Wars" wrote in the *New Republic*:

> A leaky U.S. defense would have a reverse effect on the Soviets. No one would be quite sure how leaky the American defense was. It would undoubtedly not be good enough to prevent the Soviets, if they struck first, from destroying the United States as a functioning society. But a degraded Soviet missile force— one that had sustained a first strike—might not be sufficient to overcome a leaky defense, and thus would lose much of its credibility as a deterrent. In a crisis the Soviets would find themselves pressed to use it or lose it....Uncertainty that the Soviet retaliatory force could indeed retaliate would make the nuclear balance more precarious than it is today.[7]

TRANSITION INSTABILITY

The potential for crisis instability could be particularly disturbing soon after a decision for BMD deployment is made because the system will be "leaky" at least for the initial period of time required to deploy the system, no matter how effective it eventually becomes. In short, a very effective defense cannot be built overnight, and during the "transition" phase when a ballistic missile defense system is being deployed U.S. defenses are likely to be leaky. This potential problem of a transition phase characterized by leaky defenses and crisis instability is a key concern for many. Among those concerned, for example, is James Woolsey, a well-respected member of the president's Commission on Strategic Forces, who has remarked:

> ...I have a similar attitude toward a space-based ballistic missile defense that I do toward a negotiated world that would be entirely free of nuclear weapons. Both, in a sense, are attractive objectives in a philosophical way, but the whole problem with

both is how you would manage a transition, and the transition is not some footnote to the problem. The transition is the major problem.[8]

Crisis instability is not the only potential "transition" problem pointed to by critics of the SDI and strategic defense. Another involves the incentives for the Soviet Union to destroy U.S. space-based ballistic missile defense components before they could provide any significant protection. The U.S. defense system might seem so threatening to the Soviet leaders, that they would rather accept the risks of attacking the U.S. system than permit it to be fully deployed. Given that space-based components would likely be unmanned, a Soviet attack on them would neither strike U.S. soil nor kill any Americans. Thus, it is argued, the risk of attacking U.S. space-based components could appear low compared to the benefit if it compelled the United States to forego its defensive capability. As one critic of strategic defenses explains it:

> What would the Soviets do [in response to U.S. BMD deployment]? They would certainly develop counter measures, increase their offensive capacity, and so on. But if they found themselves facing nuclear subjugation, they might attack elements of the system when it approached completion; even more likely, during a crisis; and, almost certainly if war appeared imminent. And since it is hard to imagine an attack on American defensive installations being viewed as anything other than an act of war, a Star Wars defense, *before becoming operational*, could easily provoke an armed conflict between superpowers.[9]

In short, it is argued that the dangers of the transition period could include: (1) an incentive for the Soviet Union to launch a nuclear first-strike during a crisis for fear that a partially defended United States would feel itself compelled to strike first; and (2) the likelihood that the Soviet Union would perceive U.S. BMD as so threatening that it would not permit its deployment, i.e., it would destroy U.S. space-based BMD components before they became operational.

POST-TRANSITION INSTABILITY

Even if it were possible to proceed safely through the

"transition" phase of BMD deployment, critics of the SDI and strategic defense are worried about the potential instability even effective defenses would create once in place. The "post-transition" instability problem centers upon the current role that the U.S. nuclear threat plays in deterring a Soviet conventional attack on U.S. allies. As described in the first chapter, the United States and NATO have become highly reliant upon the nuclear threat to deter a Soviet conventional attack against Western Europe. Critics of the SDI argue that the president's vision of a world wherein nuclear weapons are made obsolete does not allow the NATO nuclear threat to compensate for NATO conventional force inadequacies. If the SDI leads to a world wherein nuclear weapons are "obsolete," how could NATO use the threat of nuclear escalation to deter the Soviet Union from exploiting its advantages in and around Eurasia? Critics of the SDI charge that removing the strategic nuclear threat through strategic defense would significantly reduce Soviet inhibitions concerning a *conventional* war against U.S. allies, thereby increasing the probability of war. In short, it is argued that effective defenses would make the world safe for conventional war. As Charles Glaser, a critic of the SDI, has asserted, the potential problem with very effective defenses

> ...is that they could increase the probability of superpower conventional wars. Today's nuclear forces greatly increase the potential costs of any direct U.S.-Soviet military confrontation. As a result, nuclear weapons increase the risk of starting a conventional war, and therefore contribute to the deterrence of conventional war. Impenetrable defenses would eliminate this contribution.[10]

In this argument, critics of BMD charge that post-transition instability would increase the risk of war for U.S. allies because the Soviet Union, given its own defenses, would be less fearful of U.S. nuclear escalation and the ensuing instability would increase the current level of threat to Western Europe. Whether this is likely to be the case is examined later in this chapter.

STABILITY: "DON'T ROCK THE BOAT"

Another stability-oriented criticism of the SDI and strategic defense is that deterrence is working, and the current condition of mutual vulnerability is stable, so why take any action that might rock the boat? This charge does not claim that BMD would necessarily be destabilizing, but that there is no reason to risk a change when the current deterrence relationship is working so effectively, and strategic defense might be destabilizing. To quote again from Charles Glaser, a critic of strategic defense:

> Even in [the] best case, defensive situations are not clearly preferable to the current assured destruction situation. In addition, many of the nuclear situations that could result from starting down the BMD route are far less desirable than our current mutual assured destruction situation. Without the possibility of a best outcome that is clearly preferable to our current situation, there is now no good reason to invest enormous resources in strategic defense and to risk creating a more dangerous world. The arguments for not drastically altering the nuclear status quo are much stronger than those that call for U.S. deployment of an area defense.[11]

This argument, in effect, follows the old adage, "if it ain't broke, don't fix it."

COMPUTERS TAKING OVER?

A final instability charge against BMD deployment is aimed specifically at the first potential layer of defense—the boost-phase tier. There are both serious and somewhat silly versions of this instability charge. The facetious version suggests that because boost-phase intercept of an ICBM would have to be accomplished very quickly (within 3-5 minutes after launch), the whole affair would be taken out of the hands of political decision-makers and placed into the "hands" of computers. That is, the president would be compelled to "predelegate" authority to an automatic boost-phase intercept system. Consequently, so the argument goes, computers, and not political authorities, would make decisions about nuclear war.

The argument, of course, equates predelegation of the authority to use nuclear weapons with automation of a boost-phase intercept system, which are two very different issues and ought not be confused. Predelegation of authority to use offensive nuclear weapons could conceivably increase the probability of a nuclear war and make its control even more difficult. Such predelegation involves nuclear weapons that could cause enormous civilian damage if involved in an accident. In contrast, automation of boost-phase interceptors would contingently authorize the use of non-nuclear defenses that would be capable of destroying nuclear weapons that *had already been launched* at the United States or its allies. Even if a boost-phase interceptor were activated somehow by mistake, a laser, particle beam, or small homing rocket launched in space accidently would hardly be likely to cause any damage to anything on Earth or in outer space. This charge—that boost-phase intercept will somehow threaten to give computers the keys to World War III—is the stuff of political campaigns, not serious discussion.

Nevertheless, there is a more serious side of the crisis-instability charge against boost-phase intercept. If a boost-phase system were automated, there could be some risk, unless precautionary measures were taken, that *nonthreatening* Soviet rockets would be intercepted. Soviet ICBM and SLBM tests might be intercepted by accident, or even a missile boosting a Soviet spacecraft into orbit. Obviously, such incidents could increase tensions and must be guarded against, although the probability that such an accident could in any way lead to a nuclear war seems remote. Fortunately, as will be discussed below, there are a number of measures that would guard against any such boost-phase intercept accident.

In summary, critics of the SDI are concerned that the deployment of strategic defense would be "destabilizing." For those SDI critics who use the term "destabilizing" analytically and not just as a political incantation, the increased risk of war they see in BMD deployment outweighs any potential benefit that might realistically be expected to come from deployment. Different critics emphasize different reasons for the instability they anticipate; but in general the charge that BMD deployment will increase the risk of war (i.e., be destabilizing) is based upon one or more of the following arguments:

1. *Crisis Instability:* BMD deployment will cause crisis instability because it will increase incentives to strike first.

2. *Transition Instability:* (a) the limited defense capability

available during a transition phase will increase crisis instability; (b) the Soviet Union will so fear U.S. defenses that it will attack U.S. space-based BMD components before they become operational, thereby triggering an acute military crisis.

3. *Post-Transition Instability:* BMD deployment leading to effective defenses will degrade the U.S./NATO nuclear deterrent and thereby increase the probability of conventional war.

4. *Maintain the Status Quo:* The current deterrence relationship is stable and acceptable while the deployment of BMD would entail potential risks; consequently the United States ought not "rock the boat" by deploying BMD.

5. *"Accidental" Boost-Phase Intercept:* Boost-phase interceptors will not have time to be under close human control. Consequently, in the absence of close human control, a peaceful Soviet space-launch could be shot down by accident, leading to an acute crisis.

The issue of stability is important: if the deployment of BMD can be shown to increase the probability of war (i.e., if it would be destabilizing), then the increased risk of war may well outweigh any of the potential benefits of defense. If that indeed is the case, then the United States ought not proceed down the road of BMD deployment. Congressman Les Aspin, chairman of the House Armed Services Committee, has rightly noted that consideration of deterrence and stability is key to the future of the SDI; and yet he questions whether the Reagan administration has examined the issue carefully. Obviously, the administration has not adequately demonstrated that the issue has received careful and detailed attention.

In fairness, it should be observed that because the SDI is indeed a research program intended to address important, but as yet unanswered, technical questions, some of the critics' instability charges cannot be addressed with any certainty, but then, nor are they based on any certainty.

The SDI should, for example, help to uncover whether defensive components placed in space would be relatively vulnerable or invulnerable to Soviet attack. The answer to that question is essential to understanding the degree to which the Soviet Union might be tempted to attack U.S. space-based systems. If those systems or components are vulnerable to easy attack the Soviets might be prompted under some circumstances to strike out at them. If they are highly survivable then it would make little sense for the Soviet leadership to risk such an attack.

Nevertheless, Congressman Aspin's questions must be addressed clearly:

> Has this administration really thought through what it is doing to the concept of deterrence?...[B]efore we discard [offensive] deterrent—which has after all helped preserve peace for 40 years—hadn't we better be sure that we have something with which to replace it?[12]

This is a reasonable question. The SDI is a research program; but if it is examining the feasibility of pursuing a course that would significantly increase the probability of war, great caution is in order.

STABILITY, THE SDI, AND STRATEGIC DEFENSE

The stability case against BMD deployment is not as one-sided as many SDI critics appear to assume. There is another side to each of the instability charges against the SDI and BMD deployment. Indeed, if pursued properly, the deployment of BMD could be stabilizing and actually reduce the probability of war.

But before examining the "other side" of the instability criticisms, allow a caveat. Stability is usually discussed with a great deal of confidence. A weapon system or concept, such as BMD often is labeled "destabilizing" by critics as if there were a precise understanding concerning what is stabilizing or destabilizing. Unfortunately, such an understanding does not and can not now exist. There is no consensus on a theory of war causation; and there is no theory—supported by the scientific method of marshaling evidence—of nuclear war causation to serve as a guide as to what is or is not stabilizing. The deductive theories of deterrence that dominate thinking about stability and nuclear war cannot be proved or disproved. The absence of war does not "prove" that deterrence has worked, while intuitively it seems that deterrence has worked, it virtually is impossible to know *why* there has been an absence of general war. Only in the event of nuclear war would we have some indication of why strategic deterrence had not worked. Even in that case, it would be unclear *exactly* why deterrence had failed unless the event could be replicated and tested under various conditions. All in all, ignorance undoubtedly is preferable to testing any such theory.

But the drawback of that ignorance is the lack of clear guidance as to what is, without doubt, stabilizing or destabilizing. Statements can be made about the instability or stability of a prospective system without being demonstrably correct or incorrect. As a result, there is little discipline in the use of the concept of stability. This in turn leads to a problem in the U.S. debate over SDI and BMD. Many in Congress and the media appear only to understand the concept of deterrence through mutual vulnerability. And, therefore, they are apt to think that anything inconsistent with that concept must be "destabilizing." Yet there may be other, more effective, approaches to deterrence that have not been popularized.

This is not to say that we are dealing in total guesswork; current theories of deterrence and stability based upon deductive logic and intuition may be valid and useful—the problem is that there can be no certainty one way or another. Very few critics or proponents of a prospective weapon system will bother to inform an audience about the weakness inherent in their charges of "instability" or "stability" (that, of course, would spoil the effect).

With the above warning in mind, the critics' charges of instability leveled at the SDI and BMD can be considered.

CRISIS STABILITY AND BMD

The first stability criticism is that BMD will cause "crisis instability," because BMD—particularly "leaky" and transitional BMD—would increase Soviet incentives to strike first. Yet even limited defenses such as those that would be available during a transition period could almost certainly provide protection for U.S. retaliatory capabilities. Even critics of the SDI note that the defense of U.S. retaliatory forces is feasible, and the defense of ICBMs could provide particularly useful advantages for the defender.[13] Reducing Soviet confidence in the military effectiveness of a first strike by defending U.S. retaliatory capabilities should be the key to *enhancing* crisis stability. The Soviet Union would be very unlikely to strike first if it were to leave many U.S. nuclear forces intact and poised to retaliate. A Soviet first strike that ensured a large-scale U.S. retaliation is hardly a useful option under any conditions, especially given the Soviet perspective. The observation by Professor John Erickson cited earlier is critical in this consideration: Soviet military opinion cautions against adventurist behavior in the absence of the capability to achieve "victory," i.e., superiority in the correlation of forces.[14] For the Soviet leadership to strike at well-defended U.S. retaliatory forces because of their fear of a U.S. first strike would be to commit suicide for fear of death. In short, if the concepts of deterrence and stability mean anything, defending U.S. retaliatory forces should help provide a condition that would maximize crisis stability.

Critics often charge that BMD for retaliatory forces would not truly enhance the U.S. deterrent because the survivability gained by defending U.S. retaliatory forces from a first strike would be nullified by the reduced capability of the surviving forces to threaten Soviet targets that would also be defended— what would be gained in increased force survivability would be lost in decreased force effectiveness. This criticism neglects the fact that Soviet defenses are already placing some targets beyond reach of U.S. retaliatory forces. But the stabilizing effect of defending U.S. retaliatory capabilities should function even when *both* the United States and the Soviet Union have BMD systems of limited effectiveness. For example, a defense system that could provide only "leaky" coverage for most types of targets could provide quite effective protection for ICBMs. This is because each ICBM need not be protected; and given the relatively large number of ICBMs, complete protection for each missile would be unnecessary. In addition, each ICBM could combine other protective measures with BMD to achieve an adequate level of defense effectiveness (e.g., silo-superhardening, deceptive ICBM basing schemes, ICBM mobility, etc.). Thus, a leaky BMD could protect ICBMs more effectively than most other types of facilities. This would provide deterrence leverage for the defender because protected ICBMs could retaliate against the opponent's more vulnerable assets, such as air bases, troop concentrations, submarine facilities, etc. As a result, even if the Soviet Union had an equally capable BMD system, defenses for U.S. retaliatory forces, especially ICBMs, should help sustain deterrence and stability.

Of course, Soviet defenses could also deny the United States a feasible first-strike option against Soviet ICBM silos. But, for a number of reasons, that is not disadvantageous for the United States. First, the declared U.S. approach to strategic doctrine and deterrence does not focus on a first strike against ICBMs as does the Soviet. The United States has not deployed offensive forces capable of a comprehensive strike against Soviet ICBM silos; if the Soviets did defend their ICBM silos against a first strike, the United States would not lose a capability that it now has or that is required by U.S. doctrine or deterrence policy. In any event, as the Soviet Union moves increasingly toward mobility for its ICBM force, those systems will become more difficult to target. Consequently, "leaky" defenses capable of protecting retaliatory capabilities, particularly ICBMs, should *reduce* Soviet incentives for a first strike, and need not debilitate the U.S. deterrent. In short, such defenses could contribute to stability, assuming the validity of the concept of deterrence and stability.

Limited BMD could enhance the survivability of other critical retaliatory assets in addition to ICBMs. For example, limited BMD could act as a "time buyer" for some critical facilities that otherwise would be subject to prompt destruction. Such sites could include fixed ballistic missile early warning radars, early warning satellite ground stations, the North American Air Defense Headquarters, Strategic Air Command (SAC) Headquarters, the National Military Command Center, the Alternate National Military Command Center, ICBM Launch Control Centers, SAC Bomber Wing Command Posts, the Emergency Rocket Communications System, air-mobile elements of the U.S. C^3 system such as the National Emergency Airborne Command Post and the Post Attack Command and Control System. Defense of such assets would help assure that a Soviet first strike could not "decapitate" the U.S. and thereby leave surviving U.S. forces beyond authorized control. This type of limited defense mission, just as defending ICBMs, would be valuable for deterrence and stability because it would help ensure that the Soviet Union could never anticipate a successful first strike. Passive defenses such as redundancy, hardening and mobility might in the future provide adequate protection; but, if the U.S. decides to pursue strategic defense the protection of retaliatory assets would be an important near-term mission that would contribute to stability during the transition period.

Interestingly, despite the fact that a majority of the public appears to support BMD even if it were only for the defense of ICBMs (see Appendix, Table 24), the Reagan administration has not strongly endorsed ICBM defense as a goal of the SDI. Indeed, the administration has stressed that "point defense" (i.e., defense for ICBMs) is not what the SDI is "about." Nevertheless, the administration has emphasized that the SDI is intended to serve deterrence and stability. But in this regard it should not be forgotten that "leaky" transitional defenses that would protect ICBMs and other retaliatory forces effectively would contribute to deterrence and stability during a defense transition period. In the absence of such defenses transitional stability may be more difficult to maintain. Consequently, given the administration's insistence upon strengthening deterrence and stability through the SDI, a greater appreciation of ICBM defense is in order. This mission may not need to rely on a BMD system capable of defending *only* ICBMs, but effective ICBM defense would contribute to stability during the transition.

Those who believe that the SDI ought not to be oriented toward near-term defense missions but should focus on more futuristic comprehensive defenses generally do not oppose near-term BMD options such as ICBM defense per se. Rather, they fear that the SDI budget and political support could not withstand the strain of both near-term BMD deployment *and* the longer-term R&D necessary for more comprehensive defenses. Thus, in a world of limited options, they would prefer to zero in on the more distant missions and BMD technologies.

There may, however, be a means of reconciling those who favor near-term BMD deployment for ICBM defense and those who favor the longer-term approach—two generically pro-SDI positions. That would be for the U.S. Army, which historically has had ground-based BMD under its auspices, to pursue the ICBM defense mission parallel with, but separate from, SDI research on more futuristic defense technologies. Indeed, pursuing an ICBM defense option as a mission distinct from a

SDI research program would seem logical given the recognized capacity of current or near-term technology to support an ICBM defense mission.

A SOVIET ATTACK ON BMD COMPONENTS?

The second transitional instability charge is that the Soviet Union would consider U.S. deployment of BMD to be so threatening that it would strike at U.S. BMD components in space rather than allow the system to become operational. In truth, no one can say with complete certainty that the Soviet Union would never commit such an act under any circumstances. But it does seem terribly unrealistic to expect the Soviet Union to commit an act of war in response to a peacetime BMD deployment, particularly given the large number of other less risky Soviet options, and the fact that the Soviet Union would undoubtedly have plans for initiating its own space-based BMD deployments.

The U.S. would assuredly respond to a purposeful act of war against a sovereign U.S. spacecraft—perhaps by striking a Soviet spacecraft, or attacking some terrestrial target. And again, as Professor Erickson has suggested, the Soviet Union is loath to commit "adventurist" acts in the absence of a winning "correlation of forces." If the Soviet Union did not see that winning condition existing before the U.S. deployed defense components, it certainly would not see it after deployment. If deterrence against war on Earth is shaky, and war appears imminent, the Soviet Union might indeed attempt an attack on U.S. space-based BMD components and other targets. But in that case—which really is the most realistic scenario for such an attack—the Soviet strike would not be prompted by U.S. BMD deployment, but by the weakness of deterrence. Assuming a very fragile deterrence and the anticipation of war, the Soviet Union *might* attack various U.S. military systems. But, recall that even leaky defenses should *strengthen* deterrence. If deterrence is functioning on Earth it should ensure a peaceful transition in space.

In short, unless deterrence is fragile and war appears imminent, the Soviet Union is very unlikely to take a high risk course, such as an act of war against the United States, in response to BMD deployment; and U.S. BMD deployment should help ensure that deterrence does not become fragile. There certainly is no precedent for U.S. peacetime deployments—even those posing a direct nuclear threat to the Soviet Union—to cause the Soviet Union to take a high-risk profile. For example, the deployment of U.S. ballistic missile-carrying submarines did not prompt any such Soviet actions; neither has the deployment of U.S. military reconnaissance satellites.

Finally, even in a condition of fragile deterrence, it is not clear that an attack on U.S. BMD components would be effective. Space-based systems may be quite capable of self-defense. Indeed, one of the conditions that administration officials have placed upon any ballistic missile defense system coming from the SDI is that it be deployed in a highly survivable mode. For example, Ambassador Paul Nitze, head of the Reagan administration's first delegation to the Intermediate-Range Nuclear Forces (INF) talks and a principal adviser to the president on arms control, recently stated:

> The criteria by which we will judge the feasibility of such technologies will be demanding. The technologies must produce defensive systems that are survivable: if not, the defenses would themselves be tempting targets for a first strike.[15]

This requirement reportedly has been reaffirmed in recent official policy guidance for the SDI.[16] If it is maintained, the Soviet Union would be unlikely to attack space-based BMD components because such an act would entail high risks with a low probability of success.

Unless, then, it appears to the Soviet leadership that the strategic balance gives the Soviet Union a "war-winning" advantage, it is highly unlikely to engage in a risky act of war against the United States, particularly if other less risky response options exist. If the Soviet Union does believe that it possesses significant advantages, and that war is imminent, then many U.S. military assets, including BMD components, could be subject to attack *if* they are highly vulnerable. But that jeopardy would be caused by the failure of deterrence, not by the deployment of BMD components—which should help stabilize deterrence. Finally, if the United States adheres to the requirement that its BMD components be survivable so as not to tempt an attack, the likelihood of such an attack appears even more remote.

POST-TRANSITION STABILITY

The post-transition instability charge suggests that mutual and highly effective defenses would weaken the U.S. capability to deter Soviet conventional attacks on U.S. allies. Stated differently, effective defenses against nuclear weapons would make the world "safe for conventional war" because the U.S. and NATO could no longer effectively use the nuclear first-use threat.

Although it is not at all controversial to suggest that NATO could not withstand a conventional onslaught for long without recourse to nuclear escalation, it does not necessarily follow that mutual strategic defenses would destroy the U.S. extended deterrent. The combination of NATO conventional force improvements and strategic defense for the U.S. and its allies could provide an improved basis for extended deterrence and "flexible response."

Obviously, if the Soviet homeland is defended comprehensively against strategic nuclear attack, a U.S. strategic nuclear threat to the Soviet homeland would be unlikely to pose a formidable threat. But, even then, it need not be the case that the world would be "safe for conventional war." For several reasons deterrence of Soviet conventional attack against U.S. allies could still function.

First, to suggest that the Soviet Union could cavalierly engage in conventional war against U.S. allies and U.S. forces because of its strategic defenses assumes that the Soviet Union would have very high confidence in its defenses. In reality, neither the Soviet Union nor the United States could have absolute confidence that their respective defensive capabilities would work perfectly; and proponents and opponents of BMD must recognize the fact. Consequently, the possibility that destructive nuclear escalation would follow from a direct U.S.-Soviet clash should always have some deterrent effect. This may or may not be adequate to deter a Soviet leadership considering conventional attack—it is impossible to know at this point—but certainly the nuclear threat would not become wholly impotent.

Second, it is absolutely essential to remember that *deterrence* is a combination of both *capability* of threat, and *credibility* of threat (i.e., the Soviet view of U.S. will to actually carry out a threat). This is obvious from everyday experience. Many people are not deterred from exceeding the speed limit by a few miles per hour because in most cases, given the infraction, no ticket will ensue. The police have the authority and *capability* to stop violators but the *credibility* of the threat is not high, so many motorists will accept the modest risk and marginally exceed the limit. This domestic example may seem remote to the issue of extending nuclear deterrence to U.S. allies, but it is not. In the post-transition condition of effective defenses, although the *capability* of the U.S. nuclear threat would be reduced by Soviet defenses, the *credibility* of the U.S. deterrent should be enhanced.

Under current conditions of absolute U.S. vulnerability to nuclear attack the credibility of the U.S. nuclear guarantee for allies is subject to severe doubt. The U.S. leadership must be perceived as being most unlikely to engage in an action that could lead to the destruction of the American homeland—such as using nuclear weapons against the Soviet Union on behalf of distant allies. Would the president order a nuclear attack against the Soviet Union in response to a Soviet conventional attack in Europe when the result of that action could lead to the destruction of the United States itself? That question is often put more informally: would a president willingly trade New York City for Bonn? The answer is, "of course not." Even though the NATO doctrine of "flexible response" commits the United States to such a threat, the threat is not credible.

Recognizing that the current condition of absolute U.S. vulnerability undercuts the credibility of the U.S. nuclear deterrent for allies is not popular given the sensitivities involved. Occasionally, however, an American statesman is willing to be straightforward about the situation, as when Henry Kissinger addressed a group of Europeans and Americans on the issue in 1979:

> If my analysis is correct we must face the fact that it is absurd
> to base the strategy of the west on the credibility of the threat

of mutual suicide...and therefore I would say—what I might not say in office—that our European allies should not keep asking us to multiply strategic assurances that we cannot possibly mean, or if we do mean, we should not want to execute, because if we execute, we risk the destruction of civilization. Our strategic dilemma is not solved by verbal reassurances, it requires redesigning our forces and doctrine.[17]

Michael Howard, the prominent British strategic theorist, made virtually the same observation in noting that:

Peoples who are not prepared to make the effort necessary for operational defense are even less likely to support a decision to initiate a nuclear exchange for which they will themselves suffer almost inconceivable destruction...[18]

Perhaps more importantly, Soviet writers pour scorn on the U.S. nuclear guarantee for allies, noting that the threat is irrational. The point is that the current U.S. deterrence policy of relying on a nuclear threat to deter Soviet conventional attack is not a credible policy; and an effective deterrent ought to combine capability *and* credibility.

The credibility of the U.S. extended deterrence guarantee would be much more credible *in the Soviet perspective* if the guarantee were not suicidal for the United States. This is a problem, the solution to which must include the reduction of American vulnerability so as to reduce the risks Americans must run in defense of overseas commitments. In a post-transition period, the United States would essentially have exchanged the current high capability/low credibility extended deterrent for a reduced capability/enhanced credibility extended deterrent. It is not clear that one type of deterrent is any more or less effective than the other; but those who assert that defenses will make the world safe for conventional war, whereas in the current situation it is not, have not thought through the incredibility of the current extended deterrent brought about by American vulnerability. (Figure 18 compares the contrasting framework of an offensive as opposed to a defensive approach to extended deterrence.)

Third, although it often is neglected, an important part of the president's "Star Wars" speech dwelt upon the need to improve U.S. non-nuclear forces. Improving U.S. conven-

FIGURE 18

Basis for Deterrence Stability

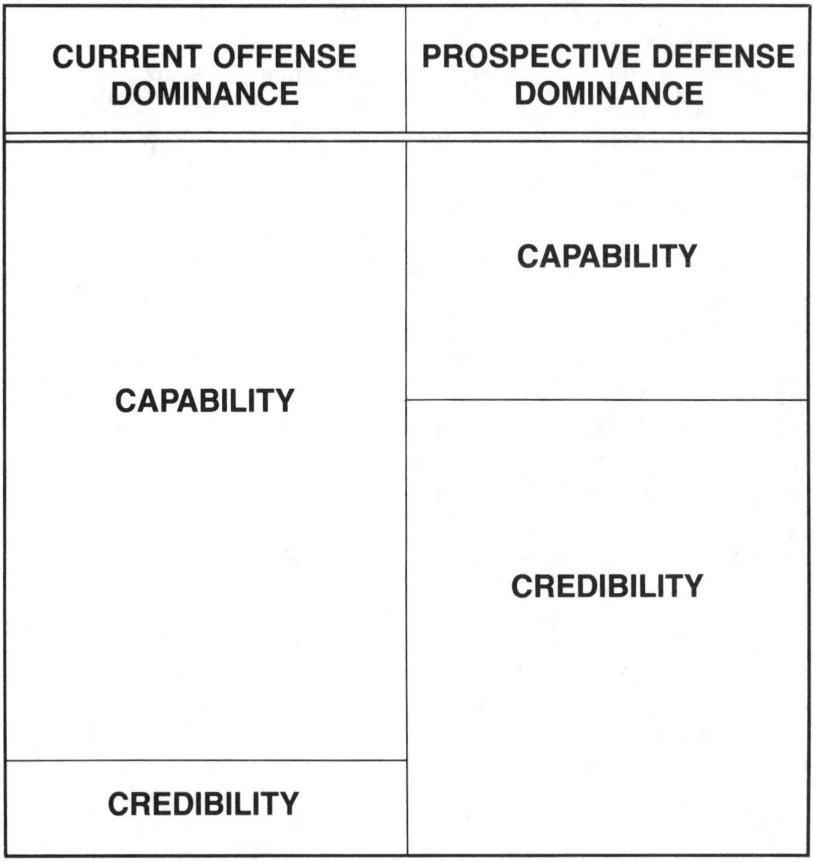

CURRENT OFFENSE DOMINANCE	PROSPECTIVE DEFENSE DOMINANCE
CAPABILITY	CAPABILITY
	CREDIBILITY
CREDIBILITY	

tional forces should help reduce the current overreliance on the nuclear threat as the basis of the American extended deterrent. Consequently, even if Soviet defenses reduce the U.S. capability for nuclear threats against the Soviet homeland, U.S. and allied conventional force improvements should help reduce reliance on that threat.

Unfortunately, a Western conventional buildup alone would be unlikely to solve the entire problem. NATO conventional force improvements are essential today, and would remain so, in a "defense dominant" world.[19] Just as strategic defenses alone would not solve all of NATO's security problems, neither would conventional force improvements alone provide a panacea. But improvements in NATO conventional force, as a complement to the deployment of strategic defenses, could vastly improve the current situation.

The improvement of NATO conventional forces *alone* would likely leave those improved forces vulnerable to nuclear attack. Indeed, very effective NATO conventional forces might increase Soviet incentives to trump NATO conventional forces through a nuclear attack. Yet the credibility of the U.S. deterrent to dissuade a nuclear attack upon Western Europe will remain low in the absence of U.S. strategic defenses. As Henry Kissinger observed as early as 1970:

> It is a different decision for the President of the United States to risk general war when the strategic balance is this, than it was throughout most of the post-war period. Therefore, the possibility of defending other countries with strategic American power has fundamentally changed and no amount of reassurance on our part can change these facts.[20]

Strategic defense and conventional force improvements, then, although not adequate individually, could together provide a significant improvement for Western European security. Strategic defense for the U.S. and Western Europe (anti-tactical ballistic missile defense - ATBM) could enhance the credibility of the U.S. extended deterrent and reduce the vulnerability of NATO forces to a ballistic missile first strike. Both of these factors should enhance deterrence of nuclear or conventional attack *and* enhance NATO's capability to protect Western Europe conventionally if deterrence fails.

Fourth, very effective defenses could also help protect the capability of the U.S. to mobilize its vast military-industrial base. Defense of the U.S. ability to mobilize men and material and move them to Europe should contribute powerfully to the deterrence of a Soviet attack on Europe. The Soviet Union saw the results, in World War II, when U.S. military-industrial potential was mobilized. The prospect of unleashing that military-industrial potential and engaging a mobilized U.S. in war should be extremely effective in deterring attack both on NATO and the American homeland. The inability of the United States now to protect its military-industrial base denies it that possible deterrent factor. Strategic defenses could provide the coverage necessary to exploit this potential for the purposes of enhancing deterrence and stability.

Defenses (even limited defenses) would help ensure that any attack on the U.S. or its allies would not result in rapid and decisive victory for the Soviet Union. That is, strategic defenses would ensure that attack on the U.S. and its allies would lead to a *prolonged* war. Soviet doctrine is clear in its preference for rapid and decisive victory, whether at the intercontinental level or in the European theater. The Soviet Union prepares for prolonged war, but clearly is highly concerned over the prospect of a long and indecisive conflict wherein the possibility of ultimate defeat would have to be considered.[21] Indeed, the Bolshevik revolution was spawned in such a context.

Mutual strategic defenses would reduce the level of strategic nuclear capability with which the West could threaten the Soviet Union. However, BMD for the U.S. and its allies would provide a less direct, but possibly more effective, deterrent through the highly credible threat of a prolonged, unwinnable conflict—i.e., denying the Soviet Union its theory for theater or strategic victory. The possibility that defenses could be so effective that conflict would be prolonged and against a U.S. capable of mobilizing its vast military potential should provide a powerful deterrent effect. This is hardly a context wherein the Soviet Union could see the world as "safe for conventional war."

Fifth, although Soviet defenses presumably would reduce the capability of the U.S. nuclear threat vis-à-vis the Soviet homeland, the same probably would not be as true of Soviet military forces sent outside the defended Soviet homeland.

Soviet ground, air, and naval forces sent outside the Soviet Union in an offensive war could still be vulnerable to nuclear attack. That vulnerability should help deter offensive projection into areas of U.S. vital interest.

Finally, if it is assumed that Soviet defenses would weaken or virtually eliminate the Western capability to target military installations in the Soviet homeland, NATO defenses should be expected to provide at least an equivalent level of protection. The Soviet strategy for a quick and decisive (Blitzkrieg) victory over NATO would be much more difficult to achieve if NATO could defend key main operating bases (MOB), command control and communications (C^3) facilities, nuclear weapon storage sites, critical resupply facilities, and so on.[22] Providing defensive coverage for important NATO facilities would be an integral part of any future decision to deploy BMD. A defended NATO more able to ward off a Soviet attack, to survive and to be supported by the United States, should provide a powerful deterrent to Soviet attack. Such a NATO capability could promise a long war that the Soviet Union would have little confidence in winning. The point is *not* that increasing the probability of war in Europe is acceptable because NATO will be more able to fight, but that being manifestly more able to fight will help deter Soviet attack in the first place.

In an important policy speech regarding European participation in the SDI, Secretary of Defense Caspar Weinberger noted:

> I know that some Europeans fear that our pursuit of the defense initiative would tend to "decouple" America from Europe. This is quite wrong. The security of the United States is inseparable from the security of Western Europe. As we vigorously pursue our strategic defense research program, we work closely with all our allies to ensure the program benefits our security as a whole.

> In addition to strengthening our nuclear deterrent, such defenses would also enhance NATO's ability to deter Soviet aggression in Western Europe by reducing the ability of Soviet ballistic missiles to put at risk those facilities essential to the conventional defense of Europe—airfields, ports, depots, and communications facilities to name just a few examples.[23]

ATBM defense for NATO-Europe would reduce the feasibility of the Soviet "theory for victory" over NATO. It should thereby help ensure that the Soviet Union would choose not to launch such an attack—that is, it would strengthen stability. It is just too simple to assert that effective defenses will free the Soviet Union to exploit its conventional military power; the situation is much more complex. For at least the above six reasons it is not at all clear that the full deployment of mutual defenses will result in instability. Mutual deployment of comprehensive strategic defenses may instead *enhance* the credibility of the U.S. commitment to defend its allies and interests, actually improve its capability to do so in some important respects, and thereby improve deterrence stability.

It should be recognized that the way the United States has chosen to support its foreign policy objectives logically *requires* a capability for strategic defense. The United States has used the threat of nuclear escalation—"extended nuclear deterrence"—as the ultimate means of preserving distant allies and interests. This is apparent particularly in the U.S. nuclear guarantee to NATO. Yet the guarantee must be highly suspect because it is potentially suicidal; and as Henry Kissinger has noted, the West should not base its security upon a policy position that presumes that the United States is willing to commit suicide for distant interests—no matter how important.

U.S. foreign policy requirements as defined in Washington have expanded since World War II, while the U.S. ability to support those requirements has been constricted. The United States has tried to sustain its global foreign policy objectives "on the cheap" through the threat of nuclear escalation, even though the threat no longer should be considered credible vis-à-vis the Soviet Union. It is quite clear that the threat of nuclear escalation is more economical than deploying the types of conventional forces around the globe that would be necessary to protect U.S. allies and interests. The benefits of economy, however, have been achieved at the cost of great danger and risk should the U.S. bluff ever be called.

There are no easy solutions to the dilemma of having grand foreign policy objectives with inadequate means of support. If the United States maintains foreign policy objectives that entail a virtually unlimited wartime commitment to distant allies (i.e., the nuclear guarantee to NATO), then the condition of U.S.

homeland vulnerability will continue to weaken the stability of deterrence. But revising that vulnerability through strategic defense, if technically feasible, would help realign U.S. commitments with U.S. capabilities.

DON'T ROCK THE BOAT?

When critics of the SDI and BMD compare the current condition of mutual vulnerability with a future condition of deployed defenses they often assume that the current condition is sound and stable. From that assumption it is easy to conclude that we ought not "rock the boat" of deterrence stability with new defensive deployments—the adage being, "if it ain't broke, don't fix it." Yet, the current deterrence relationship entails severe elements of instability and risk. For example, NATO overreliance on an implausible U.S. nuclear first-use guarantee, and U.S. reliance on the first-use nuclear threat to safeguard other vital interests outside Western Europe represent a bluff just waiting to be called. The conventional and strategic force advantages that undergirded "extended deterrence" and the U.S. bargaining position during, say, the Cuban Missile Crisis of October 1962 will not exist during any crisis in the foreseeable future. Yet U.S. commitments have increased, not diminished. In addition, the current offense-dominated approach to deterrence ensures that if deterrence fails it will "fail deadly"; that is, there will be little prospect for significant relief from the resultant nuclear holocaust. Similarly, if our deterrence theories turn out to be so much intellectual verbiage that do not apply to the real world, there will be no significant relief from the resultant nuclear holocaust under the current offense-dominated approach to deterrence.

Finally, the mutual vulnerability approach to deterrence does not offer any relief from the destruction that could be caused by the unauthorized or "accidental" use of nuclear weapons, or from the nuclear destruction that might be inflicted upon the United States by some future irrational terrorist organization or state in possession of a nuclear weapon. The current offense-dominated approach to deterrence and stability is far from comforting when put in perspective.

Those who suggest that the current approach to deterrence

is acceptable often support their position by claiming that the absence of war is proof of the effectiveness of current policy, so why risk change? But strategic deterrence is tested only very rarely in international relations. The absence of war probably reflects the fact that nuclear deterrence has not undergone the severe test of an acute military crisis in over two decades, i.e., since the Cuban Missile Crisis when the United States had significant advantages it no longer possesses. There is now little basis for confidently assuming that deterrence stability will survive the next acute military crisis, whenever it may occur. Yet the SDI may hold the answer—to enhance the stability of deterrence through strategic defense, and to provide relief should deterrence ever fail.

COMPUTERS TAKING OVER?

The charge that an automated boost-phase BMD system could fire accidently at Soviet test ICBMs or a peaceful Soviet launch must be considered. Although such an accident, if occurring during a period of political calm, would be unlikely to initiate World War III, it would still lead to increased U.S.-Soviet hostility and heightened tensions. Fortunately, there are a number of ways to guard against such accidents. For example, the boost-phase layer of a multitiered system might be shut down during normal periods of international calm. Strategic offensive forces are held at various levels of readiness during periods of calm, and increasingly readied as a military crisis develops. A defensive architecture could use a similar approach and help avoid the possibility of a boost-phase accident.

A second possible approach to guarding against a boost-phase accident would be to exempt certain Soviet launch sites from BMD coverage—such as those that are well-known Soviet sites for ICBM testing or for launching peaceful spacecraft (the Baykonu Cosmodrome near Tyuratam, the Northern Cosmodrome near Plesetsk, and the Volograd Station Cosmodrome near Kapustin Yar). Of course, there could be some small risk in exempting any Soviet launch sites from boost-phase coverage. But if the Soviet Union exploited one of these "safe" sites to launch a few genuine ICBMs, the U.S. mid-course and terminal BMD layers would safeguard the country.

Similarly, a boost-phase system could have a "safety catch" that exempted any small number of Soviet missile launches from intercept, on the assumption that if the Soviet Union launched only a few missiles they would be for ICBM testing or for placing spacecraft in orbit. If, upon inspection, the small number of missiles turned out to be nuclear armed ICBMs, then again, the midcourse and terminal layers of BMD could deal with them.

A preferable means of dealing with this problem—a solution that would have the additional benefit of helping to protect U.S. space launches from Soviet boost-phase interceptors—could be for the U.S. and Soviet Union to negotiate an agreement concerning prenotification of the time and location of all such missile launches. Such an agreement would be in the self-interest of both parties and therefore probably negotiable. Indeed, there are existing U.S.-Soviet agreements—the Accident Measures Agreement of 1971, the Incidents at Sea Agreement of 1972, and SALT II of 1979—that include commitments to prior notification of some missile launches.

In short, a system for boost-phase intercept may well require some level of automation. However it certainly appears that the United States could guard against boost-phase accidents through a variety of potential "safety catches."

A CHANCE FOR INSTABILITY FROM BMD?

Interestingly, critics of the SDI and BMD have proposed all of the instability charges discussed above, none of which appears to be beyond doubt, and several of which appear to be misguided on their own terms. Yet, there may be a more serious potential for instability generally not discussed by the critics of BMD.

As noted in chapter four, the Soviet Union already has BMD radars, launchers, and interceptors in production, and functioning models of ground-based laser BMD systems may be available within the decade. The point is that, while the United States may be ahead of the Soviet Union in some areas of high technology that could be applied to future BMD systems, the Soviet Union is, without doubt, far ahead of the United States in its capability to deploy a near-term (i.e., within ten years) operational, nationwide BMD system. If this near-term BMD deployment potential were combined with existing air defense and civil defense programs, the Soviet Union could easily have formidable deployed defenses well in advance of virtually any comparable U.S. capability. Exacerbating the problem of the Soviet capability for rapid BMD deployment, is the likelihood that the Soviet Union would consider as "acceptable" a more modest level of defense effectiveness than would the United States. American leaders talk of the need for near-perfect defenses against a Soviet first strike while the Soviet Union appears to require defenses that need "only" limit the potential damage from a weakened U.S. retaliatory force.

In short, the real potential danger of instability stems from two factors. One, the Soviet Union could "hit the ground running" with its existing BMD deployment program, and the U.S. could not; and two, the Soviet Union does not have as far to go in attaining its definition of "highly effective" defenses. Consequently, the Soviet Union probably could achieve its definition of "defense dominance" before the United States could achieve its more demanding definition of "defense dominance."

This eventuality could be highly destabilizing. This point often is misstated as a suggestion that a U.S. BMD would be stabilizing while a Soviet BMD would be destabilizing. The point rather is that a *unilateral* Soviet capability for comprehensive strategic defense would be destabilizing. It could reduce Soviet concern for the U.S. nuclear deterrent without the compensating beneficial effect of U.S. and NATO defenses. Unilateral Soviet strategic defenses, including BMD, could indeed "make the world safer," from the Soviet perspective, for conventional or even nuclear war. The Soviet Union might not choose to exploit this advantage militarily or politically, but the fact of its availability could prove highly destabilizing.

It must be recognized that the United States cannot determine whether or not the Soviet Union will deploy nationwide defenses. It simply is mistaken to assume that the Soviet Union will deploy nationwide BMD only if the United States moves in that direction first. The Soviet Union may well deploy additional BMD regardless of U.S. actions *vis-à-vis* the SDI and BMD. After all, historically the Soviet Union began deploying its BMD system when the United States had none, and it continues to operate and modernize the world's only BMD system despite the fact that the United States deactivated its only operational BMD site in 1975. In effect, the potential for instability from Soviet BMD deployment need not result from the SDI. To oppose the SDI and any future American BMD deployment on the premise that the Soviet Union would expand its BMD system *only* in response to U.S. deployment is an erroneous presumption and inconsistent with historical precedent.

Nevertheless, if the United States does decide to deploy BMD, the Soviet Union almost certainly will rapidly expand its current system. Such Soviet BMD deployment could have destabilizing consequences given their early advantage in BMD and other forms of strategic defense. Two potential solutions to the problem spring to mind. First, if the United States and Soviet Union could achieve an arms control agreement regulating BMD deployment, the probability of a destabilizing unilateral advantage could be reduced. The Soviet Union, however, is not noted for ceding any potential advantages in arms control agreements. Consequently, it may be reluctant to constrain itself to a slower U.S. BMD deployment schedule.

A second possible solution would be for the United States to maintain a manifest strategic offensive capability to penetrate Soviet defenses *until* U.S. defensive programs could achieve sufficient effectiveness to counter the likely initial Soviet defensive advantage. In effect, U.S. offensive forces would have to counter Soviet defense advantages until U.S. defenses could "catch up." This mission for U.S. strategic offensive forces would be a key to maintaining stability during the initial years of the "defense transition."

There are numerous implications of this requirement to integrate U.S. offensive and defensive programs during an initial interim period to ensure a stable transition. For example, the current U.S. ICBM modernization program includes a very small single-warhead missile for the 1990s known as "Midgetman." Yet how sensible is it for the U.S. to concentrate its efforts for the 1990s and beyond so heavily on a small ICBM that would not have the payload capacity necessary to penetrate early Soviet defenses? Clearly, the prospect for Soviet BMD and the need to maintain an interim U.S. offensive deterrent in the absence of arms control success ought to be more fully taken into consideration as the U.S. plans its future ICBM force. The larger MX-Peacekeeper ICBM planned by the U.S., if it can achieve survivability against a first strike through mobility, superhardening, and/or BMD, would be more in line with the need to maintain some offensive deterrent capability during the transition period. The greater payload capacity of the MX-Peacekeeper would help the United States counter those early defensive advantages likely to be held by the Soviet Union.

There is little doubt, however, that it would be difficult politically for the United States to pursue an SDI and BMD deployment intended to make offensive nuclear weapons "obsolete" while simultaneously modernizing strategic offensive forces, even if it were only for an interim period. The outcry from critics would be that the United States was seeking superiority by building both offensive and defensive forces. The somewhat subtle reasoning behind the genuine need to "safeguard a transition" by maintaining an offensive deterrent undoubtedly would be lost upon those already skeptical of U.S. strategic policy in general and any decision to deploy BMD in particular. Some of the same political factors that led the Reagan Administration to want to "change the ball game" toward defense and away from a continued offensive force competition (i.e., the increasingly obvious political inability of the United States to compete effectively) could make it difficult for the United States to help ensure a safe transition period. Only clear and public presentations by the president concerning what the United States would need to do defensively and offensively to maintain stability during the transition period could possibly generate the necessary public and congressional support.

A "MULTISTABLE" BALANCE THROUGH STRATEGIC DEFENSE?

The deployment of strategic defenses by the United States and the Soviet Union may be the only means to establish the stable condition characterized by Herman Kahn as a "multistable" strategic balance. Dr. Kahn observed that a multistable strategic balance could provide deterrence stability in all those areas of U.S. vital interest *without* the crisis instability that might be caused by a U.S. first strike capability.[24] Stability for allies and distant vital interests would be enhanced because, even with deployed defenses, war between the superpowers would be extremely risky and dangerous for both countries. Each country would be dissuaded from threatening the vital interests of the other—lest a risky general war result. Yet, because war would not be suicidal, both sides could make "not incredible" security commitments on behalf of their allies. The U.S. extended deterrent commitment to allies, for example, would appear much more credible to the Soviet leadership, because of the greater compatibility between the risk to the United States in extending deterrence and the "value" of the interest or ally involved. In addition, because strategic retaliatory forces would be defended, a first strike against those forces could be of little military utility, thereby negating the value of striking first.

In short, Herman Kahn created a conceptual image of a strategic balance wherein a "not incredible" extended deterrent threat could be made *without* the need for the U.S. strategic superiority that was the original basis for America's extended deterrent commitment. Indeed, in a multistable strategic balance both the United States and the Soviet Union would enjoy similar deterrence benefits and be bound by similar deterrence limitations. However, as Kahn noted over two decades ago, a multistable balance would require that both sides be capable of significantly limiting damage to their homelands in the event of war. The SDI may provide the means of escaping from the present morass of misaligned policy commitments and capabilities by moving towards Kahn's concept of a multistable strategic relationship with the Soviet Union.

SUMMARY AND CONCLUSION

In summary, there are a number of instability charges aimed at the SDI and the future possibility of BMD deployment. These, along with the contrasting reasons as to why BMD could be stabilizing, are summarized below:

Strategic Defense Would Be Destabilizing Because:	Strategic Defense Would Be Stabilizing Because:
1. It would increase incentives for striking first by reducing mutual vulnerability.	1. It would decrease incentives for striking first by initially increasing the survivability of retaliatory forces.

2. The Soviet Union would attack U.S. space-based BMD components because they would pose an unacceptable threat to the Soviet Union.

2. The Soviet Union would be most unlikely to attack U.S. BMD components during an otherwise peaceful period because there would exist many other less risky Soviet options. In the event of war, BMD components, *if* vulnerable, could be the target of attack as could many other military systems. However, deployed BMD components will be relatively survivable and will not invite attack.

3. It will increase the probability of conventional war by degrading the *capability* of the U.S. "extended deterrent."

3. It will enhance the *credibility* of the U.S. extended deterrent and increase the capability of the U.S. and Western Europe to withstand Soviet attack, thereby supporting deterrence.

4. It will alter the existing stability of mutual vulnerability.

4. It will alter the existing condition of mutual vulnerability which is extremely risky and increasingly unstable.

5. Automated boost-phase interceptors will be accident prone and place computers in control of starting World War III.

5. Automation of boost-phase interceptors is *not* the same as predelegation of the authority to use nuclear weapons; and the potential for a boost-phase accident can be guarded against through various alternative measures.

Some critics of strategic defense suggest that defenses are, by definition, "destabilizing." This opinion generally rests on the assumption that deterrence stability requires mutual vulnerability, therefore defense and stability are incompatible. There is no reason to accept such an assumption. Deterrence and defense need not be incompatible, as the prospect of protecting the U.S. military-industrial base and NATO's logistical infrastructure in Europe illustrate. An effective capability to defend territory and vital military installations, or a more limited defense capable of protecting only the latter, should reduce an opponent's incentives to pursue what would be a useless attack. Indeed, deterrence stability was maintained from the 1950s through the early 1960s when then-existing U.S. strategic forces should have functioned quite well to protect the United States in the event of war. Historically, deterrence has been based on a combined offensive-defensive capability. The notion that defense and deterrence are inconsistent is supported neither by history nor logic.

Nevertheless, all considerations of deterrence and stability should be recognized as speculative, given the many uncertainties involved. What is certain is that deterrence could fail despite our best efforts to maintain stability, particularly when viewed in the long term. In the event that deterrence fails, our current strategic policy, focused almost exclusively upon the threat of offensive nuclear forces, would likely ensure the destruction of the United States, and possibly a global climatic catastrophe. Strategic defenses may be the only solution to this danger, a danger that may encompass the entire planet.[25] The R&D program that is SDI is vital if we are to find answers to the critical questions of the feasibility and cost of strategic defense. Thus, the R&D of the SDI may suggest to a future president and Congress that deployment of defenses is advisable. If so, whether comprehensive or only limited defense options are available, their deployment could contribute significantly to stability; and the stability of a defensive-oriented deterrent would be far safer than the stability provided by the current "balance of terror."

ENDNOTES

1. U.S. Senate, Committee on Foreign Policy, Subcommittee on International Organization, *Strategic and Foreign Policy Implications of ABM Systems, Hearings,* Part I, 91st Cong., 1st sess. (Washington, D.C.: USGPO, 1969), p. 54.
2. *The President's Strategic Defense Initiative* (Washington, D.C.:

USGPO, January 1985), p. 3.

3. See for example, McGeorge Bundy, George F. Kennan, Robert S. McNamara and Gerard Smith, "The President's Choice: Star Wars or Arms Control," *Foreign Affairs*, Vol. 63, No. 2 (Winter 1984/85), pp. 269-270.

4. See for example, Hans Bethe, et. al., "Space-based Ballistic Missile Defense," *Scientific American*, Vol. 25, No. 4 (October 1984), p. 48.

5. Sidney Drell, et. al., "Preserving the ABM Treaty: A Critique of the Reagan Strategic Defense Initiative," *International Security*, Vol. 9, No. 2 (Fall 1984), p. 81.

6. Strobe Talbott, "The Case Against Star Wars Weapons," *Time* (May 7, 1984), p. 82.

7. Charles Krauthammer, "The Illusion of Star Wars," *The New Republic* (May 14, 1984), p. 16.

8. Quoted in U.S. Senate, Committee on Foreign Relations, *President's Commission on Strategic Forces, Hearings*, 98th Congress, 1st Session (Washington, D.C.: USGPO, 1983), p. 22.

9. Krauthammer, op. cit., p. 16.

10. Charles Glaser, "Why Even Good Defenses May Be Bad," *International Security*, Vol. 9, No. 2 (Fall 1984), p. 99.

11. Ibid., p. 97. The chairman of the House Foreign Affairs Committee expressed this same sentiment at a hearing concerning the SDI on April 24, 1985.

12. Speech text for delivery to: Face to Face Luncheon, *Congress, The Defense Budget, Arms Control Talks*, Washington, D.C., Jan. 16, 1985, p. 9.

13. See Harold Brown, *The Strategic Defense Initiative: Defensive Systems and the Strategic Debate*, unpublished paper, The Foreign Policy Institute, School of Advanced International Studies, Johns Hopkins University, p. 15. "The Strategic Defense Initiative: Defensive Systems and the Strategic Debate," *Survival*, Vol. 27, No. 2 (March/April 1985), pp. 59-60; and, Union of Concerned Scientists, *Space-Based Missile Defense* (Cambridge, MA: Union of Concerned Scientists, March 1984), p. 61.

14. John Erickson, "The Soviet View of Deterrence," *Survival*, Vol. 24, No. 6 (November-December, 1982), p. 246.

15. Paul H. Nitze, "On the Road to a More Stable Peace," Speech to the Philadelphia World Affairs Council (as delivered), Feb. 20, 1985, unpublished text, p. 4.

16. See the *Fact Sheet on The Strategic Defense Initiative*, released by the National Security Council in early June 1985, pp. 8-9. See also a news account of what is reported to be National Security Decision Directive 172 emphasizing this need for survivability, Jim Klurfeld, "Star Wars Plan Is Modified," *Long Island Newsday*, June 14, 1985, p. 5.

17. Reprinted in Henry Kissinger, "The Future of NATO," in *NATO the Next Thirty Years*, Kenneth Myers, ed. (Boulder, CO: Westview, 1978), p. 8.

18. "The Forgotten Dimensions of Strategy," *Foreign Affairs*, Vol. 57, No. 5 (Summer 1979), p. 983.

19. There are numerous suggestions as to how to improve NATO conventional capabilities. See, for example, General Bernard Rogers, "Greater Flexibility for NATO's Flexible Response," *Strategic Review*, Vol. 11, No. 2 (Spring 1983), pp. 11-19; "The Atlantic Alliance: Prescriptions for a Difficult Decade," *Foreign Affairs*, Vol. 60, No. 5 (Summer 1982), pp. 1145-1156; and, "Follow-on Forces Attack: Myths and Realities," *NATO Review*, No. 6 (December 1984); Kenneth Coffey, "Defending Europe Against a Conventional Attack," *Air University Review*, Vol. 31, No. 2 (January-February 1980), pp. 47-59; Franz-Joseph Schulze, "Rethinking Continental Defense," *Washington Quarterly*, Vol. 7, No. 2 (Spring 1984), pp. 51-58; Newt Gingrich, Albert Hanser, "Alternative Strategies for the Defense of Western Europe," in *Understanding U.S. Strategy*, Terry Heyns, ed. (Washington: National Defense University Press, 1983), pp. 175-195; Daniel Malone, "A Realistic Conventional Deterrent," *National Defense*, Vol. 67, No. 379 (July-August 1982), pp. 51-53; and Jeffery Record, *Revising U.S. Military Strategy* (Washington: Pergamon-Brassey's, 1985).

20. Quoted in William R. Van Cleave, "Remarks by Dr. William Van Cleave," *SALT: Foreign Policy and Strategic Policy* (Los Angeles: Pepperdine Press, 1972), p. 140.

21. For an excellent discussion of the Soviet view of, and great concern for, prolonged war see, Rebecca Strode, *The Integration of Political and Military Objectives in Soviet Strategic Arms Control Policy*, Ph.D. Dissertation (Forthcoming), Harvard University, 1985, chapter entitled, "Changes in Soviet Strategy Since SALT I."

22. See, for example, Joseph Douglas, *The Soviet Theater Nuclear Offensive*, Vol. 1 (Washington, D.C.: USGPO, 1976).

23. Quoted in Secretary of Defense Caspar Weinberger, Remarks to the Foreign Press Center, Washington, D.C., December 19, 1984.

24. See Herman Kahn, *On Thermonuclear War* (Princeton, N.J.: Princeton University Press, 1961), pp. 141-144.

25. See Colin S. Gray, "The Nuclear Winter Thesis and U.S. Strategic Policy," *Washington Quarterly*, Vol. 8, No. 2 (Fall 1985).

SEVEN
Chapter 7

"NUCLEAR WINTER," THE SDI, AND STRATEGIC DEFENSE

An important issue that should be part of any consideration of the SDI and strategic defense is the "nuclear winter" thesis. This chapter will assess the relationship between the SDI and the possibility that nuclear war would lead to a global climatic disaster, or "nuclear winter."

The "nuclear winter" thesis, in short, suggests the possibility of devastating climatic consequences following the detonation of a few hundred nuclear explosions over cities, or several thousand surface explosions (for example, against ICBM silos).[1] According to this theory, even a relatively "small" nuclear war could inject particles throughout the atmosphere, obscuring the sun, and causing global temperatures to drop rapidly, thereby plunging much of the planet into a temporary but deadly period of cold and dark.

The authors of the nuclear winter thesis recognize that many uncertainties surround the theory. Nevertheless, Professor Carl Sagan, a member of the group "discovering" the thesis, has claimed that, "...there is general agreement on the overall conclusions: in the wake of a nuclear war there is likely to be a period, lasting at least for months, of extreme cold in a radioactive gloom, followed—after the soot and dust fallout— by an extended period of increased ultraviolet light reaching the surface."[2]

Professor Sagan's conclusion is not shared by all who have analyzed the effects of nuclear war. For example, Professor George Rathjens of MIT has expressed doubt about much of the analysis supporting the nuclear winter thesis:

> ...the modelling is (admittedly) only a crude first approxima-
> tion to what would likely happen in the event of nuclear-war-
> initiated fires, and there are enormous uncertainties in some
> critical parameters—the amount of combustible materials in
> cities, the quantity and blackness of the smoke, the height to
> which it rises (and hence its persistence)—that determine just
> how cold and dark the world would likely be after a nuclear
> war.

> ....When all these concerns are combined, it appears that the
> temperature decrease may not exceed a few degrees. This
> would not add very much to the terrible destructiveness of an
> all-out nuclear war.[3]

Nevertheless, few if any analysts claim that there is no
possibility whatsoever of a "nuclear winter" following nuclear
war. Nuclear winter is of concern because, although its occurrence may be uncertain, its consequences could entail a global
catastrophe. Of course, nuclear war would be a catastrophe
for those involved whether or not it was followed by a global
climatic disaster. But the nuclear winter thesis suggests that
even a very limited nuclear conflict involving a tiny fraction
of the world's nuclear arsenal would threaten not only those
directly involved but the entire planet. The thesis may or may
not be valid; the United States, indeed the world, cannot afford
to find out through experience. Therefore, it is of some interest
to determine whether means exist to address the prospect of
nuclear winter.

NUCLEAR WINTER AND STRATEGIC DEFENSE

What is the relationship between the nuclear winter thesis,
the SDI, and strategic defense? The potential for intercepting nuclear weapons before they detonate is the least unrealistic, perhaps the only, answer to the possible threat of nuclear
winter.

Obviously, a very effective strategic defense would be
required to reduce the number of detonating weapons to
levels below the proposed "thresholds" for nuclear winter (the

authors of the thesis have indicated that the range is from a few hundred to a few thousand).[4] The SDI could be an essential contribution to achieving that capability since its purpose as a research program is to assess the feasibility and potential effectiveness of defending against ballistic missiles. Consequently, the SDI is a first step in any attempt to help counter nuclear winter through strategic defense.

The SDI and strategic defense may seem to be a long-term solution to an immediate problem. Unfortunately, that is true—just as strategic defense may be the long-term solution to the immediate problem of possible nuclear war. Unfortunately, given the relatively low level of BMD research and development pursued by the United States since 1972, there is little likelihood of much speed in American BMD deployment. But it is also true that there are no other more immediate possible solutions in sight.

Although the time for achieving a highly effective defensive capability may seem distant, there is no superior alternative for addressing the potential problem of nuclear winter. Some of the authors of the thesis have suggested that arms control is the potential solution.[5] For example, Carl Sagan suggests that the nuclear winter thesis calls for "a massive, bilateral, verifiable, decrease in the global inventory of nuclear weapons to below the threshold at which nuclear winter would be triggered,..."[6] But it is not difficult to see that arms control alone cannot address the problem of nuclear winter.

ARMS CONTROL: AN ALTERNATIVE SOLUTION?

Although arms control alone is unlikely to be the solution to nuclear winter, arms control in conjunction with strategic defense could be very helpful.

There are three reasons why arms control alone will not solve the problem: (1) the global arsenal of existing nuclear weapons already is at a high level—possibly around 50,000; (2) *all* nuclear armed powers or potential nuclear armed powers would have to cooperate; and (3) complete arms control cooperation would not necessarily be in the self-interest of each nuclear power or potential nuclear power.

The difficulties of negotiating the global arsenal of nuclear weapons from the current tens of thousands to extremely low levels are probably insurmountable. A decade of U.S.-Soviet negotiations has led to a manifold increase in the number of nuclear weapons. An arms control solution to nuclear winter would require very deep reductions in U.S. and Soviet arsenals and that at least the three additional known nuclear-armed states (Britain, China, and France) join with the U.S. and Soviet Union in achieving a very low cumulative number of nuclear weapons. Obviously, the addition of negotiating parties only makes a successful outcome more difficult.

Which country would be permitted to keep what number of weapons? Would the United States and Soviet Union be permitted more of the total than the others because they now possess most of the world's arsenal? If not, would the United States and the Soviet Union be willing to accept some type of equality with the others and descend from their current universally acknowledged positions as the nuclear superpowers? The types of problems involved in such multilateral negotiations appear insurmountable, even assuming good will on all sides.

Unfortunately, not even good will can be assumed. It could be in the interest of some of the powers not to comply with an agreement even were one negotiable. A superior means for deterrence would be available to whatever country alone retained the ability to unlease a nuclear winter. It would hold the power of life or death over all other states—a literal "doomsday device." A narrow self-interest would provide strong incentives to violate an agreement requiring deep force cuts.

In addition, even in a more cooperative environment than exists today, it would be exceedingly difficult to verify that all countries involved were abiding by the reductions and limitations. It would be relatively easy to secretly stockpile hundreds of nuclear weapons which could later be mated to aircraft or missiles. Quite reasonably, because each country could not be *certain* that all others were complying with an agreement, each would have an incentive to stockpile its own "doomsday device." In short, adequate verification of an agreement would be impossible, and states would have a reason not to comply.

The basic mistrust and lack of central control that characterizes the international system kills any possibility that multilateral arms control alone could solve the nuclear winter problem. To suggest otherwise ignores the unfortunate realities of international politics. If those realities of mistrust and state behavior based on narrow self-interest could be solved, then, of course, arms control might provide the solution. But that is like saying that if a sick man were only well he would not be in such ill health. If the international system functioned on the basis of trust and cooperation, the problem of hostile nuclear-armed states and nuclear winter would not exist in the first place.

The need to change the international system to solve the problems of nuclear weapons and nuclear winter is obvious. Unfortunately—and it has been obvious for decades—solutions to numerous international problems would require restructuring the international system away from individual sovereign nation-states. Despite the clarity of the need, and the long-term rationality of such cooperation, a fundamental change in the international system does not appear likely, to say the least.

AN ALTERATION IN WEAPON DESIGNS?

Another suggestion for a potential solution to nuclear winter involves the alteration of current weapon designs to minimize those characteristics conducive to climatic catastrophe.[7] For example, reducing the explosive power, increasing the accuracy, and perhaps delivering the weapons so they penetrate the surface deeply ("earth penetrators") might reduce the prospects for nuclear winter following a nuclear war.

Yet, redesigning weapons is not a feasible solution either. Surprisingly perhaps, this solution faces the same problem as does the arms control solution. All nuclear-armed states and potential nuclear-armed states would have to agree jointly to redesign their forces appropriately. For example, if just the United States and China went to the great expense of redesigning their nuclear arsenals, their effort would be futile (unless, of course, a future nuclear war was limited to the United States and China).

In addition, states which could not or did not want to afford the cost of redesigning their arsenals would have an incentive to maintain or acquire a "doomsday" capability against those states that had redesigned their arsenals. Unfortunately, the inability to verify compliance with a multilateral agreement on weapon redesign, and the existing mistrust of the international system put this solution outside the realm of the useful. Again, the nature of the international system works against the possibility that any international agreement or suggested multilateral cooperative action could provide a solution to the possible threat of nuclear winter.

STRATEGIC DEFENSE AND ARMS CONTROL

Despite the conclusions suggested above there is a role for arms control in reducing the risk of nuclear winter. It could work in conjunction *with* strategic defenses to limit significantly the number of nuclear weapons.

Strategic defenses could be more effective if offensive arms were capped, even at their currently high levels. The type of nuclear disarmament required to solve the nuclear winter problem through arms control *alone* is utopian. But in the realm of reality, much more modest offensive arms control could well facilitate the effectiveness of strategic defense. This is not to say that strategic defense would be impossible without the benefit of arms control (SDI research will, we hope, provide the answer to that question). But there is no doubt that ceilings on offense forces would ease considerably the defensive mission. In short, it cannot be said that offensive restrictions would be necessary for strategic defense effectiveness, but they obviously would be helpful.

A combination of offensive arms limitation and strategic defense would not require a prior miracle such as the restructuring of the international system or the putting aside of narrow national self-interest. Modest offensive arms control measures that have already been achieved in SALT, such as broad ceilings for strategic ballistic missile launchers and ceilings on multiple independently targeted reentry vehicles, might be adequately verifiable and, in the long run, could strengthen the defense considerably. Such limitations, while meaning little without a deployed defense, could mean a great deal as part of a package of strategic defense and arms control.

The combination of strategic defense and relatively verifiable offensive force ceilings would not require that states entrust their security to the unverifiable behavior of others. For example, if the Soviet Union began to violate the offensive ceilings, the United States could respond with additional offensive and/or defensive capabilities. It would, of course, be in the self-interest of the United States and the Soviet Union to abide by offensive limits to help ensure that the other continues to comply, and thereby maintain the effectiveness of both their defenses. Self-interest—not trust—is the basis of this solution, which is more realistic than the others, given the nature of international politics.

Many of the discussions concerning solutions to the nuclear winter thesis are similar to the following statement by American scientist Dr. Lewis Thomas:

> we simply must pull up short, and soon, and rid the earth once and for all of those weapons that are not really weapons at all but instruments of pure malevolence.[8]

Who does not agree that nuclear disarmament would be a marvelous development even if there were no possibility of a nuclear winter? There is little dispute about the "good" of the disarmament goal; what is lacking is a means of getting there. Even the most sincerely expressed desire for nuclear disarmament does not suggest how that goal could be achieved under the realities of international politics. Unfortunately, the nature of the international system prevents anything like the multilateral cooperation and trust required for arms reductions to be effective on their own. The nuclear winter thesis does nothing to alter this difficult condition. Yet the defense/arms control solution suggested here is a possible alternative form of disarmament, one that is more realistic politically and therefore could be effective.

ALLIES AND OTHERS

Ironically, in the absence of strategic defenses the nuclear winter thesis could actually stimulate nuclear proliferation. If only a small number of weapons and delivery systems is necessary to pose the threat of nuclear winter, then it will be relatively easy to enter into the "club" of states capable of doing so. If this were the case, the country with as few as several hundred weapons would be the nuclear equal of the current superpowers in many ways. If very limited nuclear capabilities can hold such a threat many states will want to possess them if others do. The difference from the current situation is not that nuclear weapons are not already considered awesome, but that it would be much easier for countries to acquire a deterrent on par with the existing nuclear powers. An increased incentive for proliferation could result in this case, particularly because the nuclear winter thesis suggests that abstaining from nuclear armaments and involvement would not protect a state from destruction if a conflict occurred.

In addition, the nuclear winter thesis suggests that regional conflicts in the twenty-first century could be even more dangerous than they are now. In the absence of strategic defense how would the United States or the Soviet Union respond to incoming intelligence indicating that some third party was about to initiate a nuclear strike that just might lead to a global climatic catastrophe? It could ask the third party to reconsider, but that might not work. The superpowers could also, separately or together, attempt to disarm the third party, but that could be very dangerous since the third party would be nuclear-armed (it might even ensure the use of the third party's nuclear weapons). Therefore, in the absence of adequate means to intercept offensive nuclear forces, the nuclear winter thesis suggests that regional conflicts will become more dangerous and difficult to manage.

SUMMARY AND CONCLUSION

According to the nuclear winter thesis, even a relatively "limited" nuclear war could cause a global climatic catastrophe. Nuclear war has never been envisaged as anything other than a potential disaster for those involved. Yet the nuclear winter thesis suggests that use of a very small percentage of the current global nuclear arsenal poses a danger to all mankind. The validity of the thesis is uncertain at this point; nevertheless, given the severity of its implications, it is worth considering possible solutions.

The solutions suggested by authors of the thesis generally involve some form of cooperative, multilateral nuclear disarmament, or efforts to redesign nuclear arsenals. The type of agreement necessary would require extremely deep reductions in the current number of weapons and very low ceilings on any future nuclear weapons. Such an agreement would almost certainly be unverifiable and there would be incentives for noncompliance; that is, self-interest would suggest to some states that they not comply because they could not be certain of other states' compliance—which could put them in a disadvantageous position. These disarmament proposals are ignorant of the abiding realities of the international political system. There is no powerful international authority that can enforce laws, right wrongs, and punish those who violate agreements. Consequently, states are compelled by the nature of the system to follow their self-interest in most areas, but most especially in the area of national security.

The type of disarmament necessary to address the nuclear winter thesis would require a transformation of the international political system. Such a transformation would be necessary to solve many of the fundamental problems of international politics. But as with many other pressing international problems (health, housing, food, etc.), it is much easier to identify the need than to satisfy it.

There are no apparent short-term solutions to the problem of nuclear winter. The only apparent long-term solution involves the combination of modest offensive arms control (such as has been achieved in SALT) and the extensive deployment of strategic defenses. It is not clear at this point whether strategic defense technology, especially for BMD, will provide the necessary basis for such a solution. The SDI, as a research program, will attempt to resolve such questions.

Interestingly, addressing the potential problem of nuclear winter is little different from addressing the long-standing problem of nuclear war in general. The nuclear winter thesis simply suggests that the threat is more severe and geographically more expansive than had been thought earlier. Nevertheless, the fundamental question remains: how to reduce the dangers posed by nuclear weapons. The types of answers also remain the same. The most attractive and easily understood answers are those that are impossible to implement (e.g., complete nuclear disarmament), while it is not known, as yet, whether the most realistic in terms of international politics (a combination of strategic defense and arms control) will ever be feasible technically. The SDI, if sustained, should help provide the necessary answers concerning the feasibility of defense as the necessary element in a long-term solution.

ENDNOTES

1. See Carl Sagan, "Nuclear War and Climatic Catastrophe: Some Policy Implications," *Foreign Affairs*, Vol. 62, No. 2 (Winter 1983/84), p. 267. For additional discussions of the "nuclear winter" thesis, see R. P. Turco, et al., "Nuclear Winter: Global Consequences of Multiple Nuclear Explosions," *Science*, Vol. 222, No. 4630 (Dec. 23, 1983), 1283-1292; Paul R. Ehrlich, et al., "Long-Term Biological Consequences of Nuclear War," *Science*, Vol. 222, No. 4630 (Dec. 23, 1983), pp. 1293-1300; and Richard Turco, et al., "The Climatic Effects Of Nuclear War," *Scientific American*, Vol. 251, No. 2 (August 1984), pp. 33-43. A thorough critique of the nuclear winter thesis is provided by Michael F. Altfeld and Stephen J. Cimbala "Targeting for Nuclear Winter: A Speculative Essay," *Parameters*, Vol. 15 (Autumn 1985), pp. 8-15.
2. See Sagan, op. cit., pp. 269-270.
3. See "Book Reviews," *Survival*, Vol. 27, No. 1 (January/February 1985), p. 43. See also Edward Teller, "Widespread After-Effects of Nuclear War," *Nature*, Vol. 310 (Aug. 23, 1984), pp. 58-61; S. Fred Singer, "Is the 'Nuclear Winter' Real?", *Nature*, Vol. 310 (Aug. 23, 1984), p. 62; also by S. Fred Singer, "The Big Chill? Challenging a Nuclear Scenario," *Wall Street Journal*, Feb. 3, 1984, p. 22.
4. Sagan, op. cit., pp. 267, 275, 285.
5. Sagan, op. cit., pp. 286-287, 289-292.
6. "The Chilling Aftermath of a Nuclear War," *Wall Street Journal*, Feb. 16, 1984, p. 35.
7. See for example, Theodore A. Postol, "Strategic Confusion—With or Without Nuclear Winter," *Bulletin of the Atomic Scientists*, Vol. 41, No. 2 (February 1985), pp. 14-17; and Sagan, "Nuclear War and Climatic Catastrophe," op. cit., p. 278-279.
8. Lewis Thomas, "TTAPS for the Earth," *Discover* (February 1984), p. 34.

EIGHT
Chapter 8

STRATEGIC DEFENSE:
ARMS CONTROL AND THE ABM TREATY

Arms control is another issue close to the SDI controversy. While the Reagan administration views the SDI as supporting arms control, critics of the SDI insist that the two cannot be pursued simultaneously and that the Reagan administration must choose *between* arms control and the SDI.[1]

The contention that the SDI is inconsistent with progress in arms control is based upon a particular concept of the U.S.-Soviet arms competition. The argument is that the Soviet Union reacts to specific U.S. strategic programs with offensive countermeasures, and the SDI will prove no exception. If the United States deploys BMD, the Soviet Union will build up its offensive forces in order to penetrate U.S. defenses. In this view, American BMD will serve only to increase Soviet incentives to deploy more offensive forces. Consequently, it is argued that deployment of BMD will ruin any future prospect for arms control. This view holds that the most important means of gaining control of offensive forces is to keep strict restraints on BMD. Based upon this particular line of reasoning, several well-known critics of the SDI have stated:

> Star Wars, in sum, is a prescription not for ending or limiting the threat of nuclear weapons, but for a competition unlimited in expense, duration and danger.

> ...it is possible to reach good agreements, or possible to insist on the Star Wars program as it stands, but wholly impossible

to do both.[2]

— The notion that BMD deployment would put success in offensive arms control virtually beyond reach is not new. The same line of reasoning was used to argue against the U.S. *Sentinel* and *Safeguard* BMD programs of the late 1960s and early 1970s.[3] The view—that BMD would destroy the prospects for offensive arms control—became established wisdom in the early 1970s, and was the primary rationale for the strict BMD limits of the 1972 Anti-Ballistic Missile (ABM) Treaty. As current critics of the SDI have observed concerning the assumed relationship between BMD and offensive arms control:

> A competition in building ABM systems would inevitably instigate an uncontrolled build-up in offensive nuclear forces, as each sought to ensure its ability to penetrate its opponent's defense shield.

And:

> The SALT I and II negotiations were premised on the assumption that limitations on strategic offensive forces would not be possible without extensive constraints on strategic defenses.[4]

Once again, it is not clear that established wisdom is all that wise. Indeed, the history of the U.S.-Soviet arms competition since 1972 has demonstrated that these early views about the relationship between BMD and offensive arms control are extremely questionable.

At a general level, the sentiment is often expressed at public forums concerning the SDI that, instead of building defenses against ballistic missiles, nuclear weapons ought simply to be abolished, thereby removing the need to defend against them. It is impossible to fault the sentiment, or for that matter, the logic of that position. Nevertheless, that position really offers no useful insight because, besides stating the obvious, it does not address the fundamental problem that under current conditions very deep reductions in offensive nuclear forces appear not to be negotiable. Suggesting that nuclear disarmament is the solution to the nuclear threat is like suggesting that widespread wealth is the solution to poverty. It is true, of course, but the question remains how can widespread wealth be achieved?

The reductions that would be required to end the vulnerability of the United States to nuclear attack are well beyond anything considered even remotely feasible through SALT. Such virtual nuclear disarmament would be a superior alternative to strategic defense in many respects. The problem is that it appears to be impossible to get there from here. In the meantime we must somehow survive in a world heavily armed with nuclear weapons. There are many reasons why, short of the creation of a world government with enforcement power, none of the nuclear-armed states could agree to nuclear disarmament. The most obvious is that no side of such a multinational agreement could be confident that others were complying with nuclear disarmament, given the existing numbers of nuclear weapons and the relative ease with which a few nuclear weapons could be concealed. In a world of sovereign states, where there does not exist a world organization with the power to stop or punish international lawbreakers, each state ultimately must ensure its own security as best it can—that is, unfortunately, the nature of the international system.[5] In such a system it is virtually inconceivable that all nuclear armed states would be willing, simultaneously, to trust one another enough (and all other states with the potential for nuclear arms) actually to cede all their nuclear forces. Such trust, if it proved unwarranted, could mean the end of the state willing to take the risk. Consequently, and understandably, states voice their hope for future complete and total nuclear disarmament, while knowing full well that such an event is unlikely ever to take place.

In short, most would agree that a world without nuclear weapons is preferable to one with many weapons, and with the resultant need to build defenses. Without the ability, however, to trust other states always to follow their commitments, and without an international authority to enforce them, the problem is not imagining a better world but getting from here to there. Despite the attractive notion of a future world armed with so few nuclear weapons that they do not pose a threat to the United States, there unfortunately is no indication whatsoever that such a future is a realistic alternative in the search for a method to end the nuclear threat.

There may be *no* means to ease the nuclear threat and the search could prove fruitless. A comprehensive defense against nuclear weapons may prove not to be feasible; but we should not, for lack of trying, fail to investigate the potential for highly effective defenses based upon the belief that nuclear disarmament is a possible alternative.

WILL THE SDI CONTRIBUTE TO ARMS CONTROL PROGRESS AND SUCCESS?

The SDI already has contributed to movement in the arms control process. The Soviet Union walked out of negotiations in November 1983, yet it has returned to the negotiations for the expressed primary purpose of limiting or halting the American SDI. U.S. plans for offensive force modernization undoubtedly also played an important part in convincing the Soviet Union to negotiate. Nevertheless, it appears that the SDI was the determining factor in the renewed Soviet willingness to return to negotiations.

Linkage of U.S. defensive programs with offensive force reductions could become increasingly important. For example, the prospects for deep offensive arms reductions are likely to be nonexistent *in the absence* of U.S. and Soviet strategic defenses. This preliminary requirement for strategic defenses stems from two considerations.

First, Soviet strategic doctrine, put simply, places great importance on the capability to limit damage to the Soviet homeland in the event of war. Under current conditions, this "damage-limitation" mission would be carried out not only by the extensive Soviet air defense network and civil defenses, but also by initial offensive strikes against U.S. retaliatory forces. One of the primary rationales for the modernization of the Soviet ICBM force appears to be to increase the capability to destroy U.S. retaliatory forces. The Soviet Union has repeatedly refused to accept effective limitations on the counterforce potential of its ICBMs, illustrating how important the offensive damage-limitation mission is to the Soviet Union. It must be understood that the Soviet Union will not accept significant reductions in its offensive prowess without acquiring some alternative method of pursuing its damage-limitation mission.

The deployment of BMD by the U.S. and Soviet Union would provide that alternative.

Second, defenses would allow the U.S. to maintain its commitment to verification as an intrinsic principle of arms control even in the context of deep offensive force reductions. It is clear that in the absence of BMD the U.S. cannot agree to deep strategic offensive reductions if Soviet compliance could not be monitored closely, most particularly given the Soviet Union's undistinguished record. *At the current high levels of strategic offensive forces* the U.S. can accept a degree of uncertainty in its ability to monitor compliance with treaty provisions. This is so because a significant change in the strategic balance would require treaty violations on a large (and thus presumably noticeable) scale. Consequently, some ambiguity in the data provided by our monitoring assets is considered acceptable because modest violations that might go unseen would be unlikely to be militarily significant in the context of high offensive force levels.

Deep reductions in offensive forces could easily render even modest violations militarily significant. A small number of hidden weapons may not be important when both sides possess thousands of weapons; however, if both sides only have a small number of nuclear forces then currently insignificant covert deployments could take on great meaning. As a result, deep force level reductions would require almost "perfect" verification capabilities, which will likely remain beyond reach as forces become increasingly mobile.

Strategic defense could provide the only solution to this otherwise intractable verification problem. Deployment of BMD by the U.S. and the Soviet Union could establish the necessary condition wherein illegal deployment of offensive weapons on a large scale would be required before the strategic balance would be affected seriously. More modest covert deployment of offensive forces that might go undetected would be rendered less significant by strategic defenses.

Because of the Soviet commitment to damage-limitation, and the U.S. sensitivity to the issues of compliance and verification, it is extremely unlikely that deep offensive force reductions will ever take place in the absence of ballistic missile defenses. To the extent that SDI research facilitates the U.S. ability to make an informed commitment to such defenses, it will enhance the prospects for deep reductions in offensive forces.

Critics of strategic defense insist that the deployment of BMD would simply cause the Soviet Union to expand its offensive forces, thereby escalating the arms race. Exactly the same claim was made during the BMD debate of the late 1960s and early 1970s. Confident predictions were made that if the U.S. negotiated strict limitations on BMD the Soviet Union would have no incentive to further buildup its offensive forces. In 1972 the U.S. accepted this reasoning and put strict limitations on BMD in the form of the SALT I Anti-Ballistic Missile (ABM) Treaty. On the basis of the argument that U.S. BMD must drive the Soviet strategic offensive arms build up, it was presumed that the ABM Treaty cap on BMD would facilitate offensive force reductions. Critics of BMD repeatedly made the promise before Congress of a "freeze" or reductions of offensive weapons as a result of the ABM Treaty; the belief that strict limitations on BMD would produce the needed basis for achieving U.S. goals in offensive force limitations became accepted wisdom.

BMD limitation was presented to Congress as the measure which would end or reduce Soviet incentives to further build up offensive forces on the grounds that the Soviet Union would not have to increase offensive forces to penetrate U.S. defenses. Confident assertions were made that limiting BMD would stop the "spiraling arms race." For example, writing in support of an ABM Treaty in 1969, Professor George Rathjens stated:

> Actually, with the right kind of ABM agreement incentives for either side to expand its offensive missile forces or to put MIRVs on them would be much reduced since, in the absence of concern about adversary ABM deployment, each side could be confident that it had an adequate deterrent...That of course is why an ABM agreement is so important.[6]

Dr. Herbert Scoville made the same point, claiming that in the absence of an American BMD the Soviet Union would have little incentive for a continued buildup of offensive forces because in such a condition of "frozen stable deterrence, they would not be needed."[7] In 1970 Dr. Wolfgang Panofsky presented the same assumption as fact at SALT I hearings:

> The agreed level of ABM deployment which might arise from

the SALT talks will control more than any other single factor the total level of strategic armament at which we might be able to *freeze the weaponry of the world* as a result of SALT. (Emphasis added)[8]

At the time, many other *current* critics of the SDI echoed assurances of the benign effect of halting BMD.[9]

The history of Soviet offensive deployments since 1972 illustrates clearly that the proponents of strict BMD limits were at the least confused in their understanding of the driving force behind Soviet strategic arms racing. The Soviet offensive nuclear buildup *increased dramatically following the signing of the ABM Treaty.* In 1972 the Soviet Union possessed 1,547 ICBM warheads, 497 SLBM warheads, and 145 long-range bombers. Those numbers in 1985 were, respectively, 6,420, 2,122, and 303; and Soviet offensive production continues apace— hardly the "freeze" in offensive weapons the ABM Treaty was promised to facilitate. (See Figures 19-25 for comparisons of U.S. and Soviet offensive deployments since 1972.)

Many aspects of Soviet activity are difficult to understand and predict. However, it is clear that numerous factors drive the Soviet Union to continue its arms buildup. What we do know is that the absence of U.S. BMD did *not* have the effect predicted by critics of BMD. Indeed, the certainty of having undefended U.S. ICBM silos to target may have spurred the Soviet buildup of its "counter-silo" capable ICBMs after 1972 (SS-18 and SS-19 "hard-target killers" were tested and deployed *after* the signing of the ABM Treaty). Critics who still tie Soviet offensive arms racing to the presence or absence of American BMD have learned little over the last fifteen years about the dynamics of the arms competition. We now realize, at a minimum, that the assumptions presented as facts during the earlier BMD debate concerning the reasons behind Soviet arms racing were mistaken. We should avoid being taken twice to the same dry well.

Finally, arms control does not exist as an end unto itself. Rather, it is intended to serve two primary objectives: (1) to reduce the probability of war; and, (2) to minimize the level of destruction in the event of war. These are the two classic goals of arms control. The SDI, and, if appropriate, the deployment of strategic defenses, should help both to facilitate arms control

FIGURE 19

U.S. and USSR Strategic Offensive System Since 1960

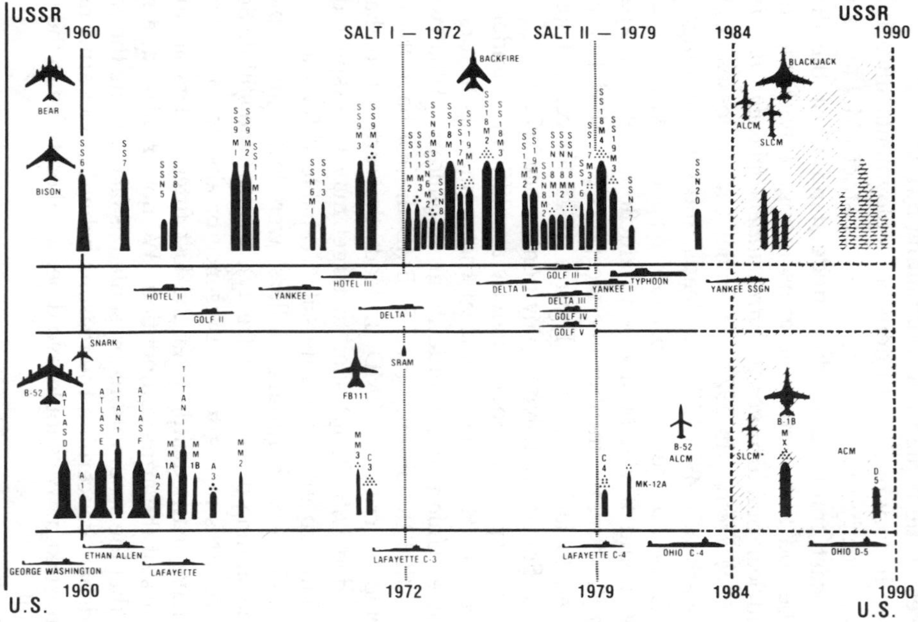

Statement by the Honorable Richard D. DeLaver, Under Secretary of Defense, Research, and Engineering, to the 98th Congress, Second Session, 1984, *The FY 1985 Department of Defense Program for Research, Development and Acquisition.*

FIGURE 20

On-Line SALT-Accountable ICBM Warheads

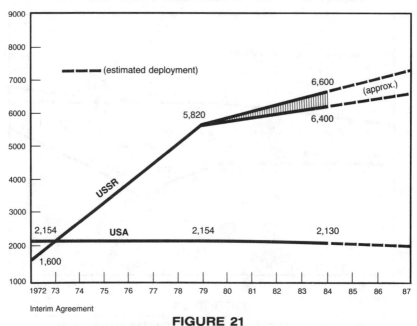

FIGURE 21

ICBM Throwweight (Millions of Pounds)

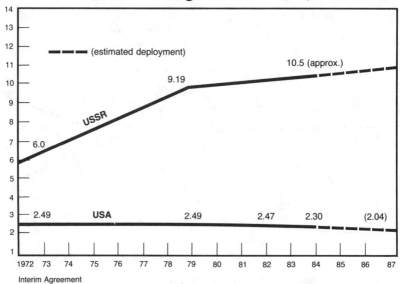

Charles Tyroler, II, *Alerting America: The Papers of the Committee on the Present Danger* (Washington: Pergamon-Brassey's, 1984)

149

FIGURE 22

"Deployed" SALT-Accountable SLBM Launcher

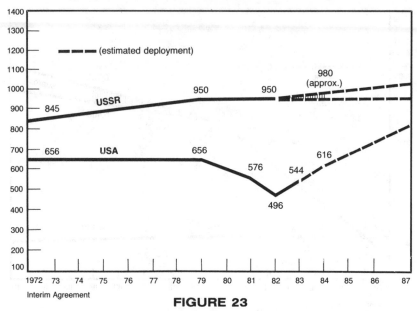

FIGURE 23

On-Line, SALT-Accountable SLBM Warheads

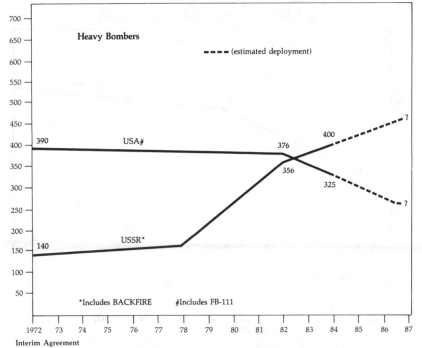

Can America Catch Up? The U.S.-Soviet Military Balance (Washington, D.C.: Committee on the Present Danger, 1984).

FIGURE 24

US and USSR Stockpile Yields

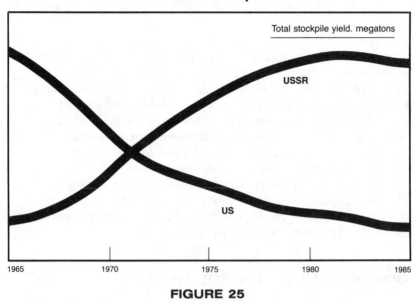

Total stockpile yield. megatons

USSR

US

| 1965 | 1970 | 1975 | 1980 | 1985 |

FIGURE 25

US and USSR Nuclear Stockpiles

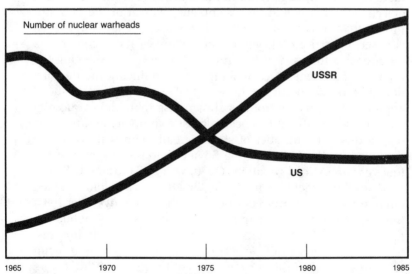

Number of nuclear warheads

USSR

US

| 1965 | 1970 | 1975 | 1980 | 1985 |

Presentation of Secretary of Defense Weinberger to Senate Armed Services
Committee in *Hearings: Department of Defense Authorization for Appropriations for
Fiscal Year 1985.*

151

negotiations and to support directly the goals of arms control.

In regard to these two goals, strategic defenses, whether partial or comprehensive, could contribute to the stability of deterrence and therefore could help reduce the probability of war. In addition, if deterrence should fail despite our best efforts, strategic defense would provide perhaps the only feasible means of reducing the level of destruction. If defense proves to be feasible, it would seem to be the height of folly to remain vulnerable to attack; even a modest defense would likely cope with a limited, accidental, or third country attack. Recall that in the absence of defenses the accidental launch of even one missile could cause millions of casualties.

In short, the SDI and the subsequent possible deployment of strategic defense could support arms control by encouraging the Soviet Union to participate in negotiations and by limiting the probability and destructiveness of war.

OFFENSIVE ARMS CONTROL AND BMD

In principle, reductions in offensive forces and the deployment of BMD could go hand-in-hand in support of arms control objectives. This would be a complete reversal of the U.S. approach to arms control established at SALT. The latter approach is based on strict BMD limits and relatively loose constraints on offensive forces. But in terms of "freezing" or reducing the number of strategic nuclear weapons, or reducing the destruction that would occur in the event of war, the "established" approach to arms control has shown less than stellar success. To be more specific, it has been almost a complete failure on its own terms. The number of strategic ballistic missile weapons deployed by the U.S. and the Soviet Union at the end of the first year of SALT negotiations (1970) was 1,874 for the U.S. and 1,716 for the Soviet Union. By the time the Soviet Union walked out of the strategic arms control negotiations in November 1983, the number of Soviet weapons had grown to 8,377, while the figure for the United States had reached 7,292.[10] If this history reflects arms control success, "failure" would be difficult to define. Many of the current critics of the SDI and BMD were the authors of, or strongly endorsed, this established approach to arms control.

A new approach to arms control that reverses the "established" pattern of loose constraints on the offense and strict limits on defenses, could be a more effective means of pursuing the objectives of arms control. Limits on offensive forces could ease the burden on the defense and thereby make Soviet and U.S. BMD systems more effective. In general, the fewer the number of offensive objects the defense must try to identify and intercept, the more effective the defense. Consequently, because defenses could strengthen stability and reduce the prospective damage in the event of war, even the type of modest offensive limitations that have proved possible could facilitate the effectiveness of the defense and thus support the objectives of arms control.

This admittedly different approach to arms control could give real significance to offensive limitations that otherwise would have little meaning. For example, in America's current condition of total vulnerability to attack, and given the high numbers of strategic nuclear weapons available to both sides (approximately 10,000 for each), even a 75 percent reduction in the number of weapons would not necessarily reduce the damage that the United States would suffer in the event of war. Yet a 75 percent reduction in the number of strategic weapons is far beyond anything previously hoped for in SALT/START. That type of deep reduction has not been, and does not appear to be, negotiable. But more modest (and realistic) offensive limitations could be extremely useful if assented to as part of an arms control agreement that permitted or encouraged defenses. Indeed, an offensive arms control agreement that did not achieve reductions, but only placed ceilings on existing offensive capabilities, could facilitate the effective functioning of the defense.

In short, the history of the "established" approach to arms control does not offer hope that it can achieve much in terms of actually reducing the vulnerability of the United States to nuclear attack. Similarly, the established approach has not proved "stabilizing" in the sense of placing effective constraints on "counterforce" weapons; under SALT the number of Soviet counterforce ballistic missile weapons grew from about 300 to well over 5,000.

There is a fundamental reason—stemming from each side's strategic policy—why deep offensive reductions through arms control have been impossible to negotiate to date, and are likely to remain so in the absence of extensive BMD. The Soviet Union has pursued an offensive force posture capable of destroying U.S. retaliatory forces in a first strike, while the United States has attempted to maintain retaliatory offensive forces capable of surviving a first strike. Consequently, the Soviet Union and the United States have been working at cross-purposes with their respective deployment policies. The result has been that the Soviet Union has builtup its offensive capability to threaten U.S. forces, and the United States has attempted to deploy forces in order to offset the Soviet threat and maintain a retaliatory deterrent. This type of relationship leaves little prospect for offensive reductions as both sides continue to build up in an offensive force tango based upon the needs of their respective nuclear policies.

A new approach to arms control—one that embraces defensive deployments and does not condone a continued offensive force buildup—has been and will continue to be opposed by those architects of the established view. They cannot, however, point to anything but disappointment after almost two decades of strategic arms control negotiations under their own offense-oriented framework. Even architects of the established approach to arms control have noted its failure. As Leslie Gelb, one of the principal official authors of SALT II, rightfully has observed:

> Arms control has essentially failed. Three decades of U.S.-Soviet negotiations to limit arms competition have done little more than to codify the arms race.[11]

An arms control perspective that reverses the established pattern could render even modest offensive limits truly meaningful in terms of stability and reducing the American vulnerability to attack. The obvious question is: how can the United States persuade the Soviet Union to agree to limitations on offensive forces while encouraging defensive deployments? This question, critics of the SDI claim, cannot be answered because BMD deployment can only increase incentives for more nuclear weapons.

There are conceivable conditions, however, that might lead the United States *and* the Soviet Union to see that reversing the established, and largely failed, approach to arms control is in their self-interest. Under these conditions there would exist mutual self-interest in restraining offensive forces and deploying defenses against ballistic missiles. Unfortunately, appealing to national self-interest appears to be the only basis for achieving serious results in arms control—as SALT and previous arms control attempts have demonstrated.

To address the question—why might the Soviet Union agree to limits on offensive forces while both sides deploy defenses—one must first recall that the primary objective of Soviet strategic doctrine is to limit damage to the Soviet Union, and particularly to its military and political control structure. The Soviet Union now pursues this objective by combining counterforce offensive forces (designed to destroy U.S. retaliatory capabilities) with extensive antibomber air defenses, extensive civil defense programs, and a limited but growing BMD capability.

The Soviet strategy for damage-limitation might have achieved its goal over the long run had the United States continued to allow its retaliatory capabilities to become increasingly vulnerable. Throughout the 1970s, the United States did little to reduce the vulnerability of its land-based forces at a time when the Soviet counterforce threat was growing rapidly. Had that decade-long malaise in U.S. programs continued, the Soviet strategy of combining heavy counterforce offense with limited defenses might have worked over the long run to ensure an effective "combined arms" damage-limitation capability.

But, the U.S. offensive strategic modernization program (e.g., the B-1B bomber, the Trident submarine, cruise missiles, a prospective new and survivable MX basing mode, and a mobile ICBM program), if it is kept on track, should demonstrate to the Soviet Union that the United States will not allow its retaliatory forces to be countered effectively by the buildup of Soviet counterforce offensive weapons. It may seem ironic, but it is precisely U.S. offensive force modernization that must cause the Soviet Union to place less hope in offensive counterforce to limit damage to the homeland and turn instead increasingly toward strategic defense. The U.S. must facilitate that shift by modernizing its offensive forces properly.

"Proper" U.S. retaliatory force modernization must focus upon "survivability"—being able to withstand a Soviet first-strike and still threaten retaliation. Increased survivability for

U.S. forces should help move the Soviet Union toward relying more on strategic defense to attain its damage-limitation objectives. Survivability is not new; U.S. policy has long been to focus on a survivable, retaliatory capability for the purpose of deterrence.

During the 1970s, however, the United States did not follow its own advice and allowed its retaliatory forces to become increasingly vulnerable to the growing Soviet counterforce threat. Relative U.S. inaction gave validity to the rationale for the Soviet counterforce buildup—that is, effectively to counter much of the U.S. retaliatory force through offensive means while leaving the rest to be handled by their defenses.

To persuade the Soviet Union to agree to serious offensive arms control and move more towards strategic defense it is unnecessary to convince Soviet leaders that a damage-limitation capability is a priority goal—they have believed that for years. Rather, the U.S. must demonstrate that damage-limitation is best achieved when offensive forces are constrained and BMD deployed. This "strategy for arms control" does not require the Soviet Union to give up its damage-limitation objective. Expecting the Soviet Union to accept significant reductions in its counterforce offensive weapons without providing some alternative means of damage-limitation, is to expect the Soviet Union to give up its damage-limitation objectives in deference to the established U.S. approach to arms control and deterrence. Such an expectation has been, and almost certainly will remain, without promise.

In the future, two conditions may exist to move the Soviet Union toward limiting offensive capabilities. The first, as mentioned above, is to demonstrate that Soviet offensive counterforce strategy will not be effective. Of course, early deployment of limited BMD may help provide the needed survivability for U.S. retaliatory forces.

Second, if the maturing of BMD technology renders strategic defense a viable alternative to offensive counterforce as the primary means of achieving damage limitation, the circle will be complete. The proper modernization of U.S. retaliatory forces would deny the Soviet Union the purpose of its dramatic offensive counterforce buildup, and the technology for strategic defense, which the Soviet Union is pursuing vigorously, would offer a defensive alternative to that goal, i.e., a damage-limitation capability for the Soviet homeland.

Under the two conditions described above, neither of which is inconceivable, it would be *in Soviet self-interest* to negotiate mutual offensive force limitations in order to facilitate the effectiveness of their own strategic defense.

Mutual offensive limitations would serve U.S. interests as well because they would facilitate the effectiveness of U.S. strategic defenses. Both U.S. and Soviet self-interest could therefore be served by accepting mutual offensive force constraints and moving toward a much greater emphasis on strategic defense. If compelled to make a choice between a strategic relationship wherein the superpowers can maintain mutually devastating offensive threats, *or* they can achieve *reliable* damage-limitation through the combination of strategic defense and arms control, the latter should be much more attractive. This assumes only that under the proper conditions both the United States and the Soviet Union will be more interested in limiting damage to themselves than in inflicting damage on each other. Nothing in Soviet or U.S. strategy suggests otherwise.

Thus, the conditions necessary to place real offensive limitations in line with both U.S. and Soviet self-interest are not inconceivable; and in the absence of that self-interest significant offensive limitations will not occur. This calls for a degradation of the value of offensive counterforce capabilities by enhancing the survivability of U.S. retaliatory forces (something to which even "leaky" BMD could contribute). It obviously also requires that strategic defense be seen as a viable alternative for damage-limitation. A mutual requirement for effective defenses should compel both sides to accept offensive force limitations. The United States is already on this road in some regards—proper U.S. actions could help move the Soviet Union in the same direction.

The approach to arms control suggested above is, in principle, far superior to the established approach. If implemented, it would lead to a more defense-oriented environment and to a U.S.-Soviet strategic relationship wherein both sides could feel more secure because the prospect of a nuclear holocaust would have abated. A new framework for arms control that endorses rather than prohibits defenses, and reduces offensive forces would have several advantages over the current offense-oriented framework:

1. The U.S. *and* Soviet Union would, for the first time, have compatible self-interest in the negotiated limitation of counterforce offensive capabilities; both could more easily achieve their respective damage-limitation objectives with the benefit of mutual offensive limitations.

2. The Soviet Union would not be required to give up its priority objective of damage-limitation as a prelude to achieving deep offensive reductions—consequently such reductions would become possible.

3. The negotiated phasing down of offensive forces in parallel with the negotiated phased deployment of defensive systems would allay fears that strategic defenses could lead to strategic superiority for either side.

The problem for the United States with this approach to arms control is apparent. It will be very difficult for the United States to pursue the development of BMD meant to "rid the world of nuclear weapons" while simultaneously reducing the worth of Soviet counterforce weapons in the immediate future by improving U.S. offensive force survivability. It will be extraordinarily difficult to explain why the move toward defense, and particularly a defense aided by arms control, will require spending additional money on the strategic retaliatory forces.

In addition, many of those who criticize the SDI on arms control grounds appear to be conversant with only two concepts about "things strategic": (1) mutual vulnerability means stability; and (2) strategic defense is the enemy of stability and arms control because it threatens mutual vulnerability. Unless U.S. strategic thinking can transcend those two pervasive and probably misguided shibboleths, there will be little prospect for serious arms control or strategic defense. Some members of the arms control and "antinuclear" community appear to recognize the compatibility between strategic defense and the objectives of arms control. For example, Jonathan Schell, whose book *The Fate of the Earth* was a catalyst for the "antinuclear movement" in the early 1980s, seems to have recognized this potential benefit of strategic defense:

> Building defenses, depending on what else you do, could make it a lot easier to achieve the abolition [of nuclear arms]. I think

what arms control people are afraid of is that Star Wars is a shield that will allow Reagan to fight a nuclear war. But what if, while you build up the defenses, you reduce the offenses...Then Star Wars isn't a threat at all. If you're afraid of the sword and the shield, OK. But then you should attack the sword—not the shield.[12]

An ideal strategic defense/arms control solution to the nuclear threat would see the continuing reduction of nuclear offensive capability (down to whatever minimum level would be acceptable to the superpowers) and a corresponding increase in strategic defenses. At a future "crossover" point defensive capabilities would surpass those of the offense. This, of course, is an ideal and may not occur even if effective defenses are feasible and deployed—it certainly will not occur in the absence of deployed defenses. The illustration below reflects such an ideal process.

FIGURE 26

An Ideal Strategic Defense/Arms Control Solution to Nuclear Weapons

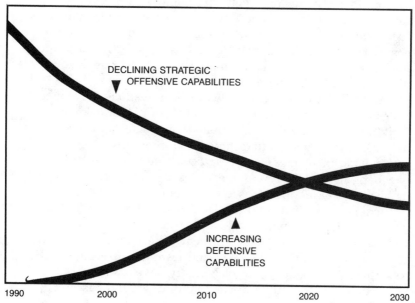

THE ABM TREATY

For the United States, the 1972 ABM Treaty was a reflection of the mutual vulnerability approach to deterrence. If abided by it ensures that there cannot be a ballistic missile defense challenge to the condition of mutual vulnerability. It was seen at the time of its signing and ratification not only as a means of halting the offensive arms race, but as a means of ensuring stability based upon mutual vulnerability. Indeed, the heart of the treaty is found in Article I, paragraph 2, which states:

> Each party undertakes not to deploy ABM systems for a defense of the territory of its country and not to provide a base for such a defense, and not to deploy ABM systems for defense of an individual region....

It might strike one as amazing that the United States signed a treaty which prohibits it from defending itself against strategic ballistic missile attack. But recall that established wisdom at the time held that mutual vulnerability was stabilizing, and probably unavoidable; the ABM Treaty was intended to perpetuate that stability based on mutual vulnerability. Interestingly, according to recent national poll data, almost 70 percent of the American public favors the development and deployment of BMD even if it requires renegotiation or withdrawal from existing arms control agreements; and less than 7 percent of the public favors current arms control agreements over deployment of defenses. (See Appendix, Table 25).

The ABM Treaty, as amended in 1974, restricts the United States and the Soviet Union to low levels of BMD deployment. Only a single BMD site is permitted each side, and that site may contain only 100 interceptors, 100 interceptor launchers, and a handful of radars. Of particular interest is Article V, which prohibits the development, testing, or deployment of mobile, air, space- or sea-based BMD components. These strict restrictions mean that if the Soviet Union or the United States decides to deploy a nationwide BMD system, the ABM Treaty will have to be revised or rescinded. The treaty does allow BMD research, full development and testing of fixed, ground-based BMD components, and laboratory development of other BMD components, and production of fixed, ground-based components. In addition, either side can suggest revisions at any time. Indeed, the treaty requires a formal review process every five years.

The SDI has generated a drive to "Save the ABM Treaty" by some of those still committed to the established anti-BMD approach to arms control.[13] From this group have stemmed recent charges that the Reagan administration's SDI threatens to violate the ABM Treaty. Ironically, however, those elements apparently of most concern, involving the placement and modernization of certain radars,[14] were not originated under the SDI Organization or by the Reagan administration; they largely were initiated years ago under the Carter administration, which had determined that they were not in violation of the treaty. After close scrutiny of these programs, the Reagan administration has endorsed the position of the Carter administration—that the programs are in compliance with the letter and spirit of the treaty. Indeed, what reportedly is the most recent and authoritative policy statement from the Reagan administration concerning the SDI, NSDD-172, mandates that the SDI program must conform to the ABM Treaty.[15]

Given the drastically changed strategic balance and the developments in offensive arms control and BMD technology since the signing of the ABM Treaty, an important question is whether it any longer serves a useful purpose. Just because conditions have changed significantly since 1972 does not necessarily mean that the ABM Treaty is now inconsistent with U.S. interests. However, the events that have occurred since 1972 give ample reason to review the value of the Treaty.

IS THE ABM TREATY IN THE U.S. INTEREST?

It is clear that the effect of the ABM Treaty, to date, has been far short of U.S. expectations. A review of U.S. hopes for the treaty at the time of its negotiation, signing, and ratification, illustrates the extent to which the treaty has failed to fulfill expectations.

At the time the ABM Treaty was signed, the U.S. saw a critical linkage between limitations on offensive and defensive arms. During the course of the negotiations the Soviet

Union gave every indication that it sought primarily to limit ballistic missile defense, and the U.S. *Safeguard* BMD program in particular. In contrast, the U.S. sought constraints on offensive forces, particularly on the Soviet ICBM force which appeared to be developing a capability to threaten American retaliatory capabilities, especially U.S. ICBMs. Consequently, in the negotiations the United States consciously used the Soviet desire for BMD limitations as a lever for achieving limitations on offensive forces. As Henry Kissinger has observed:

> ...an American ABM program was essential to any hopes for Soviet acceptance of offensive limitations.[16]

This offense-defense linkage established by the United States made good sense as a negotiating strategy, given the differing objectives of the two sides. It also was sound strategic logic. If the Soviet offensive threat to U.S. strategic forces could be reduced through arms control limitations, then the U.S. need for the *Safeguard* BMD system (intended primarily to defend U.S. strategic forces) would automatically be reduced. Consequently, the U.S. reasonably could "give up" *Safeguard* if the Soviet Union would accept constraints on the counterforce potential of its most threatening offensive forces (ICBMs). Thus the basis for agreement was established with the U.S. assuming that the five-year, interim offensive agreement of SALT I would be followed by more comprehensive offensive force limitations. It was thought in 1972 that these limitations would ensure the survivability of retaliatory forces, thereby ensuring stability even in the absence of BMD coverage for U.S. strategic forces.

Indeed, U.S. Unilateral Statement A, attached to the ABM Treaty, states specifically that the failure to achieve more comprehensive offensive force limitations within five years could be grounds for withdrawal from the ABM Treaty. Unilateral Statement A also specifies the purpose of these "more complete" offensive limitations: to "constrain and reduce on a long-term basis threats to the survivability of our respective strategic retaliatory forces."

Thus, in the process of negotiating and ratifying SALT I, the U.S. established several key assumptions as the basis for the ABM Treaty. First, it was to be accompanied by the Interim

Offensive Agreement which was to cap the Soviet counterforce threat. Second, SALT I was to be followed, within five years, by more complete offensive limitations which would reduce the Soviet threat to the survivability of U.S. retaliatory forces. The acceptance of limitations on American BMD coverage for U.S. strategic forces was reasonable, given U.S. expectations in 1972 concerning the reduction in Soviet hard-target counterforce potential.

But these optimistic U.S. expectations concerning the reduction of the Soviet offensive threat clearly have *not* been met. The Interim Offensive Agreement of SALT I did *not* diminish the Soviet threat to U.S. ICBMs. The subsequent SALT II agreement (signed in 1979) was *not* achieved within five years, and in no way reduced the Soviet threat to U.S. retaliatory forces; indeed, it lent legitimacy to the amazing increase in the Soviet counterforce threat that evolved between 1972 and 1979 and even licensed additional Soviet counterforce capabilities.

In short, the ABM Treaty has successfully denied each side effective nationwide defenses against strategic ballistic missiles. But, the primary U.S. objective for SALT I and SALT II—to reduce the growth of the Soviet offensive threat to U.S. retaliatory forces (and thereby support the U.S. deterrence concept of mutual vulnerability)—has not been achieved. The logical linkage between offensive and defensive force limitations that constituted the rationale for SALT I, and the ABM Treaty in particular, has been completely unraveled since the signing of SALT I. The conditions established by the United States concerning offensive force constraints reflected in Ambassador Gerard Smith's Unilateral Statement A have not been satisfied, and the U.S. has not abided by (and for the most part has ignored) the linkage in offensive and defensive limitation it considered vital at the time of SALT I.

Some BMD critics stated at the time of SALT I that if arms control proved inadequate to cope with the Soviet offensive buildup—as unfortunately has been the case since 1972—they would then support BMD deployment. For example, Wolfgang Panofsky stated,

> ...my view is that if the Soviet number of missiles keeps increasing at a continuing fast rate, and if we do not succeed

> in achieving a negotiated limitation of the strategic force, then defense of hardened missile sites would indeed be an objective which I would support...we may need a really effective defense of our missiles...[17]

To a large extent SALT I did not effect the expected offensive limitations because the Soviet Union chose to ignore the key U.S. provision concerning the limitation on "heavy" ICBMs (HICBMs). The U.S. understanding of the SALT I ceiling (as expressed in U.S. Unilateral Statement D of the Interim Offensive Agreement) on heavy ICBMs would have permitted Soviet deployment of no more than 313 ICBMs which are significantly larger than the Soviet SS-11 (the SS-11 useful payload capacity reportedly is approximately 2,000 lbs.). Yet the Soviet Union has circumvented this essential constraint of SALT I and has deployed over 650 heavy ICBMs since 1972. This has been accomplished by defining the SS-9 replacement, the SS-18 ICBM (reportedly 16,500 lbs. throwweight) as an HICBM and deploying 308 of these missiles; and by defining the SS-19 ICBM (reportedly 8,000 lbs. throwweight) *as a light* ICBM system, and therefore unaffected by the SALT I heavy ICBM ceiling. As a result of defining the SS-19 as a *light* ICBM, the Soviet Union has been able to deploy over 350 of these missiles. This amassing of SS-18 and SS-19 firepower has greatly increased the counterforce threat to the U.S. and undermined the core intent of SALT I as it was presented to Congress. (Compare the Soviet deployment of over 650 modern large ICBMs with the current U.S. deployment of no such missiles and future plans for deploying only 50-100 new MX ICBMs.)

The deployment of hundreds of SS-19s as light ICBMs vitiated the clear intent of SALT I and destroyed the presumed linkage between offensive and defensive force limitations. The entire rationale for the ABM Treaty, as developed during the negotiations and presented to Congress, has been undercut by the failure of SALT I to limit offensive forces as expected and the failure of SALT II to redress this inadequacy of SALT I.

It is important to note that Soviet actions regarding SS-19 deployment and the distinction between heavy and light ICBM launchers is not "just" Soviet noncompliance with a nonbinding U.S. unilateral statement. Circumvention that defeats the object and purpose of a treaty is a material breach of the agreement, according to the Vienna Convention on the Law of Treaties (1969); and Soviet behavior involving SALT I and SS-19 deployment as a *light* ICBM appears to purposeful fraudulent circumvention of the treaty.

Soviet noncompliance with the U.S. definition of the heavy/light ICBM distinction is important, given the negotiating record, because it suggests deliberate Soviet deception. During the negotiations the U.S. delegation argued that a clear dividing line should be 70 cubic meters, and later proposed that in order to keep light ICBMs from being replaced by new heavy ICBMS the volume increase not be significantly greater than the Soviet SS-11 ICBM. Yet, according to Ambassador Smith, the Soviet Union refused any definition, arguing that a clear definition was unnecessary because both sides knew what was meant by heavy and light ICBMs and could distinguish between the two.[18] During the negotiations the Soviet Union clearly had the SS-18 and SS-19 in development and *knew* the U.S. understanding of what constituted heavy and light ICBMs. It appears certain that the Soviet Union *knew* that it would violate the U.S. definition of the critical distinction between heavy and light ICBMs, yet told the United States "not to worry" about a strict definition because it was obvious. As a result of the absence of a clear definition, the Soviet Union has been able to circumvent the treaty through its deployment of over 350 SS-19s in excess of the SALT I ceiling on heavy ICBMs. Soviet deployment of the SS-19 as a "light" ICBM appears to represent misleading behavior that destroyed a primary U.S. rationale for SALT.

Unfortunately, the Soviet Union is also in direct violation of the ABM Treaty—the most obvious case being the blatantly illegal Krasnoyarsk BMD radar. According to international law, Soviet noncompliance with the ABM Treaty relieves the United States of the obligation to abide by the treaty. The United States has the prerogative to choose to void the treaty *in toto*, or to void those provisions violated by the Soviet Union or comparable provisions.

Soviet circumvention of the U.S. understanding of SALT I and its ABM Treaty violation could be extremely significant militarily. The combination of the vast counterforce capability of Soviet SS-18 and SS-19 ICBMs, and the potential—stemming in part from Soviet noncompliance—for a rapidly deployable nationwide BMD system, creates an extremely dangerous and unstable condition. The question then is: given Soviet treaty circumvention and noncompliance, does the ABM Treaty remain in the U.S. interest?

There are four obvious alternatives for the United States *vis-à-vis* the ABM Treaty: (1) continue with "business as usual"; (2) withdraw from or void the ABM Treaty in accordance with international law and deploy defenses; (3) follow a policy of selective noncompliance as a response to Soviet treaty violation; or, (4) attempt to *strengthen* the ABM Treaty in an effort to halt Soviet noncompliance. Of these options, carrying on with "business as usual" is clearly the most inconsistent with U.S. interests. It would virtually endorse Soviet noncompliance and license, perhaps even encourage, future violation and fraud. Moreover, future prospects for useful arms control are undercut when the U.S. finds the Soviet Union in violation of treaties and continually fails to achieve corrective actions.

It must be recalled that the Soviet Union appears to be reaching for the capability to deploy a nationwide BMD system relatively rapidly. As a recent government review of the Soviet BMD program observes:

> The Soviets are developing a rapidly deployable ABM system to protect important target areas in the U.S.S.R. They have been testing all the types of ABM missiles and radars needed for widespread ABM defenses beyond the 100 launcher limit of the 1972 ABM Treaty.
>
> ....The new, large phased-array radars under construction in the U.S.S.R...appear to be designed to provide support for such a widespread ABM defense system. The aggregate of the U.S.S.R.'s ABM and ABM-related activities suggests that the U.S.S.R. may be preparing an ABM defense of its national territory.[19]

Given this concern for the Soviet capability to deploy a BMD system rapidly, and the inability of the United States to do likewise, it probably would be helpful if ABM Treaty constraints could be enforced, at least until the United States is better positioned to minimize an initial Soviet BMD deployment advantage. The problem, however, is that the Soviet

Union is violating and exploiting some important terms and ambiguities of the treaty while the United States remains wholly compliant.[20] This pattern of behavior has led to an increasingly disadvantageous position for the United States *under the terms of the treaty.* We may be in the undesirable position of being harmed if the treaty is voided, and hurt if we continue with "business as usual."

A logical option for the United States at this point is to attempt to strengthen the terms of the treaty in those particular areas of concern. For example, the United States might attempt to get a better handle on the Soviet "rapid deployment" potential by negotiating clear definitions of critical yet ambiguous treaty language that has been exploited by the Soviet Union. For example, mobile BMD components are prohibited, but what about Soviet BMD components that are "transportable"? Air defense and antitactical ballistic missile defense systems are not prohibited by the treaty; but if some of the systems deployed by the Soviet Union also possess some BMD capabilities, how ought they be addressed by the ABM Treaty? Attempting to clarify exploitable ambiguities in the treaty may be a way of addressing Soviet noncompliance; or, if unsuccessful, it could at least spotlight Soviet intentions to continue their exploitation.

Attempting to strengthen the ABM Treaty by clarifying ambiguous terms and interpretations may require that the United States engage in reciprocity; that is, the United States may have to convince the Soviet Union that continued noncompliance would compel the United States to void or bend the treaty constraints it finds most binding. The Soviet Union understands politics, and is unlikely to change its behavior unless the United States makes the exploitation of the treaty a matter of high politics.

Finally, with regard to the ABM Treaty, a repeated claim has it that the treaty has saved the United States vast amounts of money that otherwise would have been spent on the *Safeguard* BMD program. Even this contention may be false. Obviously, the U.S. did not spend vast sums on the *Safeguard* BMD program—yet the net effect may not have been savings. The *Safeguard* BMD system was intended to provide protection of U.S. retaliatory forces, including silo-housed ICBMs. In the absence of BMD, the U.S. has been compelled to examine dozens of different concepts for protecting ICBMs from a Soviet first strike. The "solution" most favored of late is to develop and deploy a small, mobile ICBM (SICBM). The cost of such a system could be between $45 and $60 billion. Although unproved, it may well be that deployment of ICBM defenses would constitute a less expensive, and possibly *non-nuclear* alternative for securing ICBM survivability. There is support for such an alternative, spurred by skepticism of the ABM Treaty, from both prominent Republicans and Democrats. For example, Professor Zbigniew Brzezinski, the national security adviser for President Carter, recently noted that:

> ...the decision to go ahead with the SDI makes eminent sense....If we implement that part of the SDI program which by the mid-1990s would enable us to disrupt a Soviet first strike, we would reinforce deterrence and promote nuclear stability. That means concentrating on terminal defense and boost-phase interception.[21]

Contrasting arguments for and against maintaining the ABM Treaty in its current state are outlined below:

Maintain ABM Treaty

1. Revision of the ABM Treaty would cause an arms race between offensive and defensive weapons, thereby undercutting efforts for strategic offensive arms control.
2. Revision of the ABM Treaty would lead to BMD deployment, which would be destabilizing.

Revise ABM Treaty

1. The Soviet Union continues to violate the ABM Treaty and the U.S. should not condone such behavior by conducting "business as usual" with the Treaty.
2. After over thirteen years of negotiations the ABM Treaty has failed to produce expected results in the area of offensive arms control. Consequently, U.S. deterrent forces now are much more vulnerable to a Soviet first strike, yet the ABM Treaty prohibits the U.S. from defending those forces.

3. Without the ABM Treaty the Soviet Union would expand its BMD system nationwide well in advance of U.S. efforts.

3. Revision of the ABM Treaty would lead to BMD deployment, which would be stabilizing.

4. The ABM Treaty preserves the nuclear threats of smaller nuclear powers, thereby supporting deterrence.

4. The Soviet Union is increasing its capability to defend against ballistic missiles of all types while the U.S. adheres to the ABM Treaty. To allow this type of behavior to continue will lead to dangerous Soviet unilaterial BMD capabilities.

5. Revision of the ABM Treaty and deployment of BMD would be expensive and wasteful.

5. The U.S. should not maintain a treaty that would perpetuate its vulnerability to any country or organization that acquires an ICBM in the future.

6. Maintenance of the ABM Treaty would ensure that, in the event of war, the U.S. would be destroyed; the investment in BMD would be worth the cost.

SDI, STRATEGIC DEFENSE, AND THE NEAR-TERM PROSPECTS FOR ARMS CONTROL

The much-heralded Soviet arms control proposal of October 1985, labeled by the Soviet Union as a "radical" offer for 50 percent reductions, really is only "radical" in that it would require much deeper reductions in U.S. forces than it would in Soviet forces.[23] It is an excellent example of how an arms control proposal can be publicized as a great stride forward, but upon closer inspection turn out to be just another effort at one-upmanship. Had the United States put forth such a one-sided proposal domestic critics would have immediately dismissed it as being "insincere" and "non-negotiable."

With reference to the SDI the Soviet "radical" proposal could not reduce offensive forces as well as even a poor defensive system—yet it would ban the SDI. In effect, the U.S. would have to trade away whatever potential there is for effective defenses in return for an offensive agreement that would simply enhance the Soviet offensive advantage and leave thousands of counterforce nuclear weapons aimed at the United States.

The Soviet proposal can hardly be considered the basis for a good agreement. But it does reflect the Soviet desire to maintain its offensive counterforce approach to damage-limitation, unimpeded by the prospect that U.S. defenses might challenge the value of the enormous Soviet investment in counterforce offensive weapons.

The Soviet proposal has been publicized as endorsing 50 percent reductions on each side. Yet, there is a sharp hook in the proposal—the Soviet definition of the forces to be included and excluded from limitation. For example, the Soviet proposal includes a ceiling of 6,000 on strategic "nuclear charges." That in itself could be a step in the right direction, yet the Soviets have insisted that many U.S. forces in Europe would have to be counted under that ceiling while similar Soviet nuclear weapons would not be counted. The Soviet proposal makes for good headlines but bad arms control. It is similar to a bargain wherein one person would be required to trade 50 percent of the cash in all his pants pockets for 50 percent of what another person held in only his front left pocket.

Even a relatively incompetent four-layer defense system would reduce the quantity of the Soviet ballistic missile threat by a much greater degree than would this "radical" Soviet arms reduction proposal. For example, a four-layer system of only 30 percent effectiveness in each defensive layer would be equivalent to more than an 80 percent reduction in weapons. A four-layer system of 40 percent effectiveness in each layer would require arms reductions of almost 90 percent to achieve a comparable reduction of weapons. And defensive layers may be much more effective than the 30 to 40 percent effectiveness used here for comparative purposes. Should the U.S. be willing to trade away the SDI, and the defensive potential it may hold, in return for the grossly asymmetrical offensive reductions proposed by the Soviet Union? Of course not.

However, a question that must be considered is: what level

of offensive reductions would be required to be worth giving up the SDI? There can be no reasoned answer to that question at this point because the defensive potential of the SDI is yet to be determined. In short, how can the U.S. know what to "get" in exchange for giving up the SDI when the potential value of strategic defense is as yet uncertain? If the SDI demonstrates that comprehensive strategic defense is technically infeasible, then the U.S. will be lucky if it can use the SDI as a significant "bargaining chip" in any way. On the other hand, if a four-layer defense system could reduce the Soviet ballistic missile threat by, say, an average of 60 percent per layer, then arms reductions of 97 percent would be required to achieve an equivalent threat reduction.

This type of comparison between defense effectiveness and arms reduction ignores the potential value of limited defenses for deterrence and stability. Even if defenses offer a modest level of effectiveness overall, limited defenses capable only of protecting retaliatory forces against Soviet counterforce attack could make an extremely important contribution to stability. To achieve an equally stabilizing effect through arms control alone would necessitate substantial reductions in the Soviet ICBM force. Consequently, even very modest defenses could be extremely useful in terms of deterrence, and a major reduction of Soviet counterforce capabilities would be required to achieve the same stabilizing effect through offensive arms control alone.

This discussion of strategic defense and arms control suggests that the immediate U.S. arms control position should be four-fold:

1. protect the SDI *at least* until its potential is better known;
2. pursue offensive ceilings/reductions on destabilizing counterforce weapons—while knowing that the Soviet Union is unlikely to make significant concessions until the SDI appears to have "staying power;"
3. enhance the survivability of U.S. retaliatory forces, particularly those weapons with the potential to counter an initial Soviet defensive advantage;
4. prepare, in the mid-to-long term, to accept deep reductions in U.S. offensive forces in exchange for Soviet deep reductions—an exchange which would enhance the effectiveness of both sides' defenses.

Thus, the SDI appears to have drawn the Soviet Union back to negotiations after its sixteen month walkout. Yet SDI critics have reiterated the charge that the SDI will prevent any agreement on arms control at the Geneva talks, which deal with strategic nuclear forces, intermediate-range nuclear forces, and space and defensive weapons. The argument that no progress will be made without limits on the SDI is buttressed by the current public Soviet position that there can be no agreement limiting offensive nuclear forces unless there is a corresponding agreement limiting the SDI. Though Soviet spokesmen have on occasion observed that much SDI-type research cannot be verified effectively, the official Soviet negotiating position remains unchanged.

The U.S. public position is that reduction of real and existing offensive nuclear arsenals is most important, and agreement in this area should not be held hostage to agreement in other areas. Much of the SDI, as a research program, ought not be the object of arms control negotiations because of verification difficulties. There would be no way of verifying a ban on much of the SDI-type research, which, in any case, has long since been engaged in by the Soviet Union. The U.S. position is supported by the ABM Treaty which takes into account the difficulty of monitoring laboratory research; its prohibitions on BMD development do not, as a consequence, come into effect until the stage of actual component "field testing," which may be verified.

The U.S. public position does, however, include the prospect of discussions concerning BMD prior to any U.S. decision for deployment.[22] The ABM Treaty makes provision for such discussions and the U.S. already is trying to discuss with the Soviet Union the potential benefits of a defense-oriented, as opposed to an offense-oriented, approach to deterrence and arms control.

The United States has endorsed the ABM Treaty precedent that BMD research, which does not lend itself to adequate verification, ought not be the object of limitations. The official U.S. view—that the Soviet Union is violating earlier strategic arms control agreements—does not provide fertile ground for negotiating agreements that are "unverifiable." The positions of the United States and Soviet Union are extremely interesting because they indicate what each side is attempting to limit and protect from limitations. It should be remembered that in SALT I it was the United States that demanded a linkage between offensive and defensive limitations, while the Soviet Union eventually sought *only* BMD limitations. These positions reflected what each side wanted from the negotiations. The United States sought limits on offensive forces and, realizing that its BMD program was the leverage needed to attain this, demanded a linkage. The Soviet Union sought to limit the United States' BMD program, which at the time was technically far in advance of the Soviet Union's, but, seeking to protect its own very dynamic offensive modernization program, pushed for *only* BMD limits.

The current positions regarding offensive-defensive linkage are somewhat similar and somewhat different from the SALT I variety. Now the Soviet Union is demanding an offensive-defensive linkage. This more than likely reflects a Soviet desire to impede the U.S. movement into a high-technology arena wherein it may be feared that the United States would *ultimately* have a competitive advantage. The Soviet Union appears now to be willing to play an "offensive" card in return for nipping the SDI "in the bud." In contrast, the United States hopes to achieve offensive limitations while also protecting SDI research.

Whether this varied mixture of interests and objectives will provide suitable ground for achieving a near-term agreement is questionable at this point. But, it should be noted that previous arms control agreements have not been established upon common aims; rather, divergent aims have led to agreements on specific limitations.[24]

Nevertheless, if the Soviet Union maintains its position concerning the impossibility of offensive limitations in the absence of strict constraints on BMD research and development, then an agreement is unlikely in the near term. That said, recall that the Soviet Union has taken absolute positions in the past only to modify them significantly when it was no longer in its interest to maintain them. Whether the Soviet Union will move from its current position probably will depend upon: (1) how resolute the U.S. government appears to be in support of SDI research; (2) whether that research appears to be bearing fruit; and, (3) whether U.S. *offensive* force modernization programs will provide the Soviet Union with incentives to move increasingly toward strategic defense and come to an agreement on offensive force limitations.

SUMMARY AND CONCLUSION

In summary, there have been numerous recent charges against the SDI based upon the general view that any future U.S. BMD deployment would lead to increased Soviet arms racing. These charges are not new, they were aired extensively during earlier BMD debates. Indeed, by the time of the signing of the SALT I ABM Treaty, the view that halting BMD would facilitate a "freeze" had become established wisdom. Yet, as has become absolutely clear since 1972, even the strict BMD limits of the ABM Treaty did not lead to the fulfillment of U.S. hopes. The Soviet Union has pursued an amazing buildup of "counterforce" weapons since 1972. What is clear is that our earlier understanding of what drives Soviet arms racing was wrong. We know now for sure that U.S. BMD did not unleash that drive. Indeed, the U.S. BMD programs of the late 1960s and early 1970s appear to have been the lever by which the modest offensive limitations of SALT I were achieved.

Nevertheless, to note what we now know in this respect does not mean that the Soviet Union would not react to U.S. BMD deployment. The Soviet Union certainly would respond if the SDI leads to BMD deployment. We saw that the Soviet response to earlier U.S. BMD programs included a strong emphasis upon political and arms control initiatives. But, whether future actions would stress an even greater offensive force buildup, diplomatic political initiatives, an increased defensive buildup, a new willingness to accept mutual offensive limitations, or none of the above, will depend to a great extent upon numerous complex political, economic, and technical factors. It simply is absurd now to suggest—as was done previously and subsequently was proved incorrect—that U.S. BMD deployment would inexorably lead to Soviet offensive arms racing, while maintaining a lid on BMD deployment would lead as surely to offensive force limitations. That thesis was the basis of the "accepted wisdom" at SALT, an approach to arms control that has largely failed.

The ABM Treaty has not produced the expected effect— useful offensive force constraints. The result is that Soviet offensive forces today pose an even greater threat to U.S. retaliatory capabilities while the United States is prohibited from defending its retaliatory capabilities with BMD. This places the United States in the very position it was trying to avoid through the SALT I limitations. It is not clear that the United States should seek to void the ABM Treaty, but it is clear the treaty has failed to achieve much of what was expected. It also is evident that continued Soviet exploitation of ambiguous treaty language and outright violation could place the United States in an extremely dangerous position. A treaty that is adhered to strictly by only one party may well be worse than no treaty at all. Whether the United States will be able to "correct" Soviet misbehavior *vis-a-vis* the treaty may depend upon the extent to which the United States stops projecting a "business as usual" image and demonstrates that continued misbehavior will have undesirable consequences for the Soviet Union in terms of U.S. strategic programs—including BMD.

Despite the fact that the established "anti-BMD" approach to arms control has largely failed, the future for arms control could be bright—if we embark on a new approach that encourages strategic defense. A mutual transition toward strategic defense would serve the interests of both the United States and the Soviet Union since limiting offensive forces would help to ensure the effectiveness of defensive forces. This new defense oriented approach to arms control would require both sides to make the choice to give up some strategic offensive capabilities in order to gain reliable and less expensive defense capabilities. To believe that both sides would choose strategic defense over strategic offense, if the choice must be made, is to assume only that U.S. and Soviet leaders will see a much greater value in the capability to save the lives of their respective countrymen than in the capability to inflict destruction on the opponent. This new approach to arms control would support the true goals of arms control and provide enhanced safety for both the U.S. and the Soviet Union—goals that the established approach to arms control has failed to accomplish.

To provide a basis for this new approach to arms control the U.S. must demonstrate to the Soviet Union that its continued accumulation of offensive counterforce weapons can no longer provide an offensive route to a damage-limitation capability. Ironically, to provide the basis for a defensive approach to arms control will require that the U.S. pursue some offensive force modernization in the near-term. This is *not* to argue for a larger gross number of U.S. strategic nuclear weapons. Rather, it is to note that the U.S. retaliatory capability will require enhanced *survivability* against the Soviet counterforce threat to provide the impetus for a Soviet move away from counterforce and toward strategic defense as the primary means of damage-limitation. When both sides choose to pursue their damage-limitation objective through strategic defense because that objective can no longer be served by the continued accumulation of offensive forces, then a defensive approach to arms control will be in both sides' self-interest.

Doubt concerning the feasibility of a new approach to arms control ought not focus on the ultimate Soviet willingness to choose strategic defense over strategic offense when the choice must be made. Rather, the doubt surrounds the U.S. ability to pursue the necessary near-term offensive modernization to improve force survivability, *and* strategic defensive technologies. Although the rationale is clear, and the need for force survivability exists regardless of the SDI, an offensive/defensive "dual track" may prove politically infeasible for the United States for some of those same reasons that led the U.S. to the SDI in the first place.

ENDNOTES

1. See, for example, McGeorge Bundy, George F. Kennan, Robert S. McNamara, and Gerard Smith, "The President's Choice: Star Wars or Arms Control," *Foreign Affairs*, Vol. 63, No. 2 (Winter 1984/85), pp. 264-278.
2. Ibid., pp. 273, 277.
3. There are numerous references to this fact; for some of the more interesting see the testimony of Dr. Wolfgang Panofsky, in U.S. Senate, Committee on Foreign Relations, Subcommittee on Arms Control, International Law and Organization, *ABM, MIRV, SALT, and the Nuclear Arms Race, Hearings*, 91st Cong., 2nd sess. (Washington, D.C.: USGPO, 1970), pp. 178-180, 195-196; see also the testimony of Jerome Kahan in U.S. Senate, Committee on Foreign Relations, *Strategic Arms Limitations Agreement, Hearings*, 92nd Cong., 2nd sess. (Washington, D.C.: USGPO, 1972), p. 22; and George Rathjens, "A Breakthrough in Arms Control," *Bulletin of the Atomic Scientists*, Vol. 25, No. 1 (January 1969).

4. Thomas K. Longstreth, John Pike, and John Rhinelander, *The Impact of U.S. and Soviet Ballistic Missile Defense Programs on the ABM Treaty* (Washington, D.C.: National Campaign to Save the ABM Treaty, March 1985), pp. 3, 4.

5. This point is still best illustrated in the classic work by Kenneth Waltz, *Man, the State and War* (New York: Columbia University Press, 1954).

6. See "A Breakthrough in Arms Control," op. cit., p. 5.

7. "Next Steps in Limiting Strategic Arms," *Science and Public Affairs (Bulletin of the Atomic Scientist)*, Vol. 28, No. 3 (March 1972), p. 11.

8. U.S. Senate, Committee on Foreign Relations, Subcommittee on Arms Control, International Law and Organization, *ABM, MIRV, SALT, and the Nuclear Arms Race, Hearings*, 91st Cong., 2nd sess. (Washington, DC: USGPO, 1970), p. 179.

9. See, for example, the statement by Dr. Sidney Drell, in, *Ibid.*, p. 579.

10. See John Collins and Patrick Cronin, *US/Soviet Military Balance*, Report No. 84-163-S, Congressional Research Service, Library of Congress, Aug. 2, 1984, p. 28.

11. Leslie Gelb, "A Glass Half Full," *Foreign Policy*, No. 36 (Fall 1979), p. 21.

12. Quoted in Gregory A. Fossedal, "A Star Wars Caucus in the Freeze Movement," *Wall Street Journal*, Feb. 14, 1985, p. 30.

13. See, for example, Longstreth, Pike, and Rhinelander, op. cit.

14. As presented in testimony by John B. Rhinelander before the House Committee on Foreign Affairs, Subcommittee on Arms Control, International Security and Science, April 24, 1985.

15. See Jim Kurfeld, "Star Wars Plan Is Modified," *Long Island Newsday*, June 14, 1985, p. 5.

16. Henry Kissinger, *White House Years* (Boston: Little, Brown & Co., 1979), p. 813.

17. U. S. Senate, Committee on Foreign Relations, *Strategic and Foreign Policy Implications of ABM Systems, Hearings*, Part I, 91st Cong., 1st sess. (Washington, D.C.: USGPO, 1969), p. 332.

18. See Ambassador Gerard Smith's statement in, U.S. Senate, Committee on Armed Services, *Military Implications of Anti-Ballistic Missile Systems and the Interim Agreement on Limitation of Strategic Offensive Arms, Hearings*, 92nd Cong., 2nd sess. (Washington, D.C.: USGPO, 1972), see pp. 289, 294, 363, and 364.

19. Department of Defense, *Soviet Military Power* (Washington, D.C.: USGPO, April 1985), p. 48.

20. See Colin S. Gray, "Moscow Is Cheating," *Foreign Policy*, No. 56 (Fall 1984), pp. 141-152.

21. Zbigniew Brzezinski, "A Star Wars Solution," *The New Republic*, Issue 3677 (July 8, 1985), pp. 16-18.

22. See, for example, Michael Getler, "U.S. Official Says Deployment of 'Star Wars' May be Negotiable," *Washington Post*, January 10, 1984, p. 16.
23. For an outline of the Soviet proposal see the address by George P. Schultz before the 31st Annual Session of the North Atlantic Assembly, October 14, 1985, San Francisco, CA; the text, as prepared for delivery is presented in Department of State, Press Release, *Arms Control, Strategic Stability, and Global Security*, No. 240 (October 15, 1985), pp. 18-24.
24. See, for example, Colin Gray and Donald Brennan, "Gemeinsame Interessen als Grundlage für Rüstungskontrolle?" No. 13, in Uwe Nerlich, ed., *Sowjetische Macht und westliche Verhandlungspolitik in Wandel militärischer Kraftverhältnisse* (Baden-Baden: Nonos Verlagsgesellschaft, 1982).

NINE
Chapter 9

THE MORALITY OF THE SDI
AND STRATEGIC DEFENSE

Is the SDI moral, immoral, or is it outside such judgments? Recently, numerous American religious organizations, and individual rabbis, pastors, and priests have taken a stand on the issue—some criticizing and others endorsing the SDI.[1]

President Reagan has defended the SDI on moral grounds, arguing that defense is a morally more acceptable position than the current offensive-oriented deterrence policy. The president believes that,

> Today, the only defensive weapon we have is to threaten that
> if they kill millions of our people, we will kill millions of theirs.
> I do not think there is any morality in that at all.[2]

What strategic policy the United States should pursue certainly ought to be the subject of searching moral analyses. Since 1980 religious organizations and moral philosophers have devoted an increasing amount of consideration to U.S. strategic policy, and their pronouncements have received a great deal of attention.

The American Conference of Catholic Bishops approved their pastoral letter on nuclear weapons on May 3, 1983.[3] Other churches have taken a position on strategic policy similar to that adopted by the Catholic bishops; but the pastoral letter is the most detailed presentation of that position and has received the most attention. The pastoral letter does make general and specific recommendations concerning the character of a strategic policy that is compatible with the moral standard of the "just war" tradition. These recommendations do not include an endorsement of BMD deployment. However, it does "...welcome any effort to protect civilian populations,"[4] and specifically requests the type of studies conducted in 1983 that led to the SDI, and the research being conducted under the SDI. As the letter states:

> An independent commission of scientists, engineers and weapon experts is needed to examine if [civil defense] or any other plans offer a realistic prospect of survival for the nation's population or its cherished values, which a nuclear war would presumably be fought to preserve.[5]

The SDI research program is largely intended to examine precisely that question. This is *not* to imply that the bishops have endorsed the SDI; but their pastoral letter certainly appears to endorse what the SDI is.

There is little difficulty in recognizing the morality of the SDI research effort; the pursuit of knowledge by the United States concerning the feasibility of a comprehensive defense against strategic ballistic missiles can hardly be characterized as unethical, particularly since it is the responsibility of the U.S. government to provide for the security of the American people. SDI research could, in fact, be viewed as a moral imperative for the U.S. government.

The pastoral letter does not, however, recommend the deployment of BMD; other moral analyses specifically reject it.[6] The pastoral letter, rather than endorsing BMD deployment as a moral response to the threat of nuclear war, points to a different potential solution. The failure of the pastoral letter to endorse BMD deployment is reasonable given that it is unclear at the present whether technology will permit effective strategic defenses. But it is extremely doubtful that the alternatives favored by the American Catholic bishops could ever provide security and protection for civilian populations. Consequently, the question must be asked, why did the bishops choose their particular (yet implausible) solution, and might strategic defense provide a better (i.e., a more effective *and* moral) response to the threat of nuclear war? This chapter will focus on those questions.

THE PASTORAL LETTER:
WHAT DID IT CONCLUDE AND WHY?

The bishops endorsed a combination of limited deterrence and arms control as the immediate means of addressing the threat of nuclear war. These means are to provide a path to the long-term solution, i.e., the establishment of an international authority which could exercise central control over nuclear arms. As the letter observes:

> Looking ahead...we feel that a more all-inclusive and final solution is needed. We speak here of a truly effective international authority...The hope for such a structure is not unrealistic, because the point has been reached where public opinion sees clearly that, with the massive weaponry of the present, war is no longer viable. There is a substitute for war. There is negotiation under the supervision of a global body realistically fashioned to do its job. It must be given the equipment to keep constant surveillance on the entire earth. Present technology makes this possible. It must have the authority, freely conferred upon it by all the nations, to investigate what seems to be preparations for war by any one of them. It must be empowered by all the nations to enforce its commands on every nation. It must be so constituted as to pose no threat to any nation's sovereignty.[7]

The bishops reached this position through a sophisticated chain of logic. Their position was based largely upon the "just war" tradition. Accordingly, they assessed whether the use of nuclear force possibly could fit within the boundaries established by that tradition. According to just war standards any morally acceptable use of nuclear weapons must seek to avoid civilian destruction: it must discriminate between combatants and noncombatants; the destruction caused by nuclear weapons must be proportional to the good served by their use; and there must exist a reasonable hope of success in limiting suffering and restoring peace through nuclear use.

The bishops' judgment was that the use of nuclear weapons very likely would be uncontrollable; the bishops argued that even if a nuclear conflict began in a limited fashion it would escalate and cause massive destruction to civilian centers. Consequently, even though it is the intention of the United

States to avoid targeting civilians in a nuclear exchange, the result would involve such a level of civilian suffering that effective discrimination between combatants and noncombatants would be infeasible, and the damage done by nuclear arms could not be proportional to any good achieved. As the pastoral letter states:

> The location of industrial or militarily significant economic targets within heavily populated areas or in those areas affected by radioactive fallout could well involve such massive civilian casualties that in our judgment such a strike would be deemed morally disproportionate, even though not intentionally indiscriminate.[8]

Finally, given the view that use of nuclear weapons would escalate to uncontrolled destruction, the bishops concluded that there would be little probability of achieving an objective that could be defined as success:

> One of the criteria of the just war tradition is a reasonable hope of success in bringing about justice and peace. We must ask whether such a reasonable hope can exist once nuclear weapons have been exchanged. The burden of proof remains on those who assert that meaningful limitation is possible.[9]

Consequently, according to the bishop's analysis, because the use of nuclear weapons was likely to be uncontrollable it could not satisfy three primary just war principles: discrimination, proportionality, and probability of success. The pastoral letter itself implies strongly that no nuclear use could be moral. For example, it is replete with such statements as:

> The political paradox of deterrence has also strained our moral conception. May a nation threaten what it may never do? May it possess what it may never use?...Our no to nuclear war must in the end be definitive and decisive...there must be no misunderstanding of our profound skepticism about the moral acceptability of any use of nuclear weapons.[10]

Despite numerous such statements, since publication of the pastoral letter, bishops and consultants to the bishops have indicated that the pastoral letter did *not* contain an outright rejection of nuclear retaliation. Rather, nuclear retaliation might be morally acceptable if it could be accomplished in a fashion that minimized the prospect for escalation. In June 1984 Archbishop John O'Connor of New York stated that nuclear use might be justified if noncombatants would be exposed to minimal risk, such as in the tactical use of nuclear weapons at sea. Archbishop O'Connor noted, "could a nuclear weapon ever be used? I think we could say, if the conditions of discrimination and proportionality can be met, I say yes."[11] Such a position is not inconsistent with the pastoral letter, but neither does it acknowledge that the letter itself implies great skepticism concerning the possibility of limiting nuclear use and meeting those "just war" conditions. Indeed, concerning the possibility of limitation, as noted in the above quote, the pastoral letter concludes that, "the burden of proof remains on those who assert that meaningful limitation is possible."[12] This is significant because the thesis of the bishops' letter is that nuclear war could not be limited and that any nuclear use that can not be constrained cannot meet the conditions of discrimination or proportionality.

In short, the bishops appear to have rejected as exceedingly unlikely the notion that the operational use of nuclear weapons could morally be justified. Nevertheless, they do recognize that deterrence currently is based upon the threat of using nuclear weapons, and that offensive-oriented deterrence appears necessary (at least until replaced by some alternative means of preserving security and stability) to ensure that neither side considers nuclear conflict acceptable.

The bishops confronted a dilemma: how to maintain the necessary deterrent until the long-term solution of an international authority can be established, while simultaneously rejecting the basis of the current form of deterrence, i.e., the threat of devastating nuclear retaliation. The solution of the pastoral letter is to endorse *the possession* of nuclear weapons while virtually rejecting the possibility of any morally acceptable use. U.S. possession of strategic nuclear weapons, according to the bishops, would be an adequate deterrent even if the United States followed their moral guidelines and had no operational plans to employ them. The bishops argued that this deterrent threat would be effective because the Soviet Union would never *know* that the United States would not employ its weapons.

Soviet uncertainty concerning U.S. intentions would serve to deter even in the absence of U.S. intentions to fulfill its threat.

The pastoral letter, in effect, recommended "deterrence-by-bluff." This particular approach to deterrence, combined with arms control negotiations, a nuclear freeze, and the rejection of "destabilizing" weapons, constitute the basis of the bishops' near-term solution to the threat of nuclear war. The bishops, however, view even this limited form of deterrence as acceptable *only* as an interim step en route to an international authority that would be the "all-inclusive and final solution."

It is not surprising that the bishops recommended disarmament and world government, and not strategic defense, as the long-term moral solution to the threat of nuclear war. As discussed in chapters seven and eight, the nature of the international system constitutes a fundamental problem. The current international system, characterized by individual sovereign states pursuing their narrow self-interests in a context of mistrust and competition, does indeed set the stage for international hostility and noncooperation. The bishops, and many others before them,[13] recognize that the nature of the international system is the root problem. Consequently, it is not surprising that the pastoral letter recommended a fundamental change in the international system as the "final solution" to the threat of nuclear war. But, just as the nature of the international system precludes the level of cooperation necessary for general nuclear disarmament, so also it precludes the international cooperation necessary to establish a "freely conferred upon" international authority which "must be empowered by all the nations to enforce its commands on every nation."[14] The reasons that render general nuclear disarmament impossible in the current international system render the cooperative establishment of such a world government impossible.

WORLD GOVERNMENT: THE MORAL ANSWER TO THE THREAT OF NUCLEAR WAR?

The cooperative creation of an international authority capable of enforcing "its commands on every nation" could well address the threat of nuclear war. It certainly would, almost by definition, remove the current immoral (as defined by the bishops) U.S.-Soviet deterrence relationship. But that international authority could not ensure that nuclear weapons would never be used unless it had the coercive power necessary to preclude all potential wars and prohibit any unauthorized production or use of nuclear weapons. Such a world government would have to be very powerful indeed, perhaps totally so. It is unclear whether the possibilities of repression and coercion inherent in such a global authority would provide a safer and more secure world for its citizens. Nevertheless, the potential risks associated with a new world order may seem less threatening than the current risk of nuclear war and the existing "immoral" deterrence policies.

But even if one assumes that a world government would be benign there is a fundamental problem with any such alternative as the moral solution to the threat of nuclear war. Because, in short, such an authority is beyond any *realistic* hope of coming into being. The existing structure of the international system virtually prohibits such a change.

The problem stems from the lack of *any* central authority which could guarantee the security of sovereign states. It is beyond belief to expect the United States, the Soviet Union, or any other state to give up sovereign control of its means of security unless it could be certain that the threat posed by opponents could be handled by the central authority. Indeed, such behavior could be seen as an irrational abdication of a state's primary responsibility of providing security for its citizenry. Moreover, the level of certainty concerning the ability of the central authority to protect each state's interest could not be high, particularly during its formation. How could the United States, for example, be confident that the Soviet Union would give over control of *all* of its nuclear weapons that pose a threat to the United States? The necessary level of verification simply would be impossible. Similarly the Soviet Union would, without a doubt, be unwilling to concede sovereign control of its nuclear arsenal unless it could be certain that the United States no longer posed a nuclear threat. How could either superpower (or any nuclear-armed state) be confident that the other had not secretly stockpiled some weapons? The point is that they could not; and unless states, particularly the superpowers, conceded sovereign control of their respective forces to the central authority it would not be capable of enforcing its decisions. In effect, little would change.

The League of Nations and its successor the United Nations are excellent examples of organizations with some claim to international authority, but with only minimal enforcement power. Neither changed the nature of the international system for the very reasons that prevent the cooperative establishment of an effective global authority.

Thus, the existing lack of trust that is inherent in the sovereign state system prohibits the cooperative establishment of a central authority with genuine enforcement power. To establish such an authority virtually all states would have to agree, *simultaneously*, to concede control of their forces to the central authority, and each state would have to believe that all potential opponents would abide by that agreement and that the international authority could enforce that agreement and protect individual national interests. Unfortunately, the lack of trust among states in the international system, and the rational limitations that lack of trust places on each state's willingness to cooperate, renders virtually impossible the cooperative establishment of a new world order.

The bishops' call for a new world order as the solution to the threat of nuclear war at least recognizes the root of the problem. However, only three preconditions could lead to the *cooperative* establishment of that new order: (1) international trust and cooperation; (2) a central authority willing and able to enforce compliance with international agreements; and, (3) a common external threat to survival that would compel common action. If either of the first two preconditions existed, the new world order already would have arrived; but barring alien attack from outer space, there appear to be no common threats so persuasive as to unite the international system. As Brian Urquhart, general undersecretary of the United Nations, remarked at ceremonies celebrating the fortieth anniversary of the UN Charter, a genuine unification of the UN could not be realized "until an invasion from Mars takes place."[15]

Those who propose that a new world order is the solution to the threat of nuclear war generally recognize that its creation would not be easy. For example, one proponent of this solution, Professor Saul Mendlovitz of Rutgers University, has suggested that creation of a new world order would require the "same kind of imagination" that led to the general abolition of slavery.[16] Yet the abolition of that wretched institution in the United States did not come about through cooperative agreement; abolition was part of the bloodiest and most costly war ever fought by Americans. Similarly, the end of serfdom in Imperial Russia in 1861 did not occur through the "enlightened consciousness" of the parties concerned. Rather, it came about largely as a result of the Crimean War and was forced upon the nobility by Tsar Alexander II, not without much acrimony.

A world government could, one supposes, be established through global conquest by a superpower or an alliance of powers. In the event of such an occurrence the new political leadership presumably could enforce edicts and new policies upon the rest of the world. Yet such a conquest almost certainly would involve the use of nuclear weapons—the very threat which we are interested in avoiding.

The "moral" solutions to the threat of nuclear war proposed by the bishops (i.e., cooperative disarmament and creation of a central international authority) suffer from the same fundamental flaw—neither is feasible in the current international system. And if the system could be changed so that the necessary preconditions for these solutions existed, the solutions would no longer be necessary. In short, the bishops recognize in their pastoral letter that the fundamental problem concerning the threat of nuclear war stems from the nature of the international system. Yet the suggested solution to that problem—fundamentally changing the nature of the system—although logical, is unhelpful because we cannot get there from here without a prior, virtually simultaneous, benign transformation in the way nations behave.

STRATEGIC DEFENSE: CAN IT MEET MORAL CRITERIA?

Three alternatives—disarmament, world government, and comprehensive strategic defense—constitute the generally suggested long-term solutions to the threat of nuclear war. These three are not mutually exclusive. Indeed, as discussed in the previous chapter, if both superpowers were armed with comprehensive defenses they would more likely accept deep offensive force reductions. Similarly, as the bishops' position suggests, national disarmament and world government are complementary: an effective central authority would require a monopoly or at least superiority of power to enforce its decisions.

The SDI responds to the bishops' request for an examination of the technical prospects for population defense. Yet, despite their call for SDI-type research, the bishops moved in another direction and recommended disarmament and world government as their long term moral solution. It is curious that strategic defense did not play any role in the bishops' long term plan. One could speculate that they assumed that comprehensive strategic defense would prove impossible. *Feasibility*, however, could not have been the determining factor in their analysis given the virtual impossibility of disarmament and world government. Effective strategic defense would, after all, meet the moral conditions demanded by the just war theory without requiring a new world order for its implementation.

For example, comprehensive defenses would, by definition, protect the population and societal values in the event of war. Consequently, U.S. and Soviet deployment of effective defenses would end the current condition that the bishops rightly find morally unacceptable—the inherent vulnerability of civilian centers to nuclear attack and their likely devastation in the event of war.

Effective strategic defenses would facilitate the three conditions established by the just war theory as required by the bishops. First, defenses would ensure the minimization of civilian suffering in the event of war by protecting them directly. Consequently, the U.S. and Soviet governments would enforce through strategic defense the just war requirement for "discrimination" between combatants and noncombatants.

Similarly, strategic defenses would permit the possibility of meeting the "proportionality" requirement that the damage caused by the taking up of arms should be proportional to the good served. Obviously, such a judgment must be made case by case; but effective strategic defenses would alter the current situation and ensure that a conflict could not escalate beyond any hope of proportionality. Indeed, the key to the bishops conclusion that current policies are immoral is based upon the view that nuclear escalation would likely cause civilian suffering far outweighing any potential good served. Effective defenses would revise current conditions away from that morally unacceptable situation.

Finally, the chance of success (defined in terms of protection of the innocent) also would be facilitated by strategic defense. The current absence of defenses and the likelihood of escalation led the bishops to conclude that the resort to arms would be futile because of the inevitable massive civilian destruction. Yet an effective defense would prohibit either side from inflicting (or suffering) such destruction. In short, the deployment of comprehensive defenses could be seen as moving away from the current policies and conditions that fail to meet the moral requirements of the just war tradition.

Obviously, to satisfy these conditions it would be important that the Soviet Union possess effective defenses as well; the requirements for morality do not focus only on the protection of American civilians. This is an important point because it means that the morality of strategic defense does not depend *only* upon the United States pursuing its interest in strategic defense; it mandates that the Soviet Union continue to pursue its own obvious interests in strategic defense.

The fact that the defensive transition would be based upon the pursuit of national self-interest is the primary reason why a policy endorsing strategic defense—the transition to a more moral policy of defense—is politically more realistic than the other suggested moral alternatives of disarmament and world government. It would not require the prior transformation of the international system. The moral case for strategic defense, however, cannot rest solely upon the fact that other alternatives are infeasible; it must be demonstrated that the defensive transition is feasible. As one moral critic of SDI, Professor Henry Shue, has rightly noted:

> The moral case for SDI will not have been made until it has been shown why it will lead to the elimination of retaliation more surely than all the alternative routes, like the build-down.[17]

The reason why a transition to effective defenses could lead to the elimination of nuclear retaliation is because, in the near term, both sides' offensive forces would be less vulnerable, thereby discouraging first strikes. In the far term comprehensive strategic defenses simply would render offensive forces ineffective. Indeed, it would be in the interest of both sides to accept arms control limitations on offensive arms in order to limit the threat that their own defenses must counter. Although there exist no certainties concerning a defensive transition, what is certain is that a defensive transition is feasible politically while the alternatives are not.

It appears that a transition to effective strategic defense would satisfy moral requirements, and is politically more realistic than the alternatives of disarmament or world government. That does not mean that an effective and comprehensive defense capability is feasible technically. Fortunately, the SDI is intended to address that very question: will comprehensive defense be feasible?

SUMMARY AND CONCLUSION

The question of morality and strategic policy has become a focus of increasing debate in the United States since the publication of the American Catholic bishops' pastoral letter of May 1983. Interestingly, the bishops and the Reagan administration agree that the current strategic condition and the policies that support that condition are morally unacceptable. The pastoral letter endorses strongly the concept of a rigorous scientific examination of the technical feasibility of effective strategic defense. It appears to support research such as that pursued under the Reagan administration's SDI.

Nevertheless, the administration and the bishops differ over the appropriate short and long term solutions to the moral dilemma of nuclear weapons. For the near term, the bishops endorse a freeze in strategic force modernization and reject a policy of nuclear deterrence that cannot accommodate the moral requirement of the just war theory. The administration continues to support the modernization of U.S. strategic deterrent forces and rejects the notion that deterrence, the credibility of which depends upon the perceptions of those to be deterred, can be based largely on bluff.

The long-term solution to the nuclear threat suggested in the pastoral letter does not include strategic defense; rather, the bishops endorse the rusty and idealistic recommendations of disarmament and a new world order. Disarmament and/or a benign world government often are considered alternatives to strategic defense in the search for a moral long-term solution to the threat of nuclear war. Unfortunately, the nature of the current international system argues strongly against the possibility of nuclear disarmament or the cooperative creation of a new world order. The call for the latter is appreciated by all, but the need has not begotten a realistic strategy for achieving the goal. Expressions of the need for and rationality of international cooperation and the rejection of hostility can be inspiring, but they do not provide the route to that world.

Strategic defense appears to provide a long-term solution to the nuclear threat that can accommodate the moral guidelines set forth by the bishops. In addition, unlike the alternatives, a transition to strategic defense *is* consistent with the most basic reality of international politics—national security cannot be predicated upon the expectation of mutual trust amongst opponents. Unfortunately, the defensive solution to the nuclear threat and our moral dilemma may run afoul of technical reality. The SDI, it is fervently hoped, will help determine whether comprehensive strategic defense will prove feasible.

ENDNOTES

1. See, for example the discussion in "1,000 clergymen back 'Star Wars' defense plan," *Washington Times*, Aug. 23, 1984, p. 4; and, "Group Opposes 'Star Wars' Funding," *Washington Post*, May 14, 1985, p. A-8.
2. Quoted in "Keep Space Defense Option," *Colorado Springs Gazette Telegraph*, Dec. 30, 1984.
3. See "The Challenge of Peace: God's Promise and Our Response," *Origins*, Vol. 13, No. 1 (May 19, 1983), pp. 1-32.
4. Ibid., p. 18.
5. Ibid., p. 21.
6. See Henry Shue, "Are Nuclear Defenses Morally Superior?" *QQ: Report from the Center for Philosophy and Public Policy* (University of Maryland), Vol. 5, No. 2 (Spring 1985), pp. 6-8.
7. "The Challenge of Peace," op. cit., p. 30.
8. Ibid., p. 18.
9. Ibid., p. 16.
10. Ibid., pp. 14, 19.
11. Quoted in "Nuclear Arms Can Be Justified Archbishop Says,"

Washington Post, June 17, 1984.
12. "The Challenge of Peace," op. cit., p. 16.
13. See, for example, Jonathan Schell, *The Fate of the Earth* (New York: Alfred Knopf, 1982); most recently this suggestion was renewed in, "Is There A Way Out?" *Harper's*, Vol. 270, No. 1621 (June 1985), pp. 43-44.
14. "The Challenge of Peace," op. cit., p. 30.
15. Quoted in George Spieker, Deutsche-Presse Agentur, "Einigkeit in der UNO erst bei einer Invasion vom Mars," *Washington Journal*, July 5, 1985, p. 1.
16. "Is There A Way Out?" op. cit., p. 44.
17. See Shue, op. cit., p. 9.

TEN
Chapter 10

SDI: BRINGING IN THE ALLIES?

President Reagan's "Star Wars" speech of March 23, 1983, was as much of a surprise to allied governments as it was to most Americans. Apparently only British Prime Minister Margaret Thatcher was informed about the orientation of the speech prior to its delivery. This lack of consultation irritated the NATO allies, who tend to see their security as directly affected by shifts in U.S. strategic policy. The United States often is criticized in the Western European press for an absence of "sensitivity" to its allies; the introduction of the SDI was viewed as yet another example of this insensitivity.

The position of the NATO allies in regard to the SDI is important politically and, perhaps to a lesser degree, technically. It would be easier for any administration to sustain such a program at home if our allies were in support of it. In addition, in future arms control negotiations involving defensive forces the U.S. position would be strengthened significantly if it were clear that America's major allies backed the program. Given the U.S. position in most areas of high technology, it may seem that little European help would be needed. But if the SDI leads to the development and deployment of an extensive BMD system, European personnel will most likely participate. In addition, participation in the SDI by Britain, France, and Germany may be considered important by the United States because of advanced European work in particle physics, electro-optics, and the building of large, highly accurate space-based pointing systems, which would be necessary for some space-based weapons.[1]

THE WEST GERMAN RESPONSE

The initial response of major NATO allies ranged from cool to cold, although several NATO allies subsequently have indicated tentative support for SDI research. For example, official German statements and unofficial commentary following the president's March 23 speech expressed deep skepticism toward "Star Wars" based upon several key concerns. First, German officials expressed concern that the SDI would lead to U.S. isolationism because a defended America would be less interested in the security of Western Europe. This fear concerned Germany in particular given the obvious desire of the German government to keep the hundreds of thousands of U.S. troops intended to help deter a Soviet attack in Germany. For example, German Defense Minister Manfred Woerner repeatedly warned that a defended America could become a "fortress America."[2]

A second criticism of the president's proposal that particularly concerned Germany involved the deployment of U.S. intermediate range nuclear forces (INF) on German territory. The German government of Chancellor Helmut Kohl was striving to hold to its commitment to deploy U.S. INF (Pershing II ballistic missiles and ground-launched cruise missiles) despite vocal and sometimes violent domestic opposition. President Reagan entered into this difficult political climate with his moral condemnation of nuclear weapons and a proposal to render them obsolete. The mixture of the United States encouraging Germany to maintain its commitment to deploy American nuclear forces while the president simultaneously proposed to render nuclear weapons obsolete appeared to be another example of U.S. "insensitivity" to European politics. It was feared that this new U.S. proposal would render even more difficult the already politically perilous INF deployment program.[3] Of course, the SDI as a long-term research program is not inconsistent with modernization of INF in NATO-Europe. But much of the initial German commentary appeared not to have understood that the SDI is a research program and *not* a deployment program.

Third, following the president's speech, German Defense Minister Woerner stated that President Reagan's goal of strategic defense "would lead not to stability, but just the opposite."[4] The concern for stability was based upon the same fear expressed by American critics of SDI; if the U.S./NATO nuclear threat were rendered obsolete, the Soviet Union would be at liberty to exploit its conventional force advantages. Germany faces an entire spectrum of military threats ranging from conventional to nuclear arms. Consequently, even a perfect defense against ballistic missiles would "only" address part of the spectrum of threat confronting Germany. Mutual defenses against ballistic missiles might protect the Soviet Union from much of NATO's deterrent threat but leave Germany vulnerable to Soviet short range nuclear and conventional arms. The nuclear threat plays a principal deterrent role in the NATO "flexible response" policy that is Germany's security. Thus, a program to render nuclear weapons obsolete and thereby undercut that "flexible response" was certain to cause concern in Germany about the future of stability.

Following its initial skeptical response, the German position concerning the SDI became more supportive. German officials have, in effect, offered a limited endorsement of the SDI. For example, at an international conference in Munich in February 1985 Chancellor Kohl appealed to West Europeans to participate in SDI, stating, "I strongly advise participating."[5] At the same conference Bavarian Minister President Franz Josef Strauss spoke out enthusiastically in favor of the SDI.[6] Defense Minister Woerner, initially quite skeptical of the SDI, offered some encouragement, saying, "It's very clear that the first power to use space for military purposes was the Soviet Union. It's legitimate that the United States catch up." And, again, "It is legitimate, and even necessary, that the United States reach parity in research and development [in defensive weapons]."[7] Although Bonn has not formally agreed to participate in the SDI, in May 1985 Chancellor Kohl underlined Germany's readiness to examine "eventual" collaboration in SDI research. In September 1985, Horst Teltschik, national security advisor to Chancellor Kohl, announced after an 11-day fact-finding mission to the United States that participation in the SDI would be in Germany's "vital interest."[8]

There appears to be a distinction between Chancellor Kohl's personal support for SDI research and the continuing reluctance of the German government to respond clearly and positively to the U.S. invitation for allied participation in the SDI. The apparent official German reluctance to endorse participation in the SDI, despite support from Kohl and Woerner, may be an effort to avoid, to the extent possible, a hot domestic and NATO debate over the SDI. Political reality may have constrained the German government to state, in effect, that the decision "requires further study."

Although the position of the German Social Democratic Party remains in opposition to the SDI,[9] official German statements have become much more sympathetic since the initial reaction. This shift appears to be traceable, at least in part, to U.S. clarification for the allies of the nature and scope of the SDI. The following points appear to have been of particular importance in the reorientation of the German position:

1. the SDI is a research program, not a deployment program;
2. any move toward defense would include protection for U.S. allies;
3. the Soviet Union for years has been pursuing energetically its own R&D program for strategic defense.

An additional German consideration appears to be swaying German officials in the direction of the SDI. Chancellor Kohl highlighted this in a speech to the German Bundestag:

> In view of the magnitude of funding...with which the U.S. Government plans to support its [SDI] research program, it is quite evident to everyone even now that important and far-reaching results will be achieved—results whose significance, including the economic importance, will go far beyond the sphere of strategic defense.
>
> ...we will and must also be interested in utilizing research results in our industry that will have revolutionary civilian applications. ...we must ensure that the FRG [Federal Republic of Germany] and West Europe are not outdistanced technologically and thus become second rate.[10]

Chancellor Kohl had earlier urged European participation in the SDI to ensure that Germany and the other NATO countries would not become "technologically disconnected."[11]

How German participation in the SDI ultimately will take shape is unclear at this point. It appears, however, that the German position is supportive of some type of eventual participation in SDI research—although probably under specified conditions, which most likely will include: no technological "one-way street" (i.e., Europeans would share in all technological benefits of SDI research); and no "automatic" transition of the research stage to the deployment of weapons.[12] The recent endorsement of anti-tactical ballistic missile defense by high-ranking German officials reflects the developing German position regarding defensive objectives.

THE BRITISH RESPONSE

The British government initially was quite subdued in its response to the SDI proposal. Indeed, officially it was silent on the issue. In private, it is reported that British officials were not pleased with the president's speech.[13] The Conservative government of Prime Minister Margaret Thatcher was pursuing a $13 billion modernization program for the British sea-based independent deterrent. Consequently, the British government was coping with domestic political controversy involving its offensive force modernization program when the president condemned offensive forces morally and proposed rendering them obsolete.

The British government avoided significant public comment on the SDI for almost fourteen months. Some British officials apparently hoped that the "Star Wars" proposal would just go away quietly. According to one noted British commentator, "British officials, who had not been consulted in advance, were horrified...The basic hope was that as the announcement had so obviously slipped through the policy filter, that the machine would now correct the mistake and the plan would soon die without a trace."[14]

Unofficial British commentary on the SDI was muted in comparison to the situation in Germany, though the concerns about the SDI expressed in the German press and official German statements were reflected in the unofficial British commentary. But an additional fear appeared to be worrying the British. The British independent nuclear deterrent—consisting primarily of sea-launched ballistic missiles (SLBMs)—would be degraded by the Soviet deployment of BMD. Because the number of British nuclear forces is much smaller than the American, even a limited Soviet defense, relatively ineffective against the United States, might be quite effective against British offensive forces. Consequently, some British writers expressed their concern that a move toward strategic defense by the superpowers would compel the British to deploy expensive countermeasures to maintain an independent nuclear deterrent.[15] The possibility that the SDI could reduce the potency of the British independent nuclear force raised not only security concerns among the British, it also threatened to tread upon feelings of national pride and prestige.

This British fear is not new. Indeed, the consideration was paramount during SALT I negotiations when the British made clear "at high levels" their position regarding BMD. The British apparently urged very low limits on BMD so as not to degrade significantly the capability of British SLBM warheads to penetrate Moscow defenses.[16] This concern regarding the continuing effectiveness of the British nuclear deterrent will, almost certainly, affect the British position regarding any eventual deployment of BMD.

The initial British reaction to the SDI was nevertheless not entirely negative. The point was made in unofficial commentary, and later by Defense Secretary Michael Heseltine, that the American SDI, as a research program, was fully justified by the Soviet BMD R&D program.[17] In addition, Gerald Frost, director of the Institute for European Defense and Strategic Studies in London, has argued that BMD could facilitate offensive arms control by undercutting the value of offensive forces, and that BMD should enhance extended deterrence by making the U.S. commitment to Europe more credible.[18]

After a long period of silence the British government endorsed the SDI program. Britain evidently asked to participate in SDI research before the United States extended a formal invitation to its allies. Prime Minister Thatcher endorsed the SDI before a joint session of the American Congress, expressing enthusiasm for the project and promising British support.[19] Thatcher reportedly agreed to support the SDI under four conditions: the Western objective must not be strategic superiority; actual BMD deployment would be an issue for negotiation; deterrence must be enhanced, not degraded; and East-West negotiations should focus on the reduction of offensive forces.[20] The Reagan administration has indicated that it is agreeable to each of these conditions—each, indeed, reflects the American position.

Lord Chalfont presented a defense of the SDI in the *Times* (London), concluding that:

> President Reagan would be abdicating his responsibility not only to the citizens of his own country but to those of the West as a whole if he were now to be deflected from the course he outlined in the Strategic Defense Initiative.[21]

Despite public endorsement of the SDI by Prime Minister Thatcher, official skepticism continued. In a strongly worded speech at the Royal United Services Institute in London, British Foreign Secretary Geoffrey Howe offered a barely disguised critique of the SDI that probably reflected the doubts about SDI prevalent in Whitehall.[22] Howe observed that it would be "myopic" and "dangerous" to ignore the BMD *research* taking place in the Soviet Union for years. But Sir Geoffrey underlined four concerns regarding BMD *deployment* that had long been part of the domestic American criticism of the SDI as well as that of Germany and France:

1. BMD deployment could be destabilizing;
2. BMD deployment could be overly expensive and absorb funding for needed military programs;
3. BMD deployment would be inconsistent with the SALT I ABM Treaty and would threaten the prospects for arms control;
4. a comprehensive defense might be infeasible technically.

Of course, none of these concerns was new; they all had been cited repeatedly by American critics of the SDI soon after the president's March 23 speech. But, that this critique was presented publicly by the British foreign secretary following Prime Minister Thatcher's endorsement of the SDI appeared to reflect a continuing deep-seated official skepticism toward BMD deployment. The secretary's speech resulted in an even more sharply worded *Times* editorial defending the SDI and criticizing Howe. The *Times* editorial praised the SDI and described Sir Geoffrey's speech as "mealy-mouthed, muddled in conception, negative, Luddite, ill-informed and, in effect if not intention, a 'wrecking amendment' to the whole plan."[23]

Thus, the British government has offered the strongest endorsement of the SDI. But the support is limited to BMD *research*. There obviously exist doubts and fears about the prospect of moving away from the offensive deterrence of the past toward a more defensive-oriented relationship with the Soviet Union.

THE FRENCH RESPONSE

The French reaction to the SDI has been both the most critical and, in a sense, the most encouraging. France is the only major European ally emphatically to reject participation in the SDI. But the French so like the concept of SDI-type research that they have proposed as a quasi-alternative to the SDI, a European high-technology, space-oriented research effort labeled "Eureka."

As early as February 1984 French President Mitterrand expressed the desire for a cooperative "European Space Community" as "the most appropriate answer to the military realities of the future."[24] Former French Prime Minister Pierre Mauroy emphasized the importance of a European effort similar to the SDI:

> We Europeans cannot ignore the research on laser beam weapons in space being conducted by the Soviets and Americans...We would be wrong to attempt to defend the Europe of tomorrow with yesterday's means and organization.[25]

But despite the enthusiasm for such research, in May 1985 during the Bonn economic summit, President Mitterrand rejected French participation in the SDI. Mitterrand said at a news conference that Europeans should concentrate on their own research program rather than "wasting their talent" on a non-European undertaking.[26] Consequently, the French have developed the "Eureka" project and have blocked full NATO endorsement of the SDI. During the June 1985 spring meeting of NATO foreign ministers in Portugal the United States hoped to acquire NATO endorsement for the SDI but gave up because of stiff French opposition.[27] In a March meeting of NATO defense ministers in Luxembourg, in which the French did not participate, NATO endorsed the SDI as "in NATO's security interest."

The French have rejected the SDI on grounds generally parallel to those of the German, British, and American critics of the program. For example, French Defense Minister Charles Hernu has stressed that the SDI would threaten to upset the stability of deterrence by retaliatory nuclear threat.[28] French Foreign Minister Claude Cheysson expressed the fear that the SDI would lead to an isolationist America unconcerned about European security. Cheysson asked rhetorically, "could they [Europeans] still have faith in American protection from a United States believing itself to be protected by an anti-missile network?"[29] The French also worry that increased BMD deployment by the Soviet Union would degrade the French independent deterrent and compel them to take offensive countermeasures.[30] Official French spokesmen have further criticized the SDI for being, potentially, the means of escalating the arms race, which would lead to the "militarization of space."[31] Indeed, on June 12, 1984, the French proposed at the Geneva disarmament talks a five-year moratorium on the testing or deployment of laser BMD systems.

Finally, the French appear to perceive the SDI as an arrangement wherein the U.S. would dominate Western Europe in the area of high technology. According to the French, the SDI would relegate Europeans to the role of "subcontractors" to the United States. The French fear that such an arrangement would deny the Europeans full access to the potential civilian technological benefits of SDI. The anticipated role of "subcontractor" also appears to be an affront to French prestige and national independence.[32]

To date five allies in addition to France have rejected SDI participation: Canada, Denmark, Australia, the Netherlands and Norway. Other allies are adopting a "wait and see" attitude. Nevertheless, it appears that Germany, Great Britain, Japan, Israel, Turkey, and possibly Italy will participate formally in some fashion in SDI research.[33] Participation by private industry from countries not involved formally in the SDI, including French industry, also is likely to take place.

There are several reasons why U.S. allies may remain skeptical of the SDI and BMD deployment. There also exist sound reasons why U.S. allies will want to participate in the SDI. Each of these can be examined briefly.

1. *Effective defenses would degrade the Western nuclear threat that is intended to deter Soviet conventional or nuclear attack.*

The most fundamental reason for Western European concern *vis à vis* the SDI may be somewhat difficult for Americans to understand. The NATO allies rely excessively upon deterrence through nuclear retaliatory threat. The Western threat of nuclear escalation is viewed as compensation for Soviet advantages in conventional forces. Because the United States does not face a similar conventional force threat it may be difficult for Americans to sympathize with the European desire to maintain a nuclear threat against the Soviet Union. Very effective defenses for North America would, in effect, return the United States to the relative invulnerability it enjoyed during much of the nineteenth and twentieth centuries. In contrast, Europeans fear that a very effective BMD might result in the inability of the West to threaten the Soviet Union with nuclear attack. Such a condition could leave NATO-Europe vulnerable to Soviet conventional attack. Europeans tend to fear that even comprehensive defenses against nuclear weapons would simply "make the world safe for conventional war." This defense would require Europeans to spend more money on conventional forces because the nuclear threat "compensation" for Soviet conventional advantages would no longer be available.

In addition, Europeans are sensitive to endorsements of the SDI as the potential solution to a morally unacceptable policy of deterrence. This moral posturing makes more difficult the task of maintaining popular support for NATO, British, and French nuclear modernization programs—programs which are considered necessary for the near term because defenses, even if feasible, would not be available until the mid-to-late 1990s or beyond.

In short, a fundamental problem is that the United States and Western Europe face a different spectrum of threat. The defensive solution to the nuclear threat which confronts the United States could, in the view of many Europeans, simply increase the conventional risk Western Europe must face directly. Consequently, Europeans have criticized the SDI because, they believe, BMD cannot fully protect them while nuclear deterrence has. As Colonel Jonathan Alford of the London-based International Institute for Strategic Studies observed:

> Europeans actually tend to like nuclear weapons. They don't say we want more and more of them, but they say it is nuclear weapons on the whole, their existence, the fear they induce, which has made it impossible to contemplate war.[34]

Europeans fear that the long-term objective of the SDI—rendering nuclear weapons impotent—would, if achieved, end or reduce the Soviet fear that Western Europe now relies upon for its security.

2. *A defended America would be unconcerned about West European security.*

A second fundamental reason for European skepticism of the SDI is based on the concern that if the United States could defend itself against the nuclear threat it would become isolationist and uncommitted to the protection of Western Europe. It should be recalled that the United States maintains well over 200,000 troops in NATO-Europe and commits about 50 percent of its military spending to NATO. That is a significant contribution to West European security by Americans (especially when one considers that only 12 percent to 14 percent of U.S. defense spending is committed to U.S. strategic programs) and many Europeans already are concerned that the United States will reduce its European commitment. They fear that the SDI could lead to a situation wherein the United States would lose interest in Western Europe because BMD would ensure America's security against nuclear attack.

U.S. Secretary of Defense Caspar Weinberger has repeatedly reassured the NATO nations that the SDI would never lead to American isolationism. In a speech to the allies in February 1985 Weinberger stated emphatically, "there exists no fortress and retreat is impossible."[35] In addition, in the formal request for allied participation in the SDI, Secretary Weinberger stressed that any decision for BMD deployment would be made in close consultation with the allies and in full awareness of their security needs.[36] Nevertheless, the fear persists that a defended America would be an isolationist America given the asymmetry of threats faced by the United States and Western Europe.

It should be noted, however, that it is not American vulnerability to Soviet nuclear attack that binds together Western Europe and the United States. Reducing American vulnerability to Soviet strategic attack could not make the viability of the European free democracies any less important to the United States. Cultural ties aside, we have a vital interest in seeing to it that the Soviet Union does not conquer or control the technological and highly-skilled human resources of Western Europe. That is the "tie that binds"; it ensures that the United States remains vitally interested in the fate of Western Europe in times of relative invulnerability (such as through the mid-1960s) and times of drastic strategic defenselessness. Alterations in the level of American vulnerability cannot alter the "vital interest" status of Western Europe.

3. *The SDI and strategic defenses would reduce the potency of French and British independent nuclear deterrent forces.*

This concern obviously is relevant to the British and French. But to the extent that other NATO allies believe that their security is enhanced by the British and French nuclear deterrents they also share this concern. There has been increasing discussion within France, for example, of extending the French nuclear deterrent to West Germany.[37]

Interestingly, neither the British nor the French appear to believe that Soviet BMD could completely counter their nuclear threat. Rather, they appear to fear that additional Soviet BMD would compel them to take costly offensive countermeasures to maintain their retaliatory nuclear threats.[38] The absence of widespread Soviet defenses permits the British and French to wield a nuclear threat with relatively small forces. Widespread Soviet defenses would necessitate expensive British and French offensive modernization programs—an expense both would prefer to avoid.

The asymmetry in threats faced by the United States and Western Europe is, once again, the ultimate root of the British/French concern. Their independent deterrents are important for reasons other than merely national pride and prestige. Their primary role, for instance, is to compensate for the lack of U.S. credibility in extending deterrence to Western Europe. The French in particular expressed the concern that the United States would not risk strategic nuclear war on behalf of Western Europe. As the argument runs, the defeat of Western Europe would threaten long-term U.S. security interests, but a strategic war could destroy the United States immediately. Many Europeans logically doubt that the United States would risk its own immediate nuclear destruction on behalf of Western Europe, even if NATO-Europe faced imminent defeat. Consequently, independent nuclear capabilities are considered essential for deterrence, and implicitly, to provide a European-controlled trigger to the threat of strategic nuclear escalation. Deployment of BMD by the Soviet Union, it is feared, could reduce or eliminate that trigger.

> 4. *Strategic defense will be too expensive for Western Europe and will draw funds away from conventional military needs.*

The expense of deploying defenses concerns West Europeans in two ways. First, they fear that while the United States may be able to absorb the financial burden of strategic defense, European economies could not.[39] Second, Europeans fear that financing for strategic defense would come at the expense of conventional force improvements; and that the Europeans could not compensate for the loss were the United States to reduce its contribution to NATO conventional forces in order to fund strategic defense.[40] Consequently, Europeans fear that the SDI could lead to a situation where: (1) conventional forces would become more important because the Western nuclear threat would be less potent; yet, (2) the alliance would be less willing to provide conventional force improvements given the cost of deploying BMD.

> 5. *The SDI and deployment of strategic defenses will not provide a technical solution to European security problems and will hinder political solutions, such as arms control.*

This concern is at the heart of much of the European criticism of SDI. Europeans appear skeptical that strategic defense could adequately counter the ballistic missile threat confronting them; and, if it could, Western Europe still would face a spectrum of Soviet conventional threats. Consequently, it is argued that SDI technology does not hold the potential for solving European security problems. Worse still, it is feared that deployment of strategic defenses would undercut any prospect of reducing the Soviet threat through a political arms control process.[41] A great deal of political value is seen in the arms control process. For example, German Foreign Minister Hans-Dietrich Genscher stated at a meeting of NATO foreign ministers that the value of SALT and the ABM Treaty is so high that the United States should abide by their restrictions *even though* the Soviet Union is "adopting an attitude contrary to their spirit and letter."[42] In general, Genscher's statement reflects the allies' fear that termination of the ABM Treaty and deployment of strategic defenses would bar future more amicable relations with the Soviet Union and would compel the Soviet Union to expand its offensive forces.

This European apprehension obviously mirrors the view of many in the U.S. "arms control community." It assumes that Soviet arms racing is an "action-reaction" process. In this case, the "action" would be U.S. BMD deployment and the "reaction" would be an increase in Soviet offensive forces. Europeans fear that this "action-reaction" process will destroy any future potential for détente and arms control.

The generally skeptical European attitude toward BMD deployment is based upon the five considerations described above. Several of them are "structural," that is, they are almost inherent in the nature of the NATO alliance. Because of the geographic proximity of Western Europe to the Soviet Union, and the distance of the United States, the spectrum of threat facing NATO-Europe and the United States are distinct. Because the United States confronts primarily a strategic nuclear threat, BMD is very attractive to Americans. Because Europeans face a massive conventional and nuclear threat—and rely significantly upon the threat of nuclear retaliation for their security—Europeans believe that BMD offers them less potential benefit and entails some potential risk. The European case for the SDI and strategic defense follows:

1. *Europe should participate in the SDI to ensure that the high-technology "gap" between the United States and Europe does not widen.*

Interestingly, the consideration of advanced technology and access to the potential civilian "spin-offs" of SDI research appears to provide an extremely strong incentive for participation in the SDI.[43] Even if effective defenses are never achieved the civilian benefits in computer, telecommunications, and laser technology could be tremendous. NATO-Europe does not want to be excluded from such civilian commercial benefits resulting from major high-tech research programs. As one European commentator noted about European participation in SDI, "the certain prospect for high research profit of a general economic nature seems to be a bait which makes them all willing to spend money."[44] Similarly, Europeans have expressed the fear of a "brain drain" if they do not participate in such large, high technology research projects. Indeed, both German and British defense ministers have indicated that the commercial (nonmilitary) technological considerations are the primary incentives for European participation in the SDI.[45]

2. *The level of Soviet BMD R&D necessitates the U.S. SDI.*

This rationale for the SDI is accepted widely by the allies.[46] Europeans are concerned that the Soviet Union has been pursuing extensive BMD research for years. The SDI is justified, even necessary, many believe, given the advanced level of Soviet BMD R&D. The North Atlantic Assembly, which consists of representatives for NATO countries, endorsed the SDI in October 1983, for the following reasons:

> However undesirable some feel an American ballistic missile defense system would be, the presence of solely a Soviet system would be still less desirable. Thus while Soviet missile defense research continues, there is every reason for American research to continue also.[47]

Further supporting the SDI, NATO Secretary General Peter Carrington observed, "...the U.S.S.R. has definite capabilities in this sphere and, if the West abandoned any effort, it would expose itself dangerously."[48] This indicates European recognition that a surprise Soviet breakthrough in BMD technology would be dangerous for the West. Indeed, given the state of Soviet BMD R&D it should not be assumed that only the American SDI could cause the Soviet Union to deploy BMD; in many ways the SDI is a program to "catch up" with over a decade of steady Soviet R&D progress. There is little doubt that if the United States were to deploy BMD the Soviet Union would expand its BMD system; but the level of Soviet BMD activity indicates that the Soviet Union may well expand its BMD system whether the United States pursues the SDI or not. To criticize the SDI because Soviet BMD would degrade the Western scheme of nuclear deterrence is, to a large extent, misplaced criticism.

3. *The SDI has proved helpful in the arms control process and should be maintained to provide arms control leverage.*

This argument for supporting the SDI is based on the view that the SDI brought the Soviets back to the negotiating table following their November 1983 walkout. German Minister of Defense Manfred Woerner has said that it would be "very stupid" to halt research on the SDI because it (along with NATO INF deployment plans) had compelled the Soviet Union to return to negotiations.[49]

It should be noted, however, that the arms control "bargaining chip" rationale for the SDI does not indicate that Europeans would support BMD deployment. Indeed, arms control "bargaining chips" are to be expended as necessary to gain concessions from the other party. Consequently, while Europeans may support the SDI as a "bargaining chip," they may well prefer that BMD deployment options be limited in exchange for Soviet concessions in the area of offensive force limitations. As German Foreign Minister Hans-Dietrich Genscher has observed,

> If it is correct—and I am convinced that it is—that the SDI has enhanced the Soviet Union's interest in returning to the negotiating table, then it is likewise correct and appropriate that we must utilize the SDI for purposes of arms control policy.[50]

4. *Participation in the SDI will provide European influence in future decisions concerning BMD deployment options.*

This rationale in support of the SDI is to ensure a long-term allied voice in matters concerning BMD deployment. Participation would mean influencing decisions regarding BMD following the research phase.[51]

5. *Effective strategic defense should enhance the credibility of the U.S. extended deterrent by rendering the U.S. deterrent threat "nonsuicidal."*

Many Europeans fear that strategic defense will lead to a

"fortress America" mentality and "decouple" the United States from Western Europe. But the argument also is made that strategic defense would enhance the credibility of the U.S. commitment to NATO-Europe. If the United States were less vulnerable to the Soviet nuclear threat it would face a reduced risk in supporting Western Europe against Soviet conventional or nuclear attack. Strategic defense should thus enhance the credibility of the U.S. commitment to Western Europe, thereby preserving extended deterrence. As Gerald Frost has noted, "with the risks to America reduced by a system of defense, the policy [deterrence] would become more credible."[52] This particular benefit for extended deterrence appears to be much more persuasive to Americans than to Europeans.

ASSESSING THE PROS AND CONS FOR EUROPE

An examination of the European arguments both for and against the SDI and strategic defense reveals a rather clear "bottom line." The allies are likely to offer continuing political support for the SDI *as a research program*, and may well seek to participate in some fashion to ensure access to the civilian technology "spin-offs" of that program. However, there will likely be great allied reluctance to support any U.S. decision *to deploy* BMD unless the Soviet Union has first blatantly and unarguably expanded its own BMD capabilities. This "bottom line" is apparent because the primary allied arguments *against* the SDI are related to the anticipated negative implications of BMD deployment. In contrast, the most persuasive allied reasons *for* participation in the SDI are relevant to the SDI as a research program.

Allied leaders who have endorsed the SDI have made plain that their support is for BMD research within the bounds of the ABM Treaty and not BMD deployment. For example, Chancellor Kohl, while supporting SDI research within the ABM Treaty, suggested strongly that any future plans for deployment be subject to arms control negotiations.[53] Similarly, German Minister of Defense Woerner, who has endorsed SDI research, has also indicated that he "...would start being concerned if the West or the Americans were the first to begin deploying such systems..."[54] In considering the SDI, NATO

Secretary General Carrington found it "reassuring" that "...the United States has only launched a research and not a production effort at this stage; it is trying to determine what is technically possible and what is not."[55] Bruce George, British Labour member of Parliament, said in a recent report to the political committee of the North Atlantic Assembly:

> The U.S. research program is reasonable and, given even minimal knowledge of Soviet programs, politically wise. But there is apprehension that the SDI, with a budget of $26-30 billion, will take on a life of its own and that the SDI will lead inevitably to deployment.[56]

In short, NATO leaders endorsing the SDI have made a point of distinguishing between research and deployment, and have specified that their support is for research. This may appear to oppose the American position—it does not. It should be recalled that the SDI *is* a research program within the limits of the ABM Treaty; it is not a deployment program. In addition, the Reagan administration has not endorsed BMD deployment. Rather, the Reagan administration's position is to provide the basis for a future president and Congress, perhaps in the early 1990s, to use the results of SDI research for an informed consideration of deployment options. It is reasonable to wait for some conclusions from SDI research concerning BMD feasibility before making decisions regarding deployment—the position of the United States and its allies simply reflects a recognition of that reasoning. Consequently, the general positions of the British and German governments, for example, are not inconsistent with that of the United States: all have drawn a clear distinction between BMD research and BMD deployment.

U.S. EXTENDED DETERRENCE DUTIES: THE POTENTIAL, PERILS, AND PITFALLS

Should the U.S. *deploy* defensive weapons to protect itself and its allies from ballistic missile attack? The divergence in U.S. and European-NATO perspectives on some security issues has become so familiar as to be tedious. Every new year seems to bring forth a new "crisis within the alliance." Yet NATO muddles through, and survives, to confront next year's crisis.

Eventually, however, both the U.S. and European members of the alliance will be compelled to recognize that NATO has an inherent structural divide that no amount of good will and quiet diplomacy can correct. The introduction of the SDI may be the issue that forces such a recognition. This is *not* to say that the SDI is the cause of this structural problem. Indeed, the SDI, complemented by conventional force improvements, may provide the long-term solution to it. But the SDI debate will pose questions, as few other issues could, that will cut to the core of NATO's security dilemma and expose the underlying fissures in current NATO policy. This "debate" promises to be much more than the usual economically motivated bickering about "who spends how much for what." The debate over the SDI reflects the contrasting perspectives within NATO that, ultimately, reflect much deeper issues.

To confront the question of whether or not to deploy strategic defenses will require the alliance to reexamine the entire structure of strategic thought that undergirds NATO's doctrine of "flexible response." If the U.S. ultimately decides to deploy comprehensive defenses it will be because it has found inadequate the deterrence condition that has supported NATO doctrine for decades. Alliance consideration of the SDI illustrates that NATO's current approach to deterrence and security is acceptable, even comfortable for Europeans, and yet has become increasing unacceptable to the United States.

As discussed above, Americans and West Europeans, although facing the same opponent, confront significantly different threats. To continue to plan and deploy forces based upon the assumption that Western European and American security concerns are identical is an anachronism. Fortunately, the SDI may be the vehicle which saves us from ourselves—saves us from our penchant to gloss over and muddle through intra-NATO conflicts of interest that should be acknowledged and resolved.

THE PROBLEM

NATO's reliance on the U.S. threat of nuclear escalation to provide deterrence "stability" is the basis of official European opposition to the call by some Americans for a nuclear "no-first-use" policy.[57] Withdrawing the explicit threat of nuclear first-use would leave NATO to fend for itself conventionally against an enemy with substantial conventional advantages. Consequently, European-NATO governments have rejected "no-first-use" proposals and have sought to gain reassurance that the U.S. threat of nuclear escalation on their behalf is real.[58]

As for the U.S., every administration for two decades has encouraged a buildup of NATO conventional forces for the purpose of "raising the nuclear threshold," that is, reducing NATO's reliance on the threat of nuclear escalation by enabling the alliance to defend itself conventionally. This objective has not been achieved. Western Europeans generally do not relish the prospect of weakening the nuclear threat by over-emphasizing NATO's conventional war-fighting capabilities. Indeed, it is understandable that focusing attention away from nuclear deterrence by concentrating instead on the conventional defense of Europe would have little appeal. The economic cost of providing such a conventional capability would undoubtedly be higher than the current burden borne by NATO, which was one reason NATO turned toward such nuclear reliance in the first place. As a result, NATO-Europe has continued to be comfortable with a deterrent posture which relies on a "short fuse" to the predominantly U.S. threat of nuclear escalation.

The problem for the United States is obvious; it has made "extended deterrence" commitments to NATO that are unreasonable and irrational. The United States threatens to initiate nuclear war against the Soviet Union in response to an attack on Europe, and that threat is relied upon for deterrence. But in the event of an attack against Western Europe, the risk to the United States would increase dramatically if it actually escalated to nuclear strikes against the Soviet Union. Such a process could result in 160 million American casualties from Soviet counterfire.[59] The defeat of NATO-Europe would be a catastrophe for the U.S., but the self-destruction likely to result from nuclear escalation would be immeasurably worse—and would be unlikely to save Western Europe in any event. The American threat to commit such an act must lack credibility in the eyes of the Soviet leadership because it could serve no U.S. interest, and would indeed place the United States in much greater jeopardy than otherwise would exist.

In short, because of the Soviet capability to retaliate and ensure U.S. destruction, it is not credible for the United States to
threaten nuclear escalation, particularly strategic nuclear escalation, on behalf of NATO-Europe. The French recognized this
problem years ago and, accordingly, developed their own independent nuclear deterrent. The Soviet Union also recognizes
this dichotomy between U.S. interests and deterrent threats.[60]

Dr. Henry Kissinger clearly described the requirements
that the U.S. commitment to NATO-Europe entails:

> A leader must choose carefully and thoughtfully the issues over
> which to face confrontation. He should do so only for major
> objectives. Once he is committed, however, his obligation is
> to end the confrontation rapidly. For this he must convey
> implacability. He must be prepared to escalate rapidly and
> brutally to a point where the opponent can no longer afford
> to experiment.[61]

The American public, however, overwhelmingly opposes escalation to nuclear war with the Soviet Union on behalf of
Western Europe—public opinion data shows popular rejection
of such a notion, which is a cornerstone of NATO's deterrent
policy.[62]

Geography has placed a limit on the convergence of West
European and American security interests. The United States is
very interested in preserving NATO's independence and denying the Soviet Union hegemony over Western Europe; it is even
more interested in avoiding self-destruction. A war in Europe
could lead to a drastic reorientation of the international political situation without posing an *immediate* survival threat to the
United States—unless the U.S. escalated to strategic nuclear
war. Consequently, threatening to initiate strategic nuclear war
in order to deter an attack on allies must lack credibility; to
continue to base deterrence policy on such a threat has become
manifestly unattractive.

On this issue the United States and NATO-Europe have
fundamentally different perspectives. The European members
of NATO appear quite comfortable with a deterrence policy that
relies on limited conventional capabilities and the relatively inexpensive threat of U.S. nuclear escalation. The U.S. has sought
to reduce reliance on nuclear escalation through increased conventional capabilities; and the long-term objective of U.S. BMD

deployment would be to degrade significantly the potency of nuclear weapons. These fundamentally different views concerning the roles of deterrence and defense shape the European and American perspectives on the SDI.

The generally negative European commentary on BMD *deployment* is related directly to the apparent European preference for a relatively inexpensive and presumably known policy of *nuclear* deterrence. As discussed above, European officials and commentators have expressed deep concern that U.S. BMD will lead to Soviet defenses and that Soviet defenses will weaken the West's deterrent threat of nuclear escalation. Europeans have also expressed concern that defenses could lead to a new "fortress America" mentality, and that, once defended, the United States would abandon Europe to its fate. It has even been suggested by some European commentators that vulnerability *should* be shared.[63] (One can imagine no better way for Europeans to encourage "fortress America" sentiment among the American people than by suggesting that it is their alliance duty to remain vulnerable to nuclear attack.)

A POTENTIAL SOLUTION

The United States could embrace strategic defense as the only plausible means of realigning its interests and security commitments. A defended America could more reasonably make security guarantees to NATO-Europe because it would face fewer risks in doing so. A U.S. deterrent threat on behalf of its allies would be much more credible if that threat did not entail the potential destruction of the U.S. Reducing the risks that the United States must accept in extending deterrence should make the U.S. deterrent more believable in the eyes of the Soviet leadership.

Revising the U.S. approach to extended deterrence is, moreover, appealing to most Americans. The American public overwhelmingly opposes the concept of U.S. nuclear escalation on behalf of NATO-Europe, and supports the objective of providing a defense against nuclear weapons—even if that defense is imperfect and deployed at great expense.[64]

It is true of course, that if the Soviet Union and the United States pursue comprehensive ballistic missile defenses the capability of the U.S. nuclear threat against the Soviet Union will be reduced and the U.S. extended deterrent threat, although more believable, could be less fearsome. In that respect, the implications of BMD for extended deterrence are not wholly beneficial. This question of whether a credible threat is necessary for extended deterrence goes back to the intellectual debate between Professor Thomas Schelling and Herman Kahn. Schelling argued that a U.S. nuclear commitment to NATO, although lacking credibility because of U.S. vulnerability to Soviet counterfire, could still provide an adequate basis for the extended deterrent commitment.[65] In contrast, Herman Kahn argued that the credibility of a threat was essential to deterrence, and that U.S. vulnerability greatly degraded the credibility of the U.S. extended deterrent commitment. As Dr. Kahn observed in 1961, the credibility of the U.S. deterrent must be low in Soviet eyes when "we have made negligible preparations to ward off, survive, and recover from even a 'small' Soviet retaliatory strike. No matter how menacing they look it will be irrational to attack and thus insure a Soviet retaliation unless we have made preparations to counter this retaliation."[66]

Obviously, official U.S. policy has reflected Professor Schelling's concept of extended deterrence. But the SDI presents the opportunity to reconsider the appropriateness of basing the U.S. extended deterrent mission upon a potentially suicidal commitment to nuclear escalation. "Defense dominance" would affect both the credibility of the U.S. commitment and the capability to make strategic nuclear threats against the Soviet Union. While credibility would improve, strategic nuclear capability would be reduced. However, it should not be assumed that deterrence is more effective when offensive nuclear capability is maximized at the expense of deterrent credibility; deterrence may be equally or more effective when credibility is maximized at the expense of nuclear capability—as in the case of defense dominance.

Fortunately, strategic defense may enable the U.S. to do both—maximize the *credibility* of its commitment to NATO-Europe and help preserve a *capability* to abide by that commitment. There would, however, be a fundamental difference from the current situation: extended deterrence under defense dominance would focus much less upon a nuclear threat to the

Soviet homeland than is the case today. Rather, the capability of the extended deterrent would rest upon: (1) the potential of NATO to deny the Soviet Union its "theory of victory" in NATO-Europe; (2) the capacity of a *defended* America to mobilize its military-industrial potential in support of NATO-Europe; (3) the prospect of a protracted war; and, (4) the residual nuclear threat that might be posed against Soviet forces outside of the defended Soviet citadel. Although the basis of such a NATO deterrent capability would be far less strategic nuclear-oriented, it could be no less fearsome than the current nuclear offensive-dominated threat.

Defense against ballistic missiles would not only enhance U.S. credibility for its commitment to NATO, it could help frustrate the Soviet Union's plans for victory in Europe. For example, active defense against Soviet ballistic missile strikes on NATO's main operating bases, air power, nuclear assets, and key command and control facilities would help to counter the Soviet theory for a rapid and decisive offensive against NATO. If the Soviet strategy for a rapid victory can be denied, the Soviet Union will likely be deterred from unleashing a dangerous war in Europe.

Defense for NATO against Soviet ballistic missile attack appears increasingly to be supported by West Germany. Anti-tactical ballistic missile defense (ATBM) could help counter the increasing ballistic missile threat to NATO—a ballistic missile threat which could be nuclear and/or non-nuclear. ATBM for NATO fits well with strategic defense for the United States and Soviet Union. The prospective reduction of the strategic nuclear threat to the Soviet Union focuses attention on means of deterrence other than the strategic nuclear threat, and ATBM could help provide the "victory denial" capability that would contribute to those means.

Complementing an enhanced NATO "victory-denial" potential with a defended U.S. mobilized in support of NATO-Europe should constitute a fearsome deterrent indeed. Of course, residual Soviet vulnerability to a nuclear threat (particularly of power projection forces) could contribute to deterrence as well. In short, given its much higher level of credibility the combination of threats pertaining to "defense dominance" may not be less deterring than the traditional strategic offensive-oriented deterrent.

In the early 1960s, when the current approach to extended deterrence was formulated intellectually,[67] the U.S. commitment was backed by a strategic superiority which rendered it credible. At that time the United States could well have initiated and survived nuclear escalation. The United States could then credibly threaten to escalate a conflict in Europe because it would not necessarily have been self-destructive. The U.S. lost its superiority by the mid to late 1960s. Yet the U.S. extended deterrence policy continued, fundamentally unchanged. Consequently, NATO now wields a doctrine divorced from reality in some important aspects. That policy is predicated upon what has become a suicidal U.S. nuclear commitment. The change in the strategic balance altered the alignment of U.S. threat and U.S. interest that existed in the early to mid-1960s. Yet that alignment became enshrined as NATO's "flexible response" doctrine in 1967, precisely at the time it was becoming anachronistic. The real dilemma facing NATO is how to resolve the security problem of Soviet conventional force advantages when a return to U.S. strategic nuclear superiority is as unlikely as is a massive increase in NATO's conventional war-fighting forces.

The SDI may offer a potential solution to this problem; comprehensive strategic defenses would permit the U.S. to realign its commitments and interests without the need for strategic nuclear superiority. Effective defenses could reestablish the credibility of the U.S. commitment to NATO that has been lost as a result of the Soviet strategic buildup. It would reestablish a credible basis for the "flexible response" doctrine. It may also help NATO to pose a local "denial of victory" threat without a massive increase in conventional forces. A highly uncertain and likely protracted war with NATO would undoubtedly be a daunting prospect for Soviet leaders. In short, defenses covering the U.S. and its allies could enhance the credibility of the extended deterrent, and do so without destroying the capability of the threat.

Although the SDI often is presented as a threat to NATO unity it is, in fact, no such thing. The challenge to NATO unity stems from the difference in security considerations that has been forced on the alliance by the Soviet military buildup of the 1960s and 1970s. Whether and how to address this problem is at the heart of NATO's long-term viability. To avoid recognition of the problem can only worsen the situation. To gloss over the different perspectives regarding the implications of strategic defense, and to perpetuate the illusion that the offensive approach to strategic deterrence enshrined in "flexible response" is reasonable would be a mistake. That approach to deterrence is built upon legs of sand and would not likely withstand any severe test. There may be time to solve the problem rather than continually to defer it. Fortunately, the SDI will compel us to consider the issue; it may also provide a major part of the solution.

SUMMARY AND CONCLUSION

In summary, U.S. allies generally are supportive of the SDI as a research program. The major exception is France, which is sponsoring its own European high technology research project called "Eureka." The Germans and British, in particular, have endorsed the need for the SDI, given Soviet BMD research efforts. But, the allies draw a clear distinction between BMD research and BMD deployment. European governments have made it a point *not* to extend their support for BMD research to an endorsement of deployment. But that apparent current limitation in allied support should not undercut the SDI. The SDI *is* a research program with no current plans for BMD deployment. In fact, the hesitation of the allies to endorse BMD deployment is consistent with the U.S. position of pursuing the SDI as a research program and evaluating the results before making any commitment to BMD deployment.

Finally, the fundamental strategic problem facing NATO is how to provide security for Western Europe against Soviet conventional force advantages when the U.S. extended nuclear deterrent has lost credibility. Concern about the credibility of the U.S. deterrent is not new, or limited to Americans. Recall that a key rationale for the deployment of French independent nuclear forces was precisely this incredibility of the U.S. strategic nuclear guarantee; and the original call by former German Chancellor Helmut Schmidt for a "Eurostrategic" balance (which ultimately led to the deployment of Pershing II and cruise missiles in Europe) was made because the advent of strategic nuclear parity had eroded U.S. credibility.

The SDI may facilitate an answer to the problem. Strategic defenses, if effective, could both enhance the credibility of the U.S. commitment to NATO and NATO's capability to counter the Soviet Union's military objectives against NATO. If so, the existence of mutual defenses need not have the negative implications for extended deterrence assumed by critics of BMD.

ENDNOTES

1. See Michael Feazel, "European Leaders Expect International Participation in Defense Initiative," *Aviation Week and Space Technology*, May 27, 1985, p. 101.
2. See James Markham, "Bonn is Worried by U.S. Arms Research," *New York Times*, April 14, 1984, p. 1.
3. See Hans Ruhle, "Löcher im Drahtverhau der Sicherheitsdoktrin," *Christ und Welt/Rheinischer Merkur*, No. 13, April 1983; and Ronald Koven, "Europe Expressing Growing Alarm over U.S. 'Star Wars' Defense Plan," *Boston Globe*, July 30, 1984, p. 2.
4. Quoted in William Broad, "Allies in Europe Are Apprehensive About Benefits of 'Star Wars' Plan," *New York Times*, May 13, 1985, p. A6.
5. See "Munich Conference Prompts Space Defense Discussion," *FBIS: Western Europe*, VII (Feb. 11, 1985), p. J-2. See also R. Moniac, "Weinberger Zerstreut Bedenken: Schutzschirm auch für Europa," *Die Welt*, Feb. 11, 1985, pp. 1, 10; and Rudiger Moniac, "Kohl definiert Wunsche der verbündeten an die USA," *Die Welt*, Feb. 9/10, 1985, pp. 1, 8.
6. "Munich Conference Prompts Space Defense Discussion," p. J-3.
7. See, respectively, Robert Ruby, "Possible U.S. Space-Based Defense Causes Some Discomfort in Europe," *Baltimore Sun*, July 11, 1984, p. 2; and Charles Corddry, "Bonn Endorses 'Star Wars' Effort," *Baltimore Sun*, July 13, 1984, p. 2.
8. See Deutsche Presse-Agentur, "Kohl steckt bei SDI zurück," *Washington Journal*, May 31, 1985, p. 1; and James Markham,"West German Backs Participation in 'Star Wars," ' *The New York Times*, October 1, 1985.
9. See, for example, Deutsche Presse-Agentur, "Schmidt gegen SDI," *Washington Journal*, June 7, 1985, p. 1; "Munich Conference Prompts Space Defense Discussion," pp. J-2, J-3; "Weinberger Zerstreut Bedenken," pp. 1, 10; "Kohl fragt nach Informationen: Weinberger verweist auf Hoffnungen," *Frankfurter Allgemeine Zeitung*, Feb. 11, 1985; Broad, op. cit., p. A-6; and "Kohl steckt bei SDI zurück," p. 1.

10. "Text of Kohl Statement to Bundestag on SDI," *FBIS: Western Europe*, April 19, 1985, p. J-4.

11. "Kohl Fragt nach Informationen; Weinberger verweist auf Hoffnungen," *Frankfurter Allgemeine Zeitung*, Feb. 11, 1985, pp. 1, 2.

12. See German Information Center, "Kohl: SDI Is Both 'Opportunity and Risk,'" *This Week In Germany*, May 24, 1985, p. 1; and German Information Center, "FDP Executive Committee: No Role In SDI Without European Partners," *This Week In Germany*, June 7, 1985, p. 2.

13. See Ronald Koven, "Europe expressing growing alarm over U.S. 'Star Wars' defense plan," *Boston Globe*, July 30, 1984, p. 2.

14. See Lawrence Freedman, "The Small Nuclear Powers," *Ballistic Missile Defense*, Ashton Carter, David Schwartz, eds. (Washington, D.C.: Brookings Institution, 1984), pp. 272-273.

15. See, for example, John Connell, "How 'Star Wars' could scuttle Polaris," *The Times* (London), Feb. 26, 1984, p. 21-C.

16. See Christopher Makins, "Bringing In the Allies," *Foreign Policy*, No. 35 (Summer 1979), p. 97.

17. See Brian Crozier, letter to *The Times* (London), April 12, 1983; and Michael Getler, "W. Europe Units to Back Talks by U.S.-Soviet on Space Arms," *Washington Post*, July 7, 1984, p. A-10.

18. See Gerald Frost, "Why a Star Wars Strategy Could Help Keep the Peace," *The Times* (London), Dec. 28, 1984, p. 10; and Frost, quoted in William Broad, "Allies in Europe Are Apprehensive About Benefits of 'Star Wars' Plan," *New York Times*, May 13, 1985, p. A-6.

19. See "Prime Minister Thatcher's Address," *Congressional Record-House*, Feb. 20, 1985, p. H485.

20. See Broad, op. cit., p. A-6.

21. *The Times* (London), Sept. 25, 1984, p. 17.

22. See "Howe underlines the risks in Star Wars," *The Times* (London), March 16, 1985, p. 5.

23. "Howe's UDI From SDI," *The Times* (London), March 18, 1985, p. 13.

24. Remarks by President Francois Mitterrand at a luncheon offered by the Council of Ministers of the Kingdom of the Netherlands, the Hague, Feb. 7, 1984, Embassy of France, Press and Information Service, Memo 84/6, p. 8.

25. In Jaques Jublin, "Interest in Laser Technology," *Les Echoes*, March 8, 1984, p. 4 in *Joint Public Research Service*, WER-84-049, p. 50.

26. See Broad, op. cit., p. A6; and "Mitterrand Rejects SDI Research Role," *Washington Post*, May 5, 1985, p. A-24.

27. See John Goshko, "NATO Support for SDI Blocked by France," *Washington Post*, June 7, 1985; and "NATO Now Cooler to Space

Weapons," *New York Times*, June 7, 1985, p. A-10.

28. See Dieter Schröder, "Reagan's Pläne für Weltraumwaffen verunsichern die Verbündeten," *Süddeutsche Zeitung*, Feb. 11, 1985; "Munich Conference Prompts Space Defense Discussion," *FBIS: Western Europe*, Feb. 11, 1985, p. J2; and, "Hernu Discusses SDI, French Deterrent in Interview," *FBIS: Western Europe*, April 19, 1985, p. K2.

29. See Koven, op. cit., p. 2.

30. Schröder, "Reagan's Pläne für Weltraum"; "Mitterrand, Kohl Meet on 'Star Wars'," *Washington Post*, March 1, 1985, p. A-12; and "Paris Urges Europeans to Back High-Tech Projects," *Washington Post*, April 19, 1985, p. A-30.

31. See Koven, "Europe expressing growing alarm over U.S. 'Star Wars' defense plan"; "Kohl fragt nach Informationen: Weinberger verweist auf Hoffnungen," *Frankfurter Allgemeine Zeitung*, Feb. 11, 1985, pp. 1, 2; and Dieter Schröder, "Reagan's Pläne für Weltraumwaffen."

32. See "Hernu Discusses SDI, French Deterrent in Interview," *FBIS: Western Europe*, April 19, 1985, p. K-1; and "Mitterrand Discusses Bonn Summit, SDI, FRG Ties," *FBIS: Western Europe*, May 10, 1985, p. K-1.

33. See National Institute for Public Policy, *Allied Support for the Strategic Defense Initiative* (Fairfax, VA: National Institute, May 1985), pp. 27-32.

34. Quoted in Broad, op. cit., p. A-6.

35. See Moniac, "Weinberger Zerstreut Bedenken," p. 1.

36. See "Weinberger's Letter," *The Times*, (London) April 18, 1985, p. 8. Nevertheless, the "fortress America" concern is quite real. See, for example, Hans-Heinrich Weise, "Amerikanische Pläne für ein Weltraumgestütztes Raketen-Abwehr System," *Europa Archiv* (July 10, 1984), pp. 401-406.

37. See "Paris stellt die Deutschen unter seinen Atomschirm—weil Westeuropa in der Bundesrepublik sehr verwundbar ist," *Washington Journal*, July 12, 1985, p. 1.

38. See Ruby, op. cit., p. 2; Broad, op. cit., p. A-6; "France Is Warming to 'Star Wars' Idea," *New York Times*, May 13, 1985, p. A-3; "Thatcher Discusses SDI, Bonn Summit in Interview," *FBIS: Western Europe*, May 10, 1985, pp. Q4, Q5; and Lawrence Freedman, "The Small Nuclear Powers," *Ballistic Missile Defense*, Ashton Carter, David Schwartz, eds. (Washington, D.C.: Brookings Institution, 1984), pp. 272-274.

39. See Schröder, "Reagan's Pläne für Weltraumwaffen"; Ruby, op. cit., p. 2; and Broad, op. cit., p. A-6.

40. See Feazel, op. cit., p. 101; "NATO Allies Concern Fuel Debate on 'Star Wars'," *Washington Post*, April 4, 1985, p. A-20; and R.

Moniac, "Weinberger Zerstreut Bedenken: Schutzschirm auch für Europa," *Die Welt*, Feb. 11, 1985, pp. 1, 10.

41. See Feazel, op. cit., p. 102; Michael Getler, "W. Europe Unites to Back Talk by U.S., Soviets on Space Arms," *Washington Post*, July 7, 1984, p. A-10; Dieter Schröder, "Strategi der gegenseitigen Sicherheit?" *Süddeutsche Zeitung*, Feb. 11, 1985, p. 4; "Kohl Steckt bei SDI zurück," p. 1; and Jon Connell, "How 'Star Wars' Could Scuttle Polaris," *The Times* (London), Feb. 26, 1984, p. 21-C.

42. John Goshko, "NATO Support for SDI Blocked by France," *Washington Post*, June 17, 1985.

43. Feazel, op. cit., p. 101; Broad, op. cit., p. A-6.

44. See Enst Otto Maetzke, "Von den Schwerten zu den Schilden," *Frankfurter Allgemeine Zeitung*, Feb. 12, 1985, P. 12.

45. See "U.S. Launches Program to Bring NATO Into SDI Research Role," *Aviation Week and Space Technology*, March 11, 1985, p. 56; and, "Briton Sees Allied Interest In 'Star Wars' Research," *New York Times*, April 3, 1985, p. 10.

46. See, for example, "Prime Minister Thatcher's Address," p. H485; "Brussels Le Soir Interviews NATO's Lord Carrington," *FBIS: Western Europe*, Feb. 12, 1985, p. C-2; and "Comments by the Government of the Federal Republic of Germany on President Reagan's Strategic Defense Initiative (SDI)," March 27, 1985, p. 3 (statement provided by the German Information Center).

47. See Broad, op. cit., p. 6.

48. "Carrington Interviewed on U.S.-European Defense," *FBIS: Western Europe*, VII, July 26, 1984, p. C-2.

49. "Woerner On U.S. Hope For European SDI Role," *FBIS: Western Europe*, VII, Feb. 12, 1985, p. J-2.

50. "Text of Genscher Bundestag Address on SDI," *FBIS: Western Europe*, April 19, 1985, p. J10.

51. *Allied Support For the Strategic Defense Initiative*, op. cit., p. 25.

52. See Broad, op. cit., pp. 1, 6.

53. See Rudiger Moniac, "Kohl definiert Wünsche der Verbündeten an die USA," *Die Welt*, Feb. 9/10, 1985, pp. 1, 8.

54. Quoted in *Allied Support for the Strategic Defense Initative*, op. cit., p. 11.

55. "Carrington Interviewed on U.S.-European Defense," p. C-2.

56. Feazel, op. cit., p. 101.

57. See, for example, McGeorge Bundy, George Kennan, Robert McNamara, and Gerard Smith, "Nuclear Weapons and the Atlantic Alliance," *Foreign Affairs*, Vol. 50, No. 4 (Spring 1982), pp. 753-768.

58. See John Vinocur, "2 Bonn Parties Cool to Ban on First Use of Atom Arms," *New York Times*, April 10, 1982.

59. See, for example, the discussion in Office of Technology Assessment, *The Effects of Nuclear War* (Washington, D.C.: USGPO,

1981), pp. 94-106.

60. See, for example, V. D. Sokolovskiy, *Soviet Military Strategy*, 3rd ed., Harriet Fast Scott, ed. (New York: Crane Russak, 1975), pp. 55-57.

61. Henry Kissinger, *White House Years* (Boston: Little, Brown, 1979), p. 622.

62. See Abt Associates, Inc., *Survey on National Defense and Economic Issues October 4-10, 1984* (unpublished summary of polling data), p. 17.

63. Reportedly much of this type of thinking was reflected in the 1984 Annual Conference of the London-based International Institute for Strategic Studies, September 1984. Also Chancellor Kohl has stated, "Europe's security must not be detached from that of the United States. There must be no zones of differing security levels within NATO." See "Text of Kohl Statement to Bundestag on SDI," *FBIS: Western Europe*, April 9, 1985, p. J2.

64. Abt Associates, op. cit., pp. 20-21.

65. Thomas Schelling, *Arms and Influence* (New Haven, Conn.: Yale University Press, 1966), pp. 38-47, 97-98.

66. Quoted in *On Thermonuclear War* (Princeton, N.J.: Princeton University Press, 1961), p. 132.

67. For a history of the theoretical development of the U.S. approach to deterrence see Lawrence Freedman, *The Evolution of Nuclear Strategy* (New York: St. Martin's Press, 1982).

ELEVEN
Chapter 11

A REASON FOR HOPE?

T he president's "Star Wars" speech of March 23, 1983, set in motion a chain of events leading to the Strategic Defensive Initiative. Despite efforts by the Reagan administration to clarify the nature and scope of the SDI, it has been portrayed inaccurately in much of the public commentary. The SDI has been characterized generally as a visionary program *to deploy* beam weapons in space. This misrepresentation has begotten much criticism of the SDI. The charges are that it is not technically feasible, a violation of the ABM Treaty, destabilizing, inconsistent with future progress in arms control, and so on. Much of that criticism is based on the inaccurate portrayal of the SDI as a plan to build and deploy a BMD system. In what reportedly is the most recent policy guidance concerning the SDI (NSDD 172), strict conditions are established for SDI research: it must be consistent with the limitations of the ABM Treaty; and it must determine whether a BMD architecture would be both relatively *survivable* so as not to tempt attack, and *cost-effective* so as not to encourage an offensive-defensive arms competition.[1] A clear understanding of the SDI as a research, and not a deployment, program probably would reduce or at least change the tone of much of the criticism and negative commentary.

Since the Strategic Defense Initiative holds the potential for a genuinely new course in U.S. strategic thinking, it is the focus of legitimate controversy. It presents the possibility that a future president and Congress will attempt to alter the current condition of American defenselessness to nuclear attack. Indeed, the president's speech of March 23 put forth the hope

225

that nuclear weapons ultimately could be rendered impotent through defense. Prior to the president's speech, even the possibility that the United States might seriously seek to alter its condition of vulnerability seemed outlandish. The entire structure of established "strategic wisdom" governing U.S. deterrence and arms control policies had been built upon the view that mutual vulnerability was both inalterable and stabilizing. The president's announced vision and subsequent SDI program were regarded as a direct challenge to that established wisdom.

Predictably, then, the president's speech and the SDI have been subject to widespread criticism, particularly by those who created, endorsed, or had become accustomed to the established dogma that mutual vulnerability is inevitable and beneficial, and strategic defense is "destabilizing" and technically infeasible. In contrast, most national surveys indicate that the American public has largely been unaware of its state of defenselessness, and, not surprisingly, enthusiastically endorses the concept of being protected in the event of nuclear war.

The Soviet Union, for its part, has long endorsed the notion that strategic defense is a desirable objective. It also recognizes that it is vulnerable to nuclear attack— although possibly less so than the United States in some important respects. The Soviet Union has for years vigorously pursued programs to limit the damage it would suffer in the event of nuclear war, particularly to its leadership and control structure. These programs include extensive civil defense and hardened leadership shelters, the greatest extant antibomber system, and the world's only operational BMD system. Soviet interest and research in advanced BMD technologies has been impressive and sustained for years, and can hardly be regarded as a response to the SDI. In fact, the American program probably is mistitled. It should be the SDR—the Strategic Defense Response.

The extensive Soviet BMD program and the possible BMD potential of some Soviet air defense systems have caused genuine concern in the United States. The fear is that the Soviet Union has created a condition wherein it could "break-out" of the ABM Treaty and rapidly deploy an extensive BMD system before the United States could respond with its own defenses or improved offenses. In short, the United States will not have to convince the Soviet Union of the value of defense against nuclear weapons; the Soviet Union long has appreciated the value of strategic defense—the Soviet leadership is only unhappy about the prospect for *American* strategic defenses.

The SDI was motivated by a number of converging factors. These include the BMD potential of emerging technologies, the general dissatisfaction of the president and some of his advisers with the condition of mutual vulnerability, the president's skepticism over continuing deterrence policy based on mutual vulnerability, the disadvantageous long-term trends in the strategic offensive force competition, and the apparent growing public dissatisfaction with the nuclear threat and the offensive nuclear arms competition. These factors combined during the months preceding the speech and set the stage for the president's decision to pursue the SDI.

Criticism of the SDI has focused on a number of issues, the most prevalent being the notion that a comprehensive strategic defense capability is not technically feasible. Obviously, if there is no prospect for effective defenses then the SDI is misguided and should be discussed in different terms. There is debate within the scientific community concerning the future prospect for comprehensive defense. Some respected scientists are highly skeptical while others are optimistic about the technical potential for achieving this objective. The issue ultimately is whether sufficient potential exists to warrant increased research into BMD technologies. The Reagan administration has decided favorably and believes that the goal is so important that advanced research is warranted. Such a decision is reasonable, particularly given the relatively modest costs of the program.

A key argument against the deployment of defenses stems from skepticism concerning the technology for highly effective defenses. Near-perfect defense is necessary, the argument runs, to provide useful protection for the population and since near-perfect defense is impossible, there is no prospect for useful defense. The argument is highly questionable. It is based on the premise that if the Soviet Union could concentrate its nuclear forces to overcome U.S. defenses and destroy a limited number of targets, it would choose to destroy American cities. The assumption here is that cities are the Soviet Union's highest priority targets. Such a view almost certainly is mistaken. Soviet strategic thinking appears almost entirely at odds with the notion that nuclear weapons should be used for the militarily gratuitous purpose of killing civilians. More likely, the Soviet Union would concentrate its forces to achieve the maximum military benefit from a small number of nuclear weapons. Such an objective would suggest the targeting of those U.S. strategic retaliatory assets most valuable and most vulnerable to attack. Consequently, even a defense that was less than "near perfect" could provide protection for Americans—through direct defense and by compelling the Soviet Union to concentrate its fire power elsewhere.

Another key argument against the SDI, but more specifically against BMD deployment, is that BMD is "destabilizing," that is, its deployment would increase the probability of war. However, that argument is based on the view that deterrence stability requires mutual vulnerability. That view, again, almost certainly is mistaken. Deterrence stability appears to have prevailed in previous decades when the United States, through a combination of offensive and defensive means, would most likely have survived a nuclear war. Vulnerability to nuclear devastation *may* be inalterable, but that vulnerability should not be seen as a necessary condition for stability; nor should the consideration of ways to limit damage to the United States and its allies be opposed on such grounds. Indeed, even limited defenses should be stabilizing in that they would at least be capable of defending some retaliatory forces. Enhancing U.S. retaliatory force "survivability" should help discourage the Soviet Union from ever seriously considering a nuclear first strike.

In addition, criticism concerning the potential instability of strategic defense reflects much more faith in our collective understanding of the causes of war than is warranted. There is no consensus concerning the cause(s) or potential cause(s) of war—particularly a strategic nuclear war. The usual pat phrases concerning what is or is not "destabilizing" contain little demonstrated validity. The implications are obvious: since we cannot know for sure the cause of some future nuclear war and we cannot be certain how to prevent it or reduce its probability, it would behoove us to develop means for surviving the event. The SDI is a first step toward the potential means of survival.

The arms control process has been used both to support and attack the SDI. Almost certainly, the SDI in large part motivated the Soviet Union to return to negotiations following its walkout in November 1983. The SALT I experience suggests, similarly, that the U.S. BMD program of the early 1970s was the key to achieving the SALT I offensive limitations. However, critics of the SDI and BMD deployment contend that the prospects for offensive arms control would be ruined by BMD because defenses would cause the superpowers to build more offensive forces. This argument could be valid if defenses could easily be overcome by offensive countermeasures. If that is the case, the United States is unlikely to deploy BMD—as official policy guidance reportedly suggests. Ironically, the claim was made repeatedly by BMD opponents in the late 1960s and early 1970s that a cap on BMD would facilitate a "freeze" in offensive forces, because they would not have to be built to penetrate defenses. BMD was duly capped by the 1972 ABM Treaty but the increase in offensive forces was hardly frozen. The gross number of strategic nuclear weapons multiplied several times in the subsequent decade of strategic arms control negotiations.

The SDI appears to have facilitated the resumption of negotiations and the deployment of strategic defenses probably is the only means of achieving something useful from offensive arms control. Indeed, deployment of strategic defenses could establish the necessary basis for deep offensive force reductions. In the absence of defenses the prospects for truly deep reductions appear very low.

The extremely modest restraints that have been achieved through offensive arms control to date have not effectively reduced our vulnerability to nuclear attack. But combining even modest offensive arms limitations with the deployment of strategic defense could result in a genuine reduction in the nuclear danger. Complementing defensive deployment with negotiated restraints on offensive countermeasures would facilitate the capability of both the Soviet Union and the United States to reduce significantly their vulnerability to nuclear attack. Such an approach to arms control would be a virtual reversal of the "established approach" which brands strategic defenses as incompatible with arms control. A defense-oriented approach to arms control, however, would have the benefit of being in the self-interest of both the Soviet Union and the United States, and it would have the potential for accomplishing something useful.

The moral case for the SDI and BMD deployment seems persuasive. The protection of innocent civilian lives is the key to the "just war" theory, and research into the prospects for such protection has been endorsed by many moral leaders, including the American Conference of Catholic Bishops in their pastoral letter on nuclear war. Given the responsibility of government to protect its citizens as best it can and the clear infeasibility of other suggested solutions to the nuclear problem—disarmament and the creation of a new international order—SDI research is a moral imperative.

Finally, America's allies are cautiously endorsing the SDI as a research program, with the major exception of France. That allied endorsement does not represent support for the deployment of BMD. NATO allies are particularly wary of upsetting the current deterrence structure based upon offensive nuclear retaliation. Obviously, Soviet BMD deployment could upset it. But the threat of U.S. nuclear escalation—the basis of NATO's deterrence policy—lacks credibility because it would be suicidal for the United States to implement the threat in most situations. Consequently, the offensive deterrence structure to which the allies cling lacks a solid foundation. Strategic defense may potentially restore credibility to the U.S. "extended deterrent." It may also provide, in part, the basis for maintaining an adequate threat capability to support deterrence, although that threat would be different from the current offensive-oriented nuclear deterrent. Therefore, strategic defense need not "make the world safe for conventional war."

The pivotal question concerning the SDI is whether the United States ought to pursue the research necessary to determine the defensive potential of emerging technologies. The answer to that question clearly is, yes. We should at least have the foresight to question past dogma and examine the potential of strategic defense. Whether the United States in the future ought to deploy BMD, and strategic defenses in general, will depend in large part on the results of SDI research. If the SDI indicates that comprehensive BMD is technically feasible, then deployment would be appropriate. Even if the cost were as high as critics often charge (between $300 and $500 billion), averaged over a thirty year deployment period the cost would represent 3.3 percent to 5.5 percent of the defense budget per year at current rates. Such an expenditure for the means of defending against ballistic missile attack does not seem unreasonable.

Ultimately, if we could be *certain* that the current offense-oriented deterrence policy would always function reliably, then almost any price for strategic defense would be too high and no amount of defense "leakage" would be acceptable, for we would already have peace with security. Unfortunately, there is no such certainty about the functioning of deterrence, and the current offense-oriented policy ensures that if deterrence fails it will "fail deadly." The SDI may offer relief from this dilemma that mankind has foisted upon itself. We must not permit the examination of new defensive technologies to be prohibited by old ideas.

ENDNOTES

1. See Jim Klurfeld, "Star Wars Plan Is Modified," *Long Island Newsday*, June 14, 1985, p. 5; see also National Security Council, *Fact Sheet on the Strategic Defense Initiative*, June 6, 1985, pp. 7-9.

APPENDIX
S D I and
Public Opinion

TABLE 1

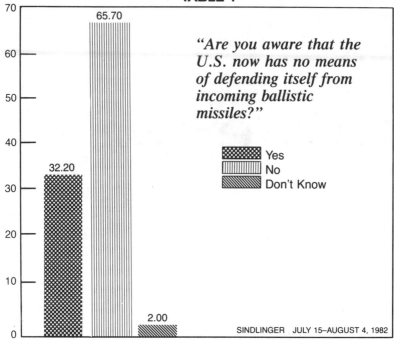

"Are you aware that the U.S. now has no means of defending itself from incoming ballistic missiles?"

Yes
No
Don't Know

65.70
32.20
2.00

SINDLINGER   JULY 15–AUGUST 4, 1982

TABLE 2

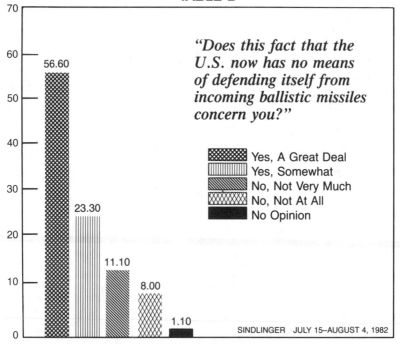

"Does this fact that the U.S. now has no means of defending itself from incoming ballistic missiles concern you?"

Yes, A Great Deal
Yes, Somewhat
No, Not Very Much
No, Not At All
No Opinion

56.60
23.30
11.10
8.00
1.10

SINDLINGER   JULY 15–AUGUST 4, 1982

TABLE 3

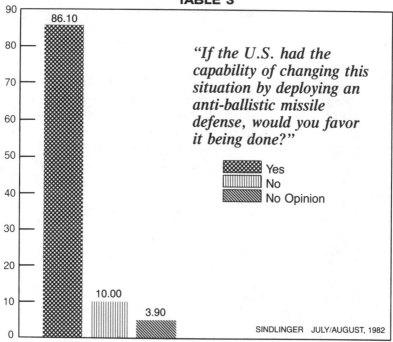

"If the U.S. had the capability of changing this situation by deploying an anti-ballistic missile defense, would you favor it being done?"

Yes
No
No Opinion

86.10
10.00
3.90

SINDLINGER   JULY/AUGUST, 1982

TABLE 4

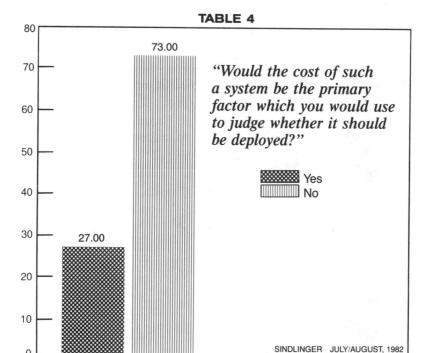

"Would the cost of such a system be the primary factor which you would use to judge whether it should be deployed?"

Yes
No

73.00
27.00

SINDLINGER   JULY/AUGUST, 1982

TABLE 5

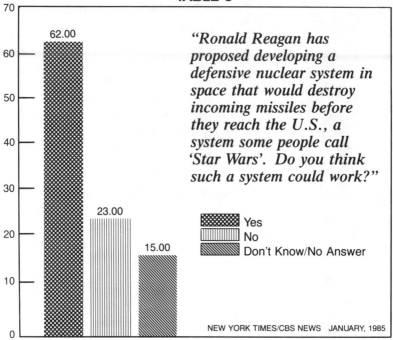

"Ronald Reagan has proposed developing a defensive nuclear system in space that would destroy incoming missiles before they reach the U.S., a system some people call 'Star Wars'. Do you think such a system could work?"

Yes
No
Don't Know/No Answer

NEW YORK TIMES/CBS NEWS   JANUARY, 1985

TABLE 6

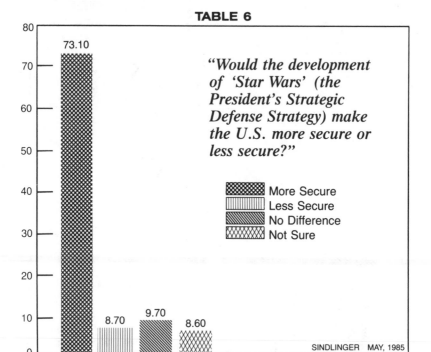

"Would the development of 'Star Wars' (the President's Strategic Defense Strategy) make the U.S. more secure or less secure?"

More Secure
Less Secure
No Difference
Not Sure

SINDLINGER   MAY, 1985

TABLE 7

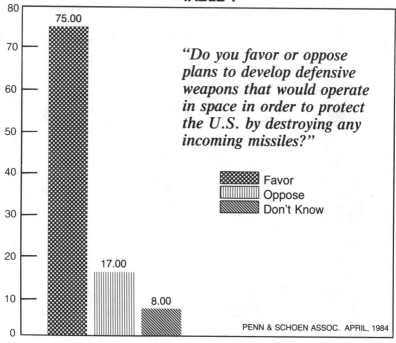

"*Do you favor or oppose plans to develop defensive weapons that would operate in space in order to protect the U.S. by destroying any incoming missiles?*"

Favor
Oppose
Don't Know

75.00
17.00
8.00

PENN & SCHOEN ASSOC. APRIL, 1984

TABLE 8

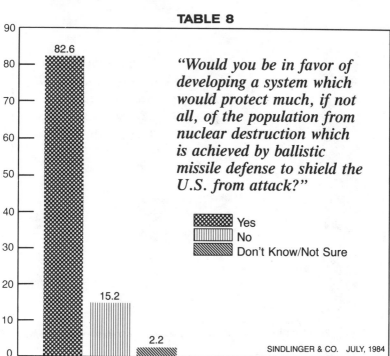

"*Would you be in favor of developing a system which would protect much, if not all, of the population from nuclear destruction which is achieved by ballistic missile defense to shield the U.S. from attack?*"

Yes
No
Don't Know/Not Sure

82.6
15.2
2.2

SINDLINGER & CO. JULY, 1984

TABLE 9

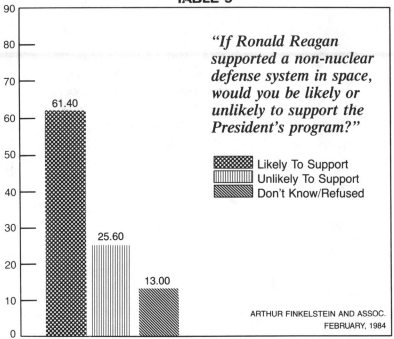

"*If Ronald Reagan supported a non-nuclear defense system in space, would you be likely or unlikely to support the President's program?*"

Likely To Support
Unlikely To Support
Don't Know/Refused

61.40

25.60

13.00

ARTHUR FINKELSTEIN AND ASSOC.
FEBRUARY, 1984

TABLE 10

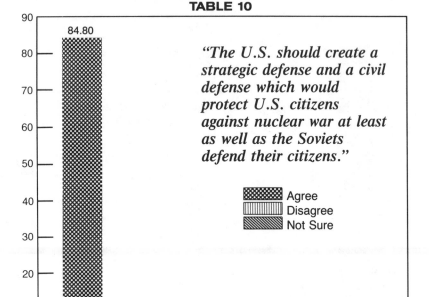

"*The U.S. should create a strategic defense and a civil defense which would protect U.S. citizens against nuclear war at least as well as the Soviets defend their citizens.*"

Agree
Disagree
Not Sure

84.80

7.60   7.60

AMERICAN SECURITY COUNCIL/OMNIBUS SURVEY
JULY, 1984

TABLE 11

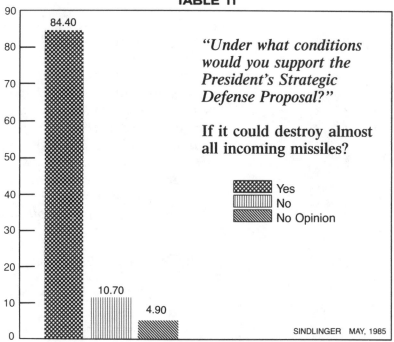

TABLE 11

"*Under what conditions would you support the President's Strategic Defense Proposal?*"

If it could destroy almost all incoming missiles?

Yes
No
No Opinion

84.40
10.70
4.90

SINDLINGER MAY, 1985

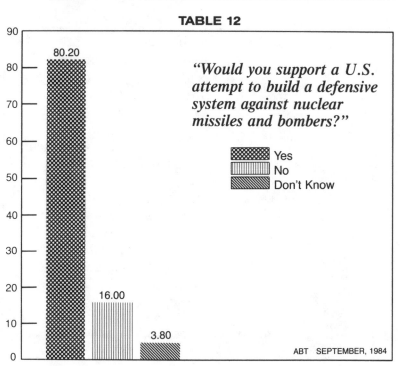

TABLE 12

"*Would you support a U.S. attempt to build a defensive system against nuclear missiles and bombers?*"

Yes
No
Don't Know

80.20
16.00
3.80

ABT SEPTEMBER, 1984

TABLE 13

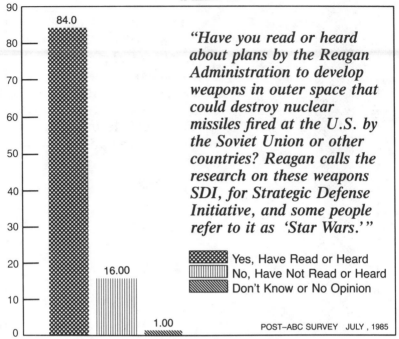

84.0

16.00

1.00

"Have you read or heard about plans by the Reagan Administration to develop weapons in outer space that could destroy nuclear missiles fired at the U.S. by the Soviet Union or other countries? Reagan calls the research on these weapons SDI, for Strategic Defense Initiative, and some people refer to it as 'Star Wars.'"

Yes, Have Read or Heard
No, Have Not Read or Heard
Don't Know or No Opinion

POST–ABC SURVEY   JULY , 1985

TABLE 14

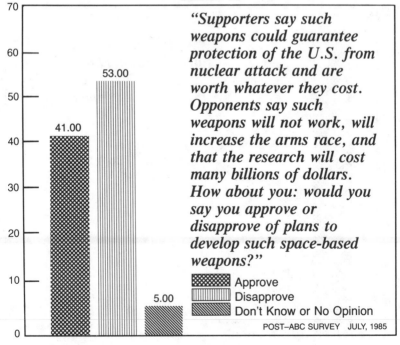

53.00

41.00

5.00

"Supporters say such weapons could guarantee protection of the U.S. from nuclear attack and are worth whatever they cost. Opponents say such weapons will not work, will increase the arms race, and that the research will cost many billions of dollars. How about you: would you say you approve or disapprove of plans to develop such space-based weapons?"

Approve
Disapprove
Don't Know or No Opinion

POST–ABC SURVEY   JULY, 1985

TABLE 15

"Do you favor or oppose plans to develop defensive weapons that would operate in space in order to protect the U.S. by destroying any incoming missiles?"

Favor
Oppose
Don't Know

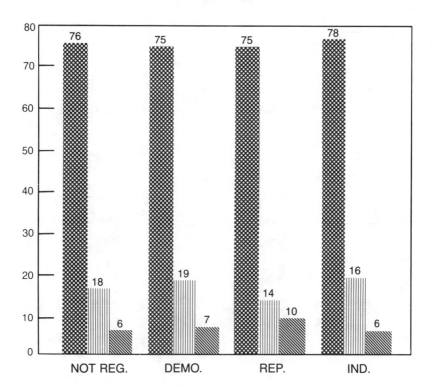

PENN & SCHOEN ASSOC.   APRIL, 1984

TABLE 16

"If a nuclear freeze were negotiated, should development of such defensive space weapons continue or should development be abandoned?"

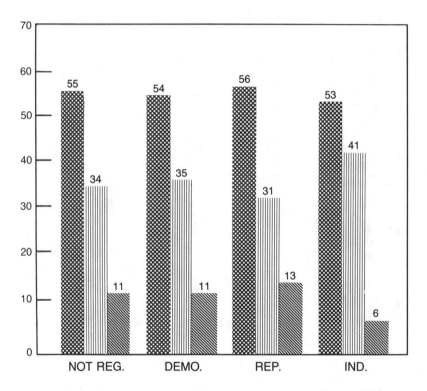

PENN & SCHOEN ASSOC.   APRIL, 1984

TABLE 17

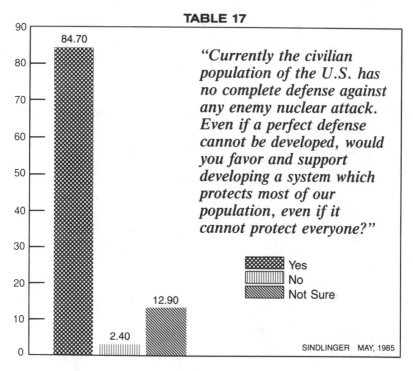

"Currently the civilian population of the U.S. has no complete defense against any enemy nuclear attack. Even if a perfect defense cannot be developed, would you favor and support developing a system which protects most of our population, even if it cannot protect everyone?"

Yes
No
Not Sure

84.70

2.40

12.90

SINDLINGER MAY, 1985

TABLE 18

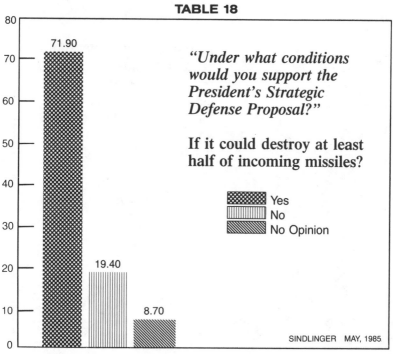

"Under what conditions would you support the President's Strategic Defense Proposal?"

If it could destroy at least half of incoming missiles?

Yes
No
No Opinion

71.90

19.40

8.70

SINDLINGER MAY, 1985

TABLE 19

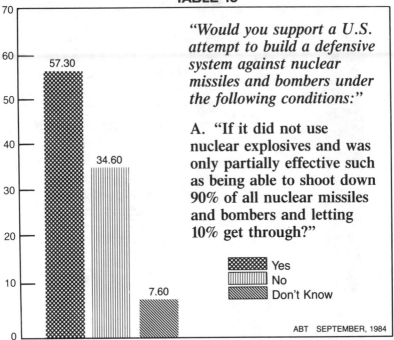

"Would you support a U.S. attempt to build a defensive system against nuclear missiles and bombers under the following conditions:"

A. "If it did not use nuclear explosives and was only partially effective such as being able to shoot down 90% of all nuclear missiles and bombers and letting 10% get through?"

Yes
No
Don't Know

57.30
34.60
7.60

ABT   SEPTEMBER, 1984

TABLE 20

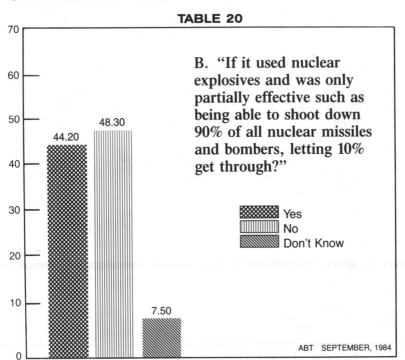

B. "If it used nuclear explosives and was only partially effective such as being able to shoot down 90% of all nuclear missiles and bombers, letting 10% get through?"

Yes
No
Don't Know

44.20
48.30
7.50

ABT   SEPTEMBER, 1984

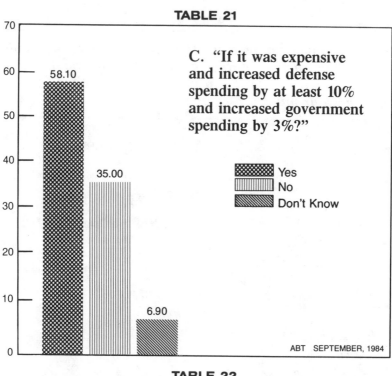

TABLE 21

C. "If it was expensive and increased defense spending by at least 10% and increased government spending by 3%?"

- Yes
- No
- Don't Know

58.10
35.00
6.90

ABT   SEPTEMBER, 1984

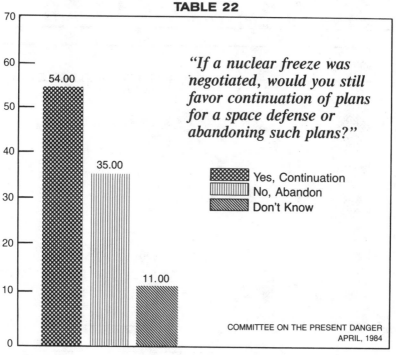

TABLE 22

"If a nuclear freeze was negotiated, would you still favor continuation of plans for a space defense or abandoning such plans?"

- Yes, Continuation
- No, Abandon
- Don't Know

54.00
35.00
11.00

COMMITTEE ON THE PRESENT DANGER
APRIL, 1984

TABLE 23

"If 'Star Wars' can be made to work, and there is a choice between the current mutual assured destruction ('Balance of Terror') strategy or the new plan of 'Star Wars,' which would be your number one choice?"

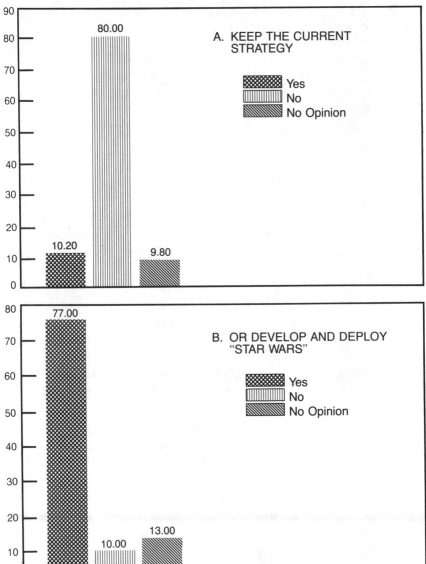

SINDLINGER   MAY, 1984

TABLE 24

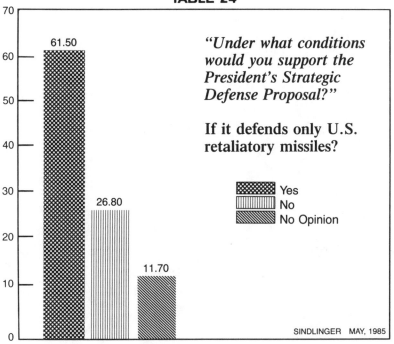

"*Under what conditions would you support the President's Strategic Defense Proposal?*"

If it defends only U.S. retaliatory missiles?

- Yes
- No
- No Opinion

SINDLINGER MAY, 1985

TABLE 25

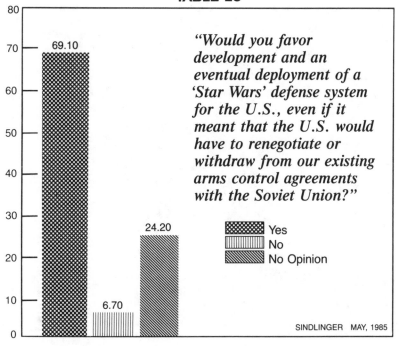

"*Would you favor development and an eventual deployment of a 'Star Wars' defense system for the U.S., even if it meant that the U.S. would have to renegotiate or withdraw from our existing arms control agreements with the Soviet Union?*"

- Yes
- No
- No Opinion

SINDLINGER MAY, 1985

Index